CONTEMPORARY GERMAN WRITERS

ZAFER ŞENOCAK

Series Editor

Rhys W. Williams has been Professor of German and Head of the German Department at University of Wales Swansea since 1984. He has published extensively on the literature of German Expressionism and on the post-war novel. He is Director of the Centre for Contemporary German Literature at University of Wales Swansea.

CONTEMPORARY GERMAN WRITERS

Series Editor: Rhys W. Williams

National University *of* Ireland, Galway
Ollscoil na hÉireann, Gaillimh

UNIVERSITY OF WALES PRESS

2003

British Library Cataloguing-in-Publication Data
A catalogue record for this book is available from the British Library.

ISBN   0–7083–1810–X paperback
            0–7083–1811–8 hardback

Cover design by Olwen Fowler.
Printed in Great Britain by Dinefwr Press, Llandybïe.

Contents

page

List of Contributors   vii

Preface   ix

Abbreviations   xi

1 Gedichte
  Zafer Şenocak   1

2 Zafer Şenocak: Outline Biography
  Karin E. Yeşilada   16

3 »Einfach eine neue Form«: Gespräch mit Zafer Şenocak
  Tom Cheesman   19

4 Wider den Exotismus: Zafer Şenocaks west-östliche
  Moderne
  Ulrich Johannes Beil   31

5 Writing Against the Grain: Zafer Şenocak as Public
  Intellectual and Writer
  Matthias Konzett   43

6 Odysseus on the Ottoman, or 'The Man in Skirts': Exploratory
  Masculinities in the Prose Texts of Zafer Şenocak
  Moray McGowan   61

7 *Der Erottomane*: Ein Vexierspiel mit der Identität
  Monika Carbe   80

8 Zafer Şenocak's Essays and Early Prose Fiction: From
  Collective Multiculturalism to Fragmented Cultural Identities
  James Jordan   91

9 Istanbul: Imagination Itself
  Pierre Pachet   106

vi

10 Poetry on its Way: aktuelle Zwischenstationen
   im lyrischen Werk Zafer Şenocaks
   Karin E. Yeşilada   112

11 Against Between: A Manifesto
   Leslie A. Adelson   130

12 Ş/ß: Zafer Şenocak and the Civilization of Clashes
   Tom Cheesman   144

13 Bibliographie
   Karin E. Yeşilada   160

Index   184

List of Contributors

Leslie A. Adelson is Professor of German Studies at Cornell University. Since *Crisis of Subjectivity* (1984) and *Making Bodies, Making History* (1993), she has focused on minority discourses, migrant cultures, and post-colonial legacies in post-war Germany. *Atlas of a Tropical Germany* (2000) introduced Zafer Şenocak as Germany's first Turkish public intellectual to an international audience. She edited *The Cultural After-Life of the GDR: New Transnational Perspectives* (2002). A book in progress addresses literary figuration and historical narrative in German literature wrought by Turkish migration.

Ulrich Johannes Beil is currently Visiting Professor of German and Comparative Literary Studies and DAAD Lektor at the University of São Paulo, Brazil. His areas of research are comparative literature, canon formation, genre theory, and modern poetry in relation to the media. His recently completed *Habilitationsschrift* is entitled *Die hybride Gattung: Gedichte im europäischen Roman bis Goethe*. His latest volume of poetry is *Aufgelassene Archive* (1998).

Monika Carbe is a poet, novelist, critic and translator of modern and contemporary Turkish literature. Recent publications include *Hundert Jahre Nâzım Hikmet* (edited with Wolfgang Riemann), *Frankfurt am Main Stadtgeschichten* and *Turbane in Venedig*, a translation of Nedim Gürsel's novel *Resimli Dünya*.

Tom Cheesman is Senior Lecturer in German at University of Wales Swansea. He directed the 'Axial Writing' research project on diaspora literatures and cultural policy in the UK and Germany, within the ESRC Transnational Communities research programme, 1998–2002. He has published several articles on German-Turkish literature and popular culture.

James Jordan is Principal Lecturer in German at Nottingham Trent University. He was co-editor of *Migrants in German-speaking Countries: Aspects of Social and Cultural Experience* (2000) and has published essays on Ota Filip, Akif Pirinçci and migrants' writing in Germany. His edition of Ernst Toller's unpublished poetry appeared in 2000.

Matthias Konzett is Associate Professor at Yale University. He is the author of *The Rhetoric of National Dissent in Thomas Bernhard, Peter Handke and Elfriede Jelinek* (2000) and the editor of *The Encyclopedia of German Literature* (2000) as well as of *A Companion to Thomas Bernhard* (forthcoming).

Moray McGowan is Professor of German at Trinity College Dublin. He has published extensively on contemporary German literature and culture, including Turkish-German writing, and is currently working on German theatre and drama of the 1990s.

Pierre Pachet teaches French and general literature at the University of Paris 7 (Jussieu). As an essayist he has written on politics in literature (for example, Naipaul), sleep in literature, literature and the politics of the individual, and on various poets. As a scholar of Greek philosophy, he translated Plato's *Republic* for a paperback edition. His books include *Autobiographie de mon père* (1987, 1994) and *Aux aguets, essais sur la conscience et l'histoire* (2002).

Karin E. Yeşilada is currently completing a Ph.D. dissertation on German-Turkish literature of the second generation. She has published several articles on this topic, as well as interviews with authors including Zafer Şenocak and Barbara Frischmuth.

Preface

Contemporary German Writers

Each volume of the Contemporary German Writers series is devoted to an author who has spent a period as Visiting Writer at the Centre for Contemporary German Literature in the Department of German at the University of Wales Swansea. The first chapter in each volume contains an original, previously unpublished piece by the writer concerned; the second consists of a biographical sketch, outlining the main events of the author's life and setting the works in context, particularly for the non-specialist or general reader. A third chapter will, in each case, contain an interview with the author, normally conducted during the writer's stay in Swansea. Subsequent chapters will contain contributions by invited British and German academics and critics on aspects of the writer's oeuvre. While each volume will seek to provide both an overview of the author and some detailed analysis of individual works, the nature of that critical engagement will inevitably depend on the relative importance of the author concerned and on the amount of critical material which his or her work has previously inspired. Each volume includes an extensive bibliography designed to fill any gaps or remedy deficiencies in existing bibliographies. The intention is to produce in each case a book which will serve both as an introduction to the writer concerned and as a resource for specialists in contemporary German literature.

Zafer Şenocak

Zafer Şenocak is widely regarded as the foremost writer and intellectual of the Turkish diaspora in Germany. This volume opens with a selection of unpublished poems, including two ('Die schlafende Generation', 'Die Pilotin') which were first drafted during his residence in the Centre for Contemporary German Literature in Swansea in May 2000. The cycle 'Wortschatzinsel' forms part of an as yet unpublished volume, titled *Schlafreflexe*. Following a biographical sketch, and an interview with Şenocak addressing both literary and political issues, different aspects and genres of his work are approached from a variety of geographical as well as professional perspectives. Fellow poet Ulrich Beil pays attentive tribute to Şenocak's wily refusal of the twin lures of exoticism and self-exoticization. Matthias Konzett explores Şenocak's essays and prose fiction as contributions of a public intellectual to debates on multicultural and international politics. Moray McGowan focuses on the theme of sexuality in Şenocak's prose work, examining the imbrication and blurring of ethnic and gender differences and desires. Monika Carbe assesses the pleasures and frustrations of *Der Erottomane*, the final work in Şenocak's prose fiction tetralogy. James Jordan tracks shifts in Şenocak's thinking on questions of identity during the 1990s. Pierre Pachet's preface to the French edition of *Das senkrechte Meer* serves as a sample of the critical enthusiasm for Şenocak's poetry in France. Closely reading the poetry published here for the first time, Karin E. Yeşilada discusses recent topographic, thematic and stylistic changes in Şenocak's verse, and underlines the omnipresence of the poetic voice in all his writing. Leslie A. Adelson frames Şenocak's work in the context of a polemic against notions of a Turkish–German 'cultural divide', which relegate his writing to a no-man's-land between national cultures, rather than seeing it as occupying space shared by both (and by others besides). Tom Cheesman considers two hybrid essay-fictions in the recent volume *Zungenentfernung*, arguing that Şenocak's use of this chameleon genre aptly conveys his efforts to reason about unreason. The final chapter comprises a detailed bibliography. Here secondary literature is organized by country, in order to highlight divergent trends in the international reception of this transcultural writer. At the start of the twenty-first century, Zafer Şenocak is held in high regard as a poet and novelist in France and Turkey, and as an essayist in the USA, but seems to be increasingly neglected in Germany. This is the first book in any language devoted to his work.

Abbreviations

Throughout the current volume, quotations from or references to primary works by Zafer Şenocak, unless otherwise indicated, will be followed by one of the following abbreviations and the relevant page number(s) in parentheses.

FT   *Flammentropfen. Gedichte* (Frankfurt am Main, Dağyeli, 1985)

RdJ   *Ritual der Jugend. Gedichte* (Frankfurt am Main, Dağyeli, 1987)

SM   *Das senkrechte Meer. Gedichte* (Berlin, Babel, 1991)

Atlas   *Atlas des tropischen Deutschland. Essays* (Berlin, Babel, 1992)

FA   *Fernwehanstalten. Gedichte* (Berlin, Babel, 1994)

Hitler *War Hitler Araber? IrreFührungen an den Rand Europas. Essays* (Berlin, Babel, 1994)

MiU   *Der Mann im Unterhemd. Prosa* (Berlin, Babel, 1995)

P   *Die Prärie* (Hamburg, Rotbuch, 1997)

GV   *Gefährliche Verwandtschaft. Roman* (Munich, Babel, 1998)

E   *Der Erottomane. Ein Findelbuch* (Munich, Babel, 1999)

ATG   *Atlas of a Tropical Germany: Essays on Politics and Culture, 1990–1998*, translated and edited by Leslie A. Adelson (Lincoln and London, University of Nebraska Press, 2000)

Zunge   *Zungenentfernung. Bericht aus der Quarantänestation. Essays* (Munich, Babel, 2001)

Ş   'Gedichte', in this volume, 1–15.

1

Gedichte

ZAFER ŞENOCAK

Wortschatzinsel

wir gehen durchs Glas
wie Sonne
sitzen hinterm Glas
wie Sonnenanbeter

sie kam auf einem Rad
und ging zu Fuß weg
sie ließ ihr Rad bei mir stehen
damit ich mich jederzeit auf den Weg machen kann

man bewegt sich nicht
in Gegenwart des Vaters
doch wie wächst man dann

das reisende Kind in mir
hat keine Spur hinterlassen
es entkam
als mein Körper in seine Fesseln wuchs

an seiner Stelle ziehe ich nun
ein gefesseltes Kind groß
vergeblich
denn es wächst nicht
aus seinen Fesseln

vielleicht wird es
ein entfesseltes Kind in mir
nie geben

niemand anders fesselt mich
als jenes Kind das verschwand

mein Lebenswiderspruch ist keinen Spruch mehr wert
er hält mich nicht auf Beinen
ich wollte nicht fort
könnte ich stehen genügte mir ein Stehplatz
ich brauche keinen Boden zum Liegen
zum Schlafen lehne ich mich an einen anderen Menschen
sollte ich auf keinen treffen habe ich Platz genug

Oft sitzt man Rücken an Rücken
und denkt über den Weg nach
der sich in Blickrichtung auftut
den man gehen könnte
ein Leben lang zu Fuß
bis man sich wiedertrifft

der Grenzsteinbesitzer
auf seinem uralten Grenzstein
auch der träumt davon
einmal wegzukommen
sieht er doch keinen wieder
den er einmal verabschiedet hat

Feigen aßen sie
vom Körper des Anderen
und wurden zu Blättern
an einem fremden Stamm
die Haut tarnte sie
das Wort trug sie ins Stammbuch ein
verriet wenig
bis jemand kam der brüllte
und das Laub fiel

Vater
ich konnte nicht bei dir bleiben
deine Augen machten mir Angst
ich konnte nicht leben in deinem Haus
in der mutterlosen Stille
du hast mich gehen lassen ohne Abschiedsworte
und irgendwann war die Schrift auf meiner Haut
nicht mehr zu lesen
Vater
lösche mich aus deiner Schrift häute mich
daß kein Wort uns erinnern kann
dein Name in mir schließt wie eine alte Wunde
niemand ruft mich mit deinem Namen
deine Augen sind schwach geworden Vater
nimm deine Hände aus meiner Sprache
damit ich mein eigenes Haus bauen kann

nicht zu Ende sprachst du
und wohntest im Halbwort
gegenüber
Lust in der Spur
des Verlusts
Knoten im Mund die Zunge
Mittlerin zwischen rohem
Fleisch und halbrohem Gedanken
die aus der Erinnerung tanzt
mit der anderen Hälfte
deines Worts

denk mich zu dir
nur bei dir kann ich denken
so viele Denkfehler unterwegs

tagsüber die Suche nach Wörtern
die in der Nacht vergraben wurden

von Seeräubern keine Spur
sie glauben nicht mehr an den Schatz
finden die Insel langweilig

mir aber sagt eine Stimme
»lies, was du nicht siehst!«

ich lese und grabe
bis ich das erste Wort greife

wenn das Mandelauge sich schließt im Baum
legt dem Baum ein paar Worte zu Füßen
damit die Wurzel nicht verwaist
und sie hören kann was zu sehen ihr versagt ist
hören wie ein Wort über das andere klagt
und eines sagt daß zu Füßen der Eiche
keine Mandelblüten zu erwarten sind
die aus dem Schatten der Zweige springen
wenn ihre Zeit gekommen ist

wen wundert's
das Kind drüben hat drei Arme
beim Aufheben ist es verschwenderisch
und zum Umarmen fehlt noch ein Arm
wen wundert's
einem solchen Kind genügt keine Mutter
den Vater hat es nie gesehen
es brachte sich selbst auf die Welt
und hat sich selbst aus der Welt geschafft

Die schlafende Generation

da Poesie keiner Worte bedarf
habe ich mich dem Schlaf hingegeben
alles um mich schlief
ich fuhr auf einer Kutsche gen Süden
der Kutscher schlief
ein Mann mit einem schmalen levantinischen Gesicht
kam mir entgegen auf einem Rad
und fragte nach dem Weg
Transsylvanien liegt schon hinter uns
und der Himalaya vor uns
ein Meer und zwei Erdteile weit
in Berlin im übrigen nehme er sich vor Fahhraddieben in Acht
also hinter mir der Himalaya
und vor mir Transsylvanien
bestätigte er meine Auskunft
auf einem Delphinrücken ritten an uns vorbei
zwei Schwarzmeerfrauen
eine von ihnen strohblond
einen vertrockneten Ast hatten sie zwischen die Beine geklemmt
Sex muß doch nicht immer so schrecklich aussehen bei Frauen
ich verpaßte an diesem Morgen den Anschlußzug nach
                                    Konstantinopel
die Zeiten wo Züge auf versprengte Reisende warten sind auch
                                    hier vorbei

auf dem Balkan schneite es
der Schnee roch nach Qualm
während ich schlief bekam ich einen Anruf
auf meinem Anrufbeantworter
eine vertraute Stimme die ferner rückte je länger sie sprach
jemand fragte mich nach der Adresse des Frühlings
er hatte sein ganzes Hab und Gut dabei
hatte sich viel gemerkt unterwegs
und las aus dem Koffer vor
da Worte keiner Poesie bedürfen
zog ich weiter und schlief
die Bäume am Wegrand rauchten ihre letzten Blätter
bevor ich mein Zimmer betrat und die Post öffnete
und weiterschlief
da Erinnern zu Hause keiner Worte bedarf

Die Pilotin

weil ich anders bin als mein Gesicht sieht man es mir nicht an aber
ich bin kein Engel
das Kind das alle gut zu kennen glauben war immer zuhause
während seine Puppen tanzen gingen unterirdisch
ich habe Köchin gelernt drei Jahre war ich in einem
Fischrestaurant Hilfsköchin
die Fische langweilten mich sie waren schon tot wenn ich sie
zubereitete
eines Nachts sperrte ich mit dem Messer nicht ein Fischmaul auf
sondern die Schatulle zwischen meinen Beinen
und jemand der immer spät in der Nacht kam dockte mit seinem
Schnabel an
ein schriller Vogel war es der tagsüber auf einer Wolke schläft
einer von meinen Zugvögeln
zu wissen ist daß es so viele Geschlechter gibt wie Vogelarten
nicht aber wie man die Flügel wechselt mitten im Flug
mein Geschlecht hatte Flugangst
ich hatte Angst mein Gleichgewicht zu verlieren
bei jedem Stoß eine andere Frau zu werden einen anderen Mann
zu töten
danach hatte ich etwas Muskelkater wie nach einem Umzug
ich wußte schon als Kind daß ich eines Tages fliegen würde
fliegen ohne Engel zu sein ich lebte ganz nach diesem Wunsch

zu wissen ist daß es keine Engel gibt die einem wehtun wenn man
                                           noch nicht fliegen kann
jeder hier wartet mit Geduld und Zurückhaltung auf den ersten
                                                Flug des anderen
Engel verpassen ihren Flug
Engel brauchen Piloten um ihre Götter zu finden
ich dagegen bin immer dann bei ihnen wenn niemand weiß wo ich
                                                             bin
ich bin nicht die Schnellste ich suche die exakte Berührung
die sorgfältig berechnete Langsamkeit
ich Lustmechanikerin vormals Hilfsköchin
geflogen bin ich noch nicht
zähle auf dem Flugplatz die Passagiere die ankommen
immer und immer wieder müssen sie an mir vorbei
um sich in mir einzutragen wie in einem großen Heft
um die zu treffen deren Liebhaber sie sind
deren Taugenichts
deren unberechenbarer Kammerspieler
die unbeholfenen Imagisten in meinem Werk
können keine Maschine warten
Engel verpassen ihren Flug

Männergeschichte

als es keine verborgenen Stellen gab
wurde die Schrift erfunden am Frauenleib
keine Stelle blieb unbeschrieben
mit groben Fingern brachten Männer
die Zeichen durcheinander
bis die Schrift unlesbar wurde
sie hatten versäumt zu lesen
wurden Zweifelnde der Schrift
auf der Suche nach der verlorenen Sprache
verbrannten sie alle Bücher bis auf ihren eigenen Körper
schufen aus Asche das Traumweib
verhüllten es tiefschwarz
blieben Analphabeten

Solitude

niemand sieht auf die Uhr
die dem Mammut eingepflanzt wurde
unter die Schädeldecke
der Jahrtausendespeicher

auf einem Röntgenbild
so groß wie eine Kinoleinwand
vermißt man die Zähne des Mammuts

sie wurden aufgestellt als Mahnmal
in einer der Brandwunden unseres Planeten
vielleicht ist der Schädel nichts wert ohne Zähne
und die Zähne sind die falschen Edelsteine der Melancholie

der Astronaut sieht die Berge in den Meeren
und hört das Ticken der Mammutuhr auf einem der Gipfel
er winkt aus seiner Kapsel
einem Ruderboot auf dem Ozean zu

wie spät ist es Bruder

Rede an die Übernächtigte

der Sterndeuter hat viele Worte gezählt
ohne Sterne zu sehen

er bildet sich ein
der Himmel sei nicht bedeckt
alles da
was das Auge nicht sieht

schau dich um
ohne aufzuwachen
laß ihn erzählen
nachts wächst ihm die Zunge aus dem Leib

er wird dich nicht finden
denn er zählt die Sterne nicht zu sich

2

Zafer Şenocak:
Outline Biography

KARIN E. YEŞILADA

1961 Born in Ankara, Turkey. His father is a journalist, his mother a teacher.

1966 The family moves to Istanbul.

1970 The family settles in Munich.

1981–7 Study of politics, philosophy and German literature in Munich.

1983 First poetry in print: *Elektrisches Blau. Gedichte*; *Verkauf der Morgenstimmungen am Markt*.

1984 Literary stipend awarded by the City of Munich, marking the 'Year of Literature'.

1985 *Flammentropfen. Gedichte.*

1986 Translations of Yunus Emre: *Das Kummerrad / Dertli Dolap. Gedichte*. Scholarship awarded by the Art Stiftung Plaas; residency in the Künstlerhaus in Lindau.

1987 *Ritual der Jugend. Gedichte.*
      Invited to read at Walter Kempowski's salon; publication of poems in the series *Literatur im Kreienhoop*.

1988 Adelbert-von-Chamisso newcomer prize ('Förderpreis') awarded by the Bavarian Academy of Fine Arts. This leads to several invitations to literature festivals in Turkey and the Netherlands. The Berlin Senate awards a scholarship at the Literarisches Colloquium. He co-founds and co-edits the multilingual literary periodical *Sirene*. His poems begin to appear regularly in German literary periodicals.

1990 Moves to Berlin, where he still lives. He starts writing political essays on German-Turkish issues. His first is the manifesto 'Deutschland – Heimat für Türken?' (co-written with Bülent Tulay, subsequently owner and editor-in-chief of the Babel publishing house, Munich) for the *Süddeutsche Zeitung*. He becomes a regular contributor to *die tageszeitung* (and from 1993 onwards to other German daily and weekly newspapers). Works freelance for the radio and television channel Sender Freies Berlin (SFB) for some time. Becomes recognized as the most important voice of German Turks in united Germany.

1991 *Das senkrechte Meer. Gedichte.*
Publishes essays on Ottoman and Turkish literature, and co-edits an anthology of contemporary Turkish authors with Deniz Göktürk: *Jedem Wort gehört ein Himmel*. From October, he co-presents the talk-show 'Berlin Mitte' for SFB television (to June 1992).

1992 *Atlas des tropischen Deutschland. Essays.*

1993 Amid German attacks on Turkish and other 'foreign co-citizens', with the political scientist Claus Leggewie he publishes a bilingual collection of articles: *Deutsche Türken – Das Ende der Geduld. Türk Almanlar – Sabrın Sonu.*

1994 *Fernwehanstalten. Gedichte.*
War Hitler Araber? IrreFührungen an den Rand Europas, the second volume of essays, comments on western perceptions of 'the Orient'. He also publishes the contributions to a Berlin conference in *Der gebrochene Blick nach Westen. Positionen und Perspektiven türkischer Kultur*. He succeeds Bahman Nirumand as the editor responsible for 'intertaz', the weekly intercultural section of *die tageszeitung*, a position he holds for two years. His poetry volume of 1987 appears in Turkish translation (*Gençlik Ayinleri*) and attracts a remarkable amount of attention.

1995 *Der Mann im Unterhemd. Prosa*. The first part of what will become the 'tetralogy'.

1996 Writer in residence at Oxford University, Ohio, and at the Villa Aurora, Los Angeles (scholarship awarded by the Feuchtwanger-Gesellschaft).

1997 *Die Prärie. Tetralogy, 2.*
Writer in residence at Massachusetts Institute of Technology. The prose fiction of 1995 and the essay volume of 1994 appear in Turkish translation, again attracting much attention: *Atletli Adam* and *Hitler Arap Mıydı?*

1998 *Gefährliche Verwandtschaft. Roman*. Tetralogy, 3.

Collaboration begins with the Munich artist Berkan Karpat, resulting in the publication of three lyrical-dramatic titles over the next three years. The first is *Nazım Hikmet: Auf dem Schiff zum Mars*.

1999   *Der Erottomane. Ein Findelbuch.* Tetralogy, 4.

Second volume with Berkan Karpat: *Tanzende der Elektrik. Szenisches Poem*.

The 1991 poetry volume appears in French translation, *La Mer verticale. Poèmes*, to be followed by translations of his prose fiction. Writer in residence at Dartmouth College, USA.

2000   Third lyrical co-production with Berkan Karpat: *wie den vater nicht töten. Ein Sprechlabyrinth*.

A millennium year of translations. The poetry volume of 1994 appears in Turkish: *Taşa ve Kemiğe Yazılıdır. Şiirler*. The novel of 1998 appears in French as *Parenté dangereuse*. It finds an immediate critical echo in leading periodicals. Across the Atlantic, a selection of his essays is published in English by Leslie A. Adelson: *Atlas of a Tropical Germany: Essays on Politics and Culture, 1990–1998*. The author is writer in residence at Oberlin College, USA, and at the Centre for Contemporary German Literature, University of Wales Swansea.

2001   His third collection of essays, *Zungenentfernung. Bericht aus der Quarantänestation. Essays*, comes out on 14 September. It goes rather unremarked in Germany.

The fiction of 1999 appears in French as *L'Érottoman*.

2002   Completion of two new manuscripts: stories (*Liebeskoma*) and poetry (*Schlafreflexe*). Articles in German newspapers and periodicals intervene in the debate on Turkey and Europe in the contexts of the 'war on terror' and the expansion of the European Union.

2003   Invitations as writer in residence to Berkeley, USA, and Villa Mont Noir, France. Forthcoming Italian translation of the 1999 fiction, *L'Erottomanno*.

3

»Einfach eine neue Form«:
Gespräch mit Zafer Şenocak

TOM CHEESMAN

TC: Den Klappentext der *Gefährlichen Verwandtschaft* fand ich ein bisschen strange; der Vergleich mit Alfred Polgar, OK, aber diese Formulierung: »Zafer Şenocak schreibt nicht nur deutsch, sondern mit einer Leichtigkeit . . . « etcetera.

ZŞ: Ja ja, das ist das Typische – aber ich finde es eine sehr richtige Feststellung. Polgar habe ich sehr gerne gelesen. Das ist ein Schriftsteller der 20er, früher 30er, stammt ursprünglich aus Wien, ist jüdischen Ursprungs gewesen, und hat einen unglaublich leichten und ironischen Stil etabliert in der deutschen Sprache, was man kaum kannte. Er ist auch nach Berlin gegangen, war Feuilletonist. Man kann also sicher eine Linie rüberziehen, wenn man will – intellektueller Humor, das ist die Grundlage. Trotzdem bleiben Vergleiche immer etwas hinkend, zeigen immer mehr die Geistesverfassung des Rezensenten, des Betrachters. Dieses 'nicht nur deutsch' ist nicht böse gemeint, sondern ist nur ein Zeichen für die Überraschung, von der ich ja immer spreche. Das überrascht die Leute, ist nicht gewöhnlich; aber vielleicht ist das auch normal. Weil die deutsche Sprache so etwas vor dem Krieg, vor dem Nationalsozialismus kennt, aber danach eben nur sehr brüchig, gebrochen – über die Exilsituation eigentlich. Da ist eine unglaubliche Homogenisierungsmaschine gewesen, Ausschaltung jeglicher Differenz, anderer Stillagen, Sprachen im deutschen Sprachraum, in ganz Europa. Und da ist es natürlich sehr schwierig, sowas als ganz gewöhnlich zu bezeichnen, wenn jemand, der in der Türkei geboren ist, deutsch schreibt. Aber das sind zwei verschiedene Ebenen.

TC: Für die einen liegt der Überraschungseffekt noch immer darin, dass überhaupt deutsch geschrieben wird.

ZŞ: Ja, und dann dass überhaupt so gut deutsch geschrieben wird, kommt als das zweite dazu.

TC: Das mit Humor und Leichtigkeit, das überrascht überhaupt in der deutschen Literaturlandschaft?

ZŞ: Mittlerweile ist das so eine Welle eigentlich. Als ich da meine ersten Sachen veröffentlicht habe, war das noch gar nicht der Fall, aber es sind jetzt mehr Autoren, die das für sich beanspruchen oder so verkauft werden auf dem Markt.

TC: Gerade wird viel von Generationen geredet, Generation Golf, Generation XY. Empfindest Du Dich als Teil einer Generation?

ZŞ: Eigentlich nicht. Weil ich von einer Zwischengeneration bin. Also ich bin natürlich nicht wie die 30-jährigen jetzt, die 78er, wiederum auch kein Endvierziger, der noch die 68er Bewegung als Wellenschlag mitbekommen hat. Ich bin dazwischen. Ich nehme mich jedenfalls so wahr. Ich habe relativ früh angefangen zu schreiben, deswegen passe ich auch nirgendwo rein. Es gibt Autoren, die jetzt anfangen, die so alt sind wie ich, und irgendwie ist das komisch, etwas schief: auch ich könnte fast noch als Anfänger gelten in der deutschen Literatur. Das ist natürlich absurd. Aber als ich angefangen habe zu schreiben, das waren die endsiebziger Jahre, Anfang Achtziger, war die herrschende Generation ganz klar die 68er und dann diejenigen, die gerade sozusagen mit der elitären Dichtung aufgeräumt hatten, also Brinkmann und Leute wie Born, und die Leute, die sich nach Amerika hin orientierten. Die waren alle 10 bis 20 Jahre älter als ich. Das war die herrschende Kunststimmung.

TC: War da irgendwas München-spezifisches?

ZŞ: Das war Deutschland-spezifisch. München war Provinz, ist Provinz, wird Provinz bleiben, nur eine Ecke von Deutschland. Ich würde sogar München hinter Frankfurt ansetzen, was geistige Konflikte und Neuerungen angeht.

TC: Obwohl Du Dich zu keiner Generation zählen willst, Deine Figuren haben doch oft dieses Generationsbewusstsein, so zum Beispiel diese Stelle in 'Das Haus' (*MiU*): »Ich nicke zu allem, das verbindet mich mit meiner Generation, lächeln und nicken, doch wo bleibt der Hass – wen oder was hassen wir . . . ?«

ZŞ: Also das ist jetzt natürlich eine Falle gewesen, [*lacht*] weil ich auch viel über Generationen schreibe, beziehungsweise nicht über Generationen. Ich habe ja eine Figur entworfen, für diese vier Prosabände, manche bezeichnen sich als Romane, andere als Erzählungen, andere als Mischform, es ist einfach eine neue Form. Und die werden zusammengehalten von einer Figur. Sie kommt in Bänden zwei und drei als der ganz klar benannte Sascha Muhteschem raus, in eins und vier sehr verschwommen, und es ist auch nicht unbedingt die gleiche Figur, sondern in vielen verschiedenen Identitäten und Formen – aber Charakterzüge dieser Figur sind ähnlich, erkennt man. Und er ist eigentlich so ein Zwischengenerationtyp, er passt auch nirgendwo rein. Ist eigentlich kein politischer Mensch und doch immer wieder in politischen Dingen tätig oder eingefangen. Im Grunde genommen ist er innerlich sehr konservativ, und doch ist er gleichzeitig viel weiter als bestimmte linke Leute. Man kann ihn schwer einstufen, einkasteln oder eingrenzen. Und dann kommt, was erst im dritten Buch bewusst entschlüsselt oder entdeckt wird zu seiner Herkunft – das wird ja im zweiten ganz bewusst verschwiegen – und er hat eigentlich eine Grundabneigung gegen dieses Thema, fällt aber trotzdem immer wieder ins Thema rein: auch so ein Grundkonflikt . . .

TC: . . . der ihm aufgebürdet wird . . .

ZŞ: Ja, aber wenn man genau hinschaut, hat es auch etwas mit ihm zu tun. Es ist immer so widersprüchlich. Ich wollte gerade diesen Widerspruch einfangen, der viele Menschen beschäftigt oder begleitet, die in einer ähnlichen Situation sind. Also einerseits sagen zu wollen: ach, ich habe genug von diesem Herkunftsthema und so weiter, und gleichzeitig immer wieder nachts vorm Einschlafen sich damit innerlich zu beschäftigen. Das war ein Kommentar zu der deutschen Diskussion, an der ich auch teilgenommen habe eine Zeit lang. Da habe ich also meine Prosa ganz bewusst instrumentalisiert. Ich habe eine konstruierte Figur und eine Diskussionslage geschaffen, um das kritisch zu hinterfragen, und dann auch ironisch zu brechen, diese Debatte, diese sehr schwierige Debatte: wer ist ein Deutscher, was ist ein Deutscher, wie wird man deutsch, wie bleibt man türkisch. Um all das aufzubrechen mit diesen aus meiner Sicht total irreführenden

Formulierungen wie 'zwischen den Kulturen'. Ich habe versucht
zu zeigen, dass das, was 'dazwischen' ist, immer im Innern passiert, im Innern von einem selbst. Da ist das Gebrochene oder das
Vielfältige, nicht zwischen den konstruierten Gruppen oder Figuren, die gegeneinander stehen etwa wie Fussballmannschaften.
Das war also die Theorie dahinter. Aber bis auf das dritte Buch
habe ich Theorie von den Büchern immer sehr fern gehalten. Im
dritten Buch ist es bewusst drin, sehr stark, von den vier Büchern
ist das die mehr an die Abhandlung sich nähernde Form. Aber in
den anderen drei ist diese Theorie viel mehr in die Figuren einge-
flossen. Also das war der Hintergrund, und dann fliessen natürlich
sehr viele verschiedene Themen rein, weil es ja nicht nur um Identität oder um deutsch-türkisch-jüdische Verhältnisse geht. Es geht
um Männlichkeit, um Sexualität, um Fantasien, um Bezüge auch
Richtung Orient immer wieder, um die islamische Kultur. Das ist
vollkommen unentdeckt in der bisherigen Kritik. Es gab bisher nur
eine einzige Besprechung von dem *Erottomanen*, die das versucht
zu entschlüsseln, und das nicht zufällig von einer Frau, die aus
dem Türkischen übersetzt.

TC: Braucht man des Türkischen mächtig zu sein, um Deine
Bücher richtig zu lesen?

ZŞ: Muss man nicht, aber man muss sich zumindest in den islamischen Grundquellen auskennen. Im *Mann im Unterhemd* gibt es
zum Beispiel viele Anspielungen auf den Koran – 'Das Haus des
Schreibers' etwa ist voller solcher Anspielungen. Oder religiöse
Figuren, zum Beispiel die Engelfiguren, die ich einsetze: das sind,
ähnlich wie bei Rilke, moslemische Engelfiguren. Aber dass die
Engelfiguren bei Rilke moslemische sind, kann man auch nur entdecken, wenn man den Hintergrund kennt. Der Koran hat einen
grossen Einfluss auf ihn, auf seine Engelfiguren gehabt. Das kann
man nicht durch Eingebung oder Inspiration entdecken, sondern
nur über Quellenforschung. Und das ist eben die Grundfrage: was
bedeutet eigentlich Multikulturalität? Verschiedene Traditions-
stränge kommen zusammen, und man beginnt jenseits des eigenen
Traditionsstrangs – ob Christentum, griechische Antike, römische
Antike – die Überlieferungen zu entdecken. Byzanz, also das
Oströmische zum Beispiel, was auch von uns kaum beherrscht
wird, und darüber hinaus jüdische oder islamische Quellen, die
Teil des Ganzen sind, aber sehr distanziert betrachtet werden. Das

Christentum ist ja auch eine orientalische Religion. Also in diesem Bereich liegt das, diese neu entstehenden kulturellen Komponenten oder Koordinaten – sehr gut zu sehen auch bei Salman Rushdie. Wobei man das nicht sehr ernst nehmen darf, weil er, wir natürlich auch damit spielen. Denn wir sind nicht unbedingt Wissenschaftler oder Vermittler von Kultur. Ich bin kein Vermittler, der versucht, der deutschen Literaturlandschaft beizubringen, wie man den Koran zu lesen hat . . .

TC: . . . aber dass man den Koran lesen *könnte* . . . ?

ZŞ: Wenn man meine Texte verstehen will, muss man ihn wahrscheinlich lesen oder sich wenigstens ein bisschen in der Lebensgeschichte von Mohammed oder in den Überlieferungen auskennen, in der anatolischen Mystik. Ich mache das ja nicht, weil ich daran interessiert bin, dass Leute den Koran lesen oder so, das ist mir echt wurscht, sondern weil das mich selbst interessiert, weil es meine Geschichte ist. Ich kann ja nur über meine Geschichte schreiben. Wenn ich über meinen Grossvater schreibe oder über meinen Vater oder das, was ich zu Hause als Kind erlebt habe, dann bin ich automatisch darin. Im *Mann im Unterhemd* gibt es diesen kurzen autobiographischen (in Anführungszeichen) Text, 'Mein Lebenslauf', wo diese Spuren nachgezeichnet werden. Der Text dient gleichzeitig als Lebenslauf der Figur oder auch des Autors, und da sieht man schon wie der Hintergrund einfach aus der Biographie erwächst. Das war auch die Hauptargumentation in meinem Text über den Mythos des Schreibens ['Welcher Mythos schreibt mich?', *Zunge*, 97–103], wo ich versuche zu sagen, Biographie ist das, was als Thema aus dem Erlebnis erwächst, als Knotenpunkt für die Beschäftigung im Innern, was sich dann sprachlich äussert.

TC: Nehmen wir den Grossvater in *Mann im Unterhemd*, den Schreiber. Er basiert auf Deinem Grossvater?

ZŞ: Mein Vater ist Schreiber, ich habe das übertragen auf den Grossvater. Ich habe ja zwei Grossväter, wie jeder auch, und der Grossvater mütterlicherseits war ein typischer Vertreter dieser Aufbaugeneration der türkischen Republik, hat auch ein bisschen als Modell gedient für den Grossvater in der *Gefährlichen Verwandtschaft*. Im *Mann in Unterhemd* ist der Grossvater eher dem Vater nachgezeichnet, wobei da wirklich erlebte oder in Anführungszeichen erinnerte Stücke drin sind und natürlich auch völlig erfundene. Aber es ist eine Geschichte, die zumindest von den Orten her, die drin sind, nachzuvollziehen oder nachzugehen ist. Sie spielt im christlichen Teil von Istanbul, wo im Zentrum des Orts eine Kirche und keine Moschee steht, das heutige Kadiköy – also die asiastische Seite, wo ich meine ganz frühe Kindheit verbracht habe – und gleichzeitig spielt das mit der alten Schrift als Symbol für das Vergangene, das für die Gegenwart nicht mehr Lesbare – und da wiederum sind Parallelen zur Figur meines Vaters, der ein sehr altmodischer Mensch ist, ein sehr konservativer und gleichzeitig ein Kenner der osmanischen Kultur. Ich komme aus einer Familie, wo die Bruchlinie richtig in der Familie eingelegt ist zwischen den konservativen Intellektuellen und den sehr modern orientierten, fortschrittlichen Rationalisten. Meine Mutter ist Lehrerin, sehr mathematisch begabt; mein Vater ist einer der letzten Exemplare vom intellektuellen Konservatismus oder vom intellektuellen Islam eigentlich, der sich absolut von den Frommen unterscheidet. Das hat nichts zu tun mit den Moscheegängern, die man tagtäglich sieht. Später, als ich mehr darüber gelesen habe, hat mich das an jüdische Figuren erinnert, die sehr viel in der Schrift leben, aus der Schrift leben. Das habe ich sehr früh mitbekommen. Aber interessanterweise war das erste Buch, das mir mein Vater schenkte – und er schenkte mir immer Bücher – *Robinson Crusoe*, ein westliches Buch.

TC: *Der* Roman des neuzeitlichen westlichen Individualismus.

ZŞ: Ja. Und da sieht man wieder, wie diese Bilder vom Westen und Osten vorsichtig betrachtet werden müssen.

TC: Von daher vielleicht das Motiv Insel in Deiner Arbeit?

ZŞ: Höchstwahrscheinlich. Das ist etwas, was mich beschäftigt hat. Diese autonome, auf den einzelnen, auf das Individuum hin orientierte Tradition. Das ist etwas, was heute überhaupt gar nicht mehr verstanden wird, denn die Tradition der Gegend, aus der ich stamme – der Orient, dieses Gegeneuropa, das andere Ufer [*lacht*] – die ist mittlerweile im Image, in der Wahrnehmung, nur noch als Kollektiv sichtbar. Das sind immer so Massen, die irgendwo hingehen und irgendwo herkommen, irgendwie bedrohlich und unklar in ihren Motivationen.

TC: Diese Wahrnehmung hat man aber offenbar auch in der Türkei selbst, so bei Orhan Pamuk, *Die weisse Festung* zum Beispiel: da hat man diesen Kontrast zwischen dem sogenannten westlichen Individualismus und dem orientalischen Gemeinschaftlichen und Kollektiven, es wird daran gezweifelt, ob der orientalische Mensch jemals zu diesem Sinn für Individualität und Eigenverantwortung finden kann.

ZŞ: Türkische Schriftsteller haben dieses Bild übernommen. Ich lehne das ab. Das ist der Unterschied, wenn Du so willst, zwischen dem was geschieht und dem was ich versuche zu formulieren. Ich lehne das ab: nicht aus ideologischen Gründen, weil ich irgendwie als Mensch, der aus dieser Gegend stammt, beleidigt bin oder so. Sondern ich habe das Gefühl, diese Vorstellung wächst aus Unwissen. Es ist nur eine Konstruktion. Denn natürlich funktioniert der Westen auch nicht nur individualistisch, wie kann man sonst den Hitlerismus erklären, der das Kollektivste ist, in der Form, in der Praxis, was man überhaupt erlebt hat. Andererseits: wie kann man zum Beispiel die Figur des Eremiten erklären, der so stark ist in der islamischen Tradition. Damit habe ich mich immer wieder beschäftigt, mit dem absolut radikalen Einzelgänger, der – und damit eben anders als der Asket im Christlichen – nicht auf die weltlichen Dinge verzichtet sondern auf die Kommunikation. Als Eremit spricht man zum Beispiel nicht, aber man kann Sex haben: eine ganz seltsame Mischung. Aber im Christlichen ist das ja mehr auf den Leib fokussiert, Leib und Körper dürfen nicht sprechen. Da verstummt nicht unbedingt die Zunge sondern das Körperliche. Oder auch die Figur, die Goethe so begeistert hat, diese freischaffende, freischwebende Figur, die er an Hafiz zu erkennen glaubte, das, was man im Persischen 'rend' nennt. Das ist der weise freie Vogel, der über den Geboten des Koran oder der Dogmatiker steht und überall ein bisschen zweifelt und gleichzeitig lächelt: Hayam ist auch so eine Figur. Das sind alles keine westlichen Figuren, sondern Teile der Tradition, die verloren gegangen sind, die man nicht mehr im Kopf hat. Und deswegen denke ich, diese Konstruktion der Gegensätze ist zumindest zu einfach. Ich lehne sie ziemlich radikal ab. Ein gewisser kollektiver Hang ist zwar immer überall sichtbar. Aber nehmen wir zum Beispiel auch diese ganzen Beurteilungen der Sexualität und der Erotik: mittlerweile hat man ja den Eindruck, der ganze Orient besteht nur noch aus puritanischen Menschen, und das ist das Unsinnigste was sein kann, wenn

man die Geschichte betrachtet. Das ist diese seltsame Wiederer-
weckung des Islam als eine Mischung zwischen Ingenieurwissen-
schaft, amerikanischem Puritanismus und Dogmatismus, also eine
ganze seltsame Mischung. Wenn man die Figuren, die dabei tätig
sind, betrachtet, sieht man auch diese Einflüsse: das hat nichts mit
eigener Tradition zu tun, sondern mit vielfältigen modernen Ein-
flüssen.

TC: Ich wollte zu der Tetralogie noch etwas fragen. Wie ist das
gewesen, war die Gesamtform, die Architektur schon von vorn-
herein im Kopf ausgearbeitet oder ist das im Prozess der Arbeit
entstanden?

ZŞ: Beides. Es gab am Anfang eine grobe Vorstellung, und zwar
nichts als diese Figur. Ich wollte eine Figur schaffen, die sozusagen
an meinen Erfahrungen orientiert ist, aber gleichzeitig diese völlig
bricht, weil sie etwas in Erinnerung ruft, was man überhaupt nicht
mehr in Erinnerung hat. Die Möglichkeit einer deutsch-türkischen
Figur mit einem bürgerlich türkischen und einem jüdisch-
deutschen Hintergrund: das war die Grundidee am Anfang. Dann
hatte ich gewisse Begegnungen in Istanbul mit deutschen Exilan-
ten, wo ich das Gefühl immer mehr hatte, dass man eine solche
Figur aufbauen und glaubwürdig darstellen könnte. Ich hatte
meine Prosaarbeit mit den Geschichten, die im *Mann im Unterhemd*
sind, schon begonnen, und ich habe mich dann, wenn man so will,
an die Figur herangeschrieben. Es ist wie ein Weg, den man geht.
Um dann sozusagen im zweiten und dritten Buch die Figur zu
finden und im vierten wieder völlig zu verlieren. Diese Idee war
schon von Anfang an da. Aber ob das vier Bücher werden oder
drei, fünf, ist eigentlich erst klar geworden, als ich an der *Prärie*
arbeitete. Da wusste ich ganz klar, ich setze es fort, indem diese
Figur zurückkehrt nach Berlin, nach der Maueröffnung. Das ist
eigentlich der Plot des ganzen, das Verpassen des Ereignisses
schlechthin: wenn man so will, auch ein ironischer Kommentar zu
dem, was als Wende-Literatur tituliert wird. Die *Gefährliche Verwandtschaft* hatte auch eine Vorform, in der mehr die Geschichte in
der Geschichte erzählt worden war, die habe ich dann getrennt,
und werde sie vielleicht später mal in einem anderen Buch
benutzen. Die Geschichte in der Geschichte ist ja die Verhältnis des
Grossvaters zu dieser jungen Armenierin während des ersten
Weltkriegs, was zu seinem Selbstmord 1936 führt. Im Zuge der

Gestaltung dieser vier Bücher habe ich dann gesehen, dass ich diese Geschichte nicht erzählen darf, weil ich mir sonst selbst widerspreche. Ich werde oft gefragt, warum ich diese Geschichte nicht erzähle, genau das ist der Grund: es ist eben ein Symbol für das Schweigen. Allerdings wird sie letztlich angedeutet, zum Schluss des Buches, als Anfang eines Buches, das der Ich-Erzähler schreiben will. Übrigens: das ist kein Zufall, dass diese Geschichte so aufgetaucht ist, weil meine Familie sowohl mütterlicherseits als auch väterlicherseits aus Nordosttürkei stammt, das war ein total gemischtes Gebiet mit Griechen, Armeniern, Kurden, Türken, Lazen, Tscherkessen, Georgiern, Iranern ... Ich gehöre einer ethnisch gemischten Familie an, wobei das sehr verschwunden ist, sehr türkisch assimiliert, aber sowohl mütterlicher- als auch väterlicherseits gibt es sehr viel Georgisches. Die Familie meiner Mutter stammt aus Batumi, das Ajarien-Gebiet, wo die Muslime in Georgien leben, heute noch, an der Grenze zur Türkei. Väterlicherseits ist das Azerbaijanische sehr stark, weil diese Familie vor sieben oder acht Generationen aus Scheki, einer Stadt 60 Kilometer westlich von Baku, eingewandert ist. Und was sich dann noch vermischt hat, kurdisch, armenisch, tscherkessisch, das kann man überhaupt nicht mehr nachvollziehen. Diese Mischsituation ist die typische türkische Grundlage, obwohl natürlich jahrhundertelang diese Gruppen auch getrennt gelebt haben. Es gab – mein Vater spricht noch davon – das griechische Dorf, das armenische Dorf, das kurdische Dorf ... und man lebte bis Ende des neunzehnten Jahrhunderts wohl ausserordentlich friedlich in diesem Gebiet. Das ist radikal verloren gegangen.

TC: Durch den Nationalismus. Also die Kerngeschichte sozusagen, die im Zentrum des Ganzen steht und verschwiegen werden muss, handelt vom Beginn von dieser Reihe von Greueltaten, Gewalttaten ...

ZŞ: ... wobei es nur Hilflosigkeit ist, einen Beginn konstruieren zu wollen. Das ist anscheinend etwas natürlich Urmenschliches, dieser Gewalttrieb. Aber gleichzeitig wird dieser Gewalttrieb modernisiert oder auch radikalisiert durch die Moderne, einmal durch den Nationalismus, der ein noch viel grösserer Kollektivbegriff wird, als es früher die Religion oder die Stammeszugehörigkeit war, weil einfach die Macht der Mittel sich vergrössern. Das ist organisiert, durchgestylt, durchgedacht, das mündet wirklich in

Radikalform in das, was der Nationalsozialismus schafft. Ich bin kein Freund der Vergleiche, weil zwischen dem nationalsozialistischen Zerstörungswillen, diesem radikalen Rassismus, diesem dem anderen überhaupt keine Lebenschance lassen oder den anderen als 'Untermenschen' definieren, zwischen dem und dem was zum Beispiel in den letzten zehn Jahren in Jugoslavien passiert ist oder in der Türkei oder auf dem Balkan, schon ein radikaler Unterschied ist. Es ging nicht darum, die anderen als Untermenschen oder als Nichtmenschen zu definieren, sondern einfach als Kontrahenten, als Gegner: als derjenige, der den selben Hof haben wollte, der in der selben Wohnung wohnen wollte, der am selben Tisch sitzen wollte, und darum sollte der eine den anderen ausschalten. Also auch eine ungeheure Vorstellung von Gewalt und Zerstörung und Unrecht, aber nicht unbedingt auf der Grundlage von einem fundierten oder fiktiv, irrational verfassten Rassismus auf wissenschaftlichem – pseudowissenschaftlichem – Niveau. Solches Denken gab es eigentlich weder auf dem Balkan noch in der Türkei, auch heute gibt es das nicht. Da sind Rivalitäten über Jahrhunderte gewachsen, auch zwischen Türken und Griechen zum Beispiel, eher sowas wie die zwischen Deutschland und Frankreich. Also nicht so wie dieses deutsch-jüdische Problem. Die Tragik ist eine andere, die Eliminierungsgewalt ist eine ganz andere gewesen, und wenn man so einfach Vergleiche macht, versteht man nicht mehr, was da genau gelaufen ist. Aber die Verdrängung dieser Fragen ist natürlich für mich das Interessante. Ich weiss nicht, ob mir das gelungen ist, aber ich wollte das gegenüberstellen: das Beredte, dieses Darübersprechende, Es-wieder-ins-Zentrum-Rückende der deutschen Gesellschaft, Holocaust als Leitthema der deutschen Gegenwart, und dieses absolute Schweigen, dieses Verknoten im Türkischen, wo man zwar ständig damit beschäftigt ist natürlich auch, durchaus, man spricht bloss darüber nicht – das wollte ich gegenüberstellen.

TC: Im Hinblick auf Armenien oder Kurdistan oder . . . ?

ZŞ: Man kann es eigentlich auf alles beziehen. In meiner Geschichte geht es ja um Armenier, aber gleichzeitig ist es natürlich schon eine Parallelgeschichte zu verschiedenen ähnlich organisierten Gewalttaten.

TC: Eine andere Parallelgeschichte ist die Erzählung 'Die unlesbare Karte' im *Mann ohne Unterhemd*, mit dem verschollenen Schulfreund, den die Militärs mitgenommen hatten. Wobei da offenbar ein politischer Hintergrund im Spiel ist, der genau so gut die DDR sein könnte wie Türkei und Kurdistan oder was immer.

ZŞ: Spannend, dass Du das sagst. Ich habe diese Geschichte gelesen, da war das Buch noch gar nicht erschienen, Anfang 90 in Ostberlin, und es gab eine grosse Reaktion auf diese Geschichte: Leute haben das voll auf die eigene Geschichte übertragen. Ich war völlig überrascht, ich hatte das überhaupt nicht im Kopf. Ich meine, jetzt ist das klar, aber da sieht man auch meine Naivität. Bei der Geschichte merkt man ein putschartiges Szenario dahinter, und eine Exilgeschichte, aber die Leute waren ganz bewegt und gerührt, wollten mehr wissen. Ich war plötzlich in eine Diskussion eingetreten, die ich so gar nicht kannte.

TC: Du hast Dich als typischer Westdeutscher eigentlich nie so mit der DDR beschäftigt?

ZŞ: Null. Also, ein bisschen mit der Literatur natürlich, vor allem mit der Lyrik, die hat mich immer interessiert, und einige Autoren habe ich auch gerne gelesen. Aber das war wie Österreich, für meine Generation war es ein Österreich, in das man nicht fuhr. Während man nach Österreich ja fuhr [*lacht*]. So ein bisschen war das; ich glaube, da habe ich die absolute Mehrheit representiert. Es gab einige in der Schule und auch später während des Studiums, die engagiert waren und zu Kirchentagen fuhren und irgendwelche DDR-Austauschgeschichten, aber das deutet schon auf die Ausnahmesituation hin. Man musste sich engagieren um dieses Land DDR zu entdecken, genau wie man Polen entdeckte oder so. Das ist auch das Köstliche an dieser Situation jetzt, weil es natürlich eine absolute Lüge ist, in Deutschland gebe es oder hätte es eine Vereinigungsmentalität gegeben, es gab sie nicht. Es gab sie vielleicht für Helmut Kohl, aber nicht mal für ihn höchstwahrscheinlich, man muss noch weiter zurück gehen. Die Leute, die das bewusst erlebt haben, diesen Bruch, diese Niederlage 1945, die sozusagen an der Front gekämpft haben – aber für mich und meine Generation, in den 70er Jahren, nein. Auch unsere Lehrer, gerade die Sozialkunde-, Geschichtslehrer, Deutschlehrer, waren 68er, kamen direkt von dieser universitären Reformstimmung und entsprechend haben sie all das in die Schule getragen. Das hat mich auch geprägt: eine gewisse anti-autoritäre, alles hinterfragende

Grundhaltung, die möchte ich nicht missen. Die 70er waren jedenfalls eine interessante Zeit für mich.

TC: Eine letzte Frage zur Identitätsproblematik. Inwieweit würdest Du Parallelen sehen zwischen der deutsch-türkischen Situation und der afro-amerikanischen oder britisch-indischen und so weiter; und inwieweit würdest Du Dich als 'schwarzen' oder 'farbigen' Schriftsteller definieren angesichts einer 'weissen' Mehrheit?

ZŞ: Ich meine, solche Vergleiche sind irreführend. Irreführend, weil diese Zentrum-Peripherie-Mechanismen nur funktionieren, wenn die Strukturen sehr gewachsen sind. In der amerikanischen Kultur zum Beispiel – in dieser weissen amerikanischen Kultur – existiert ein bestimmtes Verhältnis zum Schwarzen, oder zu dem, was als Schwarz bezeichnet wird oder entstanden ist. Das funktioniert überhaupt nicht, wenn man es zum Beispiel auf das Jüdische überträgt – auch eine Minderheit in USA. Plötzlich wird da das Jüdische durchaus zentral oder mit der Kraft des Zentrums definiert und hat wiederum ein anderes Verhältnis zum Schwarzen. Man sieht also, dass es eigentlich immer wieder um Machtfragen geht: wo stehen die kulturellen Gruppen, wie definieren sie sich? Und das wächst auch über die Zeit. Das sieht man zum Beispiel im deutschen innerjüdischen Diskurs sehr klar, wie das assimilierte deutsche Judentum zum osteuropäischen Judentum steht, als es ab 1900 sehr stark nach Deutschland einwanderte: mit grosser Distanz, um es mal höflich zu formulieren. Da sind ganz klare Positionsbestimmungen. Jetzt die Frage, wo steht man als Mensch mit dem Ursprung oder Hintergrund Türkei in Deutschland. Das ist sehr schwer zu definieren im Moment; ich glaube, es ist zu früh um das darzustellen. Ich sehe mich eher als Autor, der versucht, möglichst nicht in diese abgrenzenden Kategorien hineinzufallen, sondern sich als schreibende Person mit der eigenen Geschichte zu präsentieren: mit dem Erlebten, mit dem Gedachten, Erträumten; und als ein Schriftsteller, der etwas Neues ausprobiert. Schwierig, mich zu positionieren. Ich weiss nicht. Das 'Gefärbte' gefällt mir, einfach weil es auch ausdrückt, dass da verschiedene Farben ineinander strömen, und weil Farben oft auch mehr sagen als Definitionen über Dinge. Mit Farben kann man mehr assoziieren als mit Gegenständen, denke ich, so gefällt mir das. Das wäre vielleicht ein interessantes Thema für ein anderes Gespräch . . . .

4

Wider den Exotismus:
Zafer Şenocaks west-östliche Moderne

ULRICH JOHANNES BEIL

Daß der Exotismus eine Verführung nicht nur für das westliche Publikum darstellt, sondern oft auch für die 'orientalischen' Betroffenen selbst, hat Irmela Hijiya-Kirschnereit in einem Buch über die japanische Kultur der Gegenwart hervorgehoben.[1] Der Vorgang des Exotisierens bestehe nicht nur darin, daß eine ferne Kultur zur ganz anderen, schlechthin fremden (auch ursprünglichen, paradiesischen) stilisiert wird; er habe vielmehr auch eine seltsame Anziehungskraft für die Exotisierten ihrerseits. Exotisierung führe zwar oftmals zu Widerstand und Kritik auf seiten der Betroffenen, ziehe aber nicht selten auch einen Effekt von 'Selbstexotisierung' nach sich, der die entsprechenden Klischees und Vorurteile noch zementiere. Selbstexotisierung in diesem Sinne wäre als eine Form der mehr oder minder freiwilligen Identifikation mit Fremdheitsmustern zu verstehen, die übereindeutige, schematische und mythische Züge trägt, aber das Verhältnis der Exotisierten zu den Exotisierenden (scheinbar) erleichtert und vorhandene Komplexitäten reduziert.

Für den türkisch-deutschen Schriftsteller Zafer Şenocak sind solche und ähnliche Fragen gleichsam das tägliche Brot. Im Anschluß an Überlegungen von Edward Said und andere wurde sich Şenocak schon früh der westlichen Orient-Projektionen bewußt.[2] Er hat sie in verschiedenen Essays herausgearbeitet, etwa in seinem Beitrag 'Das Buch mit den sieben Siegeln: Über die vergessene Tradition der osmanischen Dichtung' (*Hitler*, 34–47), in dem er das west-östliche Verhältnis als lange Zeit (auch vor Nietzsche und seinem berühmten Begriffspaar aus der *Geburt der Tragödie*) wirksame »Dialektik vom apollinisch beherrschten Okzident, dem

'Abendland', und vom dionysisch beherrschten Orient, dem 'Morgenland'«, beschrieb (*Hitler*, 39). Auch wenn Şenocak betont, daß sich in der ästhetischen Moderne die Fronten verwischen und mit Namen wie Lautréamont, Rimbaud oder Artaud eine Art von Orientalisierung (im Nietzscheschen Schema) innerhalb des Okzidents beobachtbar ist, so gilt doch auf der anderen Seite auch, daß die modernen Intellektuellen des Nahen Ostens, insbesondere der Türkei, oftmals zur »Übernahme der Orientphantasien des Abendlandes« (*Hitler*, 38) neigten, daß sie, mit anderen Worten, Selbstexotisierung betrieben.

Tendenzen zur Selbstexotisierung lassen sich in fast allen vom Okzident 'exotisierten' Kulturen beobachten, sie zählen zudem zu den naheliegendsten Versuchungen jener AutorInnen, die, mehr oder weniger zweisprachig aufgewachsen, von ihrer Herkunft und ihrer Geburt her gesehen in einer fremden Kultur leben und in der Sprache des Landes schreiben, als deren 'Gäste' sie sich seit vielen Jahren fühlen dürfen (müssen). »Dem Druck der Assimilierung von seiten der Mehrheitsgesellschaft entspricht von seiten der Minderheit ein Gegendruck der Konservierung, der meistens mit Begriffen wie *kulturelle Eigenständigkeit* und *Identität* umschrieben wird. In beiden Fällen gehen die Beteiligten von der Illusion aus, ihre Identität sei ungebrochen und ohne weiteres voneinander zu unterscheiden«, betont Şenocak in seinem Essay 'Was hat Waldsterben mit multikultureller Gesellschaft zu tun?' (*Atlas*, 39–44 [43–4]). Selbstexotisierung wird so nicht selten zu einem Ausweg für AutorInnen, die Tag für Tag um ihre Identität zu kämpfen haben und für die die Suche nach einem Tertium sich als vergeblich erwies. Dabei wäre es aber gerade dieser dritte Weg, dem Autor des *Atlas des tropischen Deutschland* zufolge, der es ihnen erlaubt, die »Fremdheit« in der »Geburtsurkunde« anzunehmen und ihre Heimat in der Sprache – Şenocak nennt es die »Suche nach einer bewohnbaren Sprache« – zu finden (*Atlas*, 101). In seiner Dankesrede anläßlich der Verleihung des Adelbert-von-Chamisso-Förderpreises 1988 umschreibt Şenocak diese Herausforderung so: »Meine Dichtung bewegt sich in einem Zwischenbereich [. . .]. Sie ist ein dritter Ort, wo sich vielleicht eine brüchige, eine flüchtige Muttersprache verbirgt, wo die Ortlosigkeit meiner Innenwelt und die Verortung meiner Außenwelt aufgehoben werden, wo Innen und Außen sich betasten und filtern« (*Atlas*, 99). Das *Tertium* ist seit Aristoteles die schwerste, wenn nicht eine unmögliche Option, und es scheint in dieser prekären Lage manchmal einfacher, auf die gegebenen Muster des 'Anderen' zurückgreifen, sich mit den oft negativen Zuschreibungen aus fremder Perspektive positiv zu identifizieren.

Auf den ersten Blick könnte es scheinen, als habe Şenocak in seiner frühen Lyrik zumindest zeitweise daran gedacht, einen tendenziell 'türkischen' Weg, eine vor allem an der türkischen literarischen Tradition orientierte Schreibweise für seine Verse zu finden und damit die deutsche Sprache auf denkbar radikale Weise zu verfremden. Jedenfalls hätte keiner der deutschen Lyriker, die wir kennen, die folgenden faszinierenden Verse (aus *Ritual der Jugend*, 1987) verfassen können, Verse, die am großen mystischen Atem der türkischen und persischen Poesie teilhaben und etwa an den (von Şenocak übersetzten) Mystiker Yunus Emre erinnern:[3]

sind das meine Beine Herr
warum gabst du mir nicht vier

ist das mein Kopf Herr
warum gabst du mir nicht zwei

sind das meine Augen
warum sind es zwei

hätte eine Nase nicht genügt
hätte ein Mund eine Zunge nicht genügt

sind das meine Münder Herr
sind das meine Zungen (*RdJ*, 63)

Hätte Zafer Şenocak nur dieses eine Gedicht geschrieben (das zu ignorieren, sehr geehrte Kritiker, der Gott der Dichtkunst nicht verzeiht), so hätte er allein dafür schon einen Platz in der deutschen Literaturgeschichte verdient, und sein Ruhm hätte nicht zuletzt darin bestanden, ein orientalisches Erbe, ein notorisch vergessenes, verdrängtes, auf denkbar subtile Weise innerhalb der deutschen Sprache aufzurufen und ihr für immer einzuschreiben. Şenocak hat freilich weitere, zahlreiche andere Gedichte geschrieben; nicht wenige kommen diesem an Intensität gleich.

Bereits in seiner Dankesrede anläßlich der Verleihung des Adelbert-von-Chamisso-Förderpreises hat er auf die Wichtigkeit der Metapher für sein poetisches Werk hingewiesen. Auch dies könnte ein Indiz für die oben genannte Tendenz des 'türkischen' Weges innerhalb der deutschen Sprache sein – geht man einmal davon aus, daß der überwiegende Teil der deutschsprachigen Lyrik in den letzten zwanzig Jahren durch eine im internationalen Vergleich auffallende Metaphernabstinenz gekennzeichnet ist. In der Rede hieß es: »Es ist somit kein Zufall, daß die Metapher das Muttermal meiner Dichtung ist. Die Metapher ist ein unverzichtbarer Ausdruck poetischer Wahrnehmung, in ihr lösen sich die Grenzen zwischen der abstrakten Sphäre des Denkens, der porösen Welt des Gefühls und der konkreten sinnlichen Wahrnehmung auf« (*Atlas*, 100). Wie ich aber andernorts bereits hervorgehoben habe, ist bei der naheliegenden Assoziation 'Bilderreichtum'–'Divanpoesie' (bei der freilich die schlichtere, volkssprachliche *Divan*-Dichtung vor allem türkischer Provenienz ausgespart bleibt) im Blick auf Şenocaks Lyrik Vorsicht geboten.[4] Denn gerade das poetische Werk Zafer Şenocaks läßt beispielhaft beobachten, wie die von ihm so genannte Erfahrung der 'Doppelzüngigkeit' auf die Schreibweise einwirkt und die Gedichte zu Zeugnissen einer kleinen ästhetischen Subversion werden – Subversion auch und gerade des Exotismus.

Da begegnen wir einmal einem elliptischen Gestus, der immer wieder den Eindruck erweckt, als seien die Verse Zitate aus einer Traumsequenz, deren Anfang und Ausgang vergessen wurden, Fetzen einer vorbewußten, nomadisierten Sprache: »Gedränge im Kopf ohne Lichtung / gebräunte Zunge im Rachen«, heißt es einmal; »selten genug kommen die Wörter an / schiffbrüchige Bilder« (*RdJ*, 14). Darüber hinaus fällt eine Neigung zum Parataktischen auf: Die Sätze emanzipieren sich einerseits von sinnstiftenden Hierarchien, andererseits wird ein Ton des 'Ist', des Unveränderlichen hörbar, der 'orientalisch' anmuten mag, aber gerade in den späteren Gedichten etwas von der Beharrlichkeit dessen gewinnt, der sich verweigert. Die Wiederbelebung des Metaphorischen wurde von Şenocak ganz bewußt, ja offensiv betrieben und stellt vielleicht die nachhaltigste Provokation der auf Nüchternheit und Bilderarmut getrimmten deutschen Poetik der 80er und frühen 90er Jahre dar. Bei genauer Lektüre freilich verlieren Şenocaks Metaphern die Aura des Exotischen oder des Anachronistischen; man entdeckt vielmehr, daß sie stark heterogenen Bildwelten entstammen, daß es sich gleichsam um entwurzelte Bilder handelt:

»entrüstet euch«, liest man im *Ritual der Jugend*, »die Rose steht /
aufrecht / ohne Erde / ohne Topf« (*RdJ*, 65). Das Gedicht wird so zu
einem Ort des Widerspruchs, der unauflösbaren Spannungen, der
sich kreuzenden Stimmen, der das oft allzu eng gefaßte Kriterium
der Stimmigkeit als zwanghafte Norm entlarvt. Nach Art einer
radikalen Auslegung des Aristoteles versteht Şenocaks verwand-
lungsfreudige Sprache die Metapher als 'fremdes', die Szenen und
Verhältnisse verfremdendes, ihre Entfremdung bloßstellendes
Wort.

Auch wenn Şenocaks Umgang mit der Metapher weit eher auf
einen 'dritten' Weg – zwischen bundesrepublikanischer Askese
und dem von Curtius so apostrophierten »asianischen Stil« –
schließen läßt als auf ein Phänomen wie Selbstexotisierung, so
scheint dieser Autor doch im alltäglichen Kampf um Wahrung der
eigenen paradoxen Situation ein wachsendes Unbehagen verspürt
zu haben: ein Unbehagen gegenüber dem von Roman Jakobson so
genannten »metaphorischen Weg«, dem Weg der Poesie. Şenocak
mag mit den Jahren mehr und mehr zu der Auffassung gekommen
sein, es schließe derjenige, der 'heute noch' Metaphern gebraucht,
im deutschsprachigen Kontext sich aus dem Bereich akzeptierter
Literatur aus und tappe unweigerlich in die Falle des Exotismus
(der 'Migrantenliteratur', des Märchenerzählers, des 'Poesie-
Clowns'). Eine solche antiexotistische Tendenz zeichnet sich ansatzweise bereits in den – noch durchaus mit Metaphern und
Paradoxien operierenden – Gedichtbänden *Das senkrechte Meer*
(1991) und *Fernwehanstalten* (1994) ab. In diesen Sammlungen zieht
es das lyrische Ich immer wieder in die Nähe öffentlicher Orte, des
'Marktes', wo es nahelläge, den Erwartungen eines westlichen Pub-
likums nachzugeben und sich auf eine Weise darzubieten, die Erfolg verspricht: Aber der Dichter, dem man hier begegnet, ist ganz
offensichtlich nicht der orientalische Zauberkünstler, der raunende
Magier, dem man im Okzident so gerne Beifall klatscht. Vielmehr
erscheint er als jemand, dem es »schwer« fällt, »die Haut zu
Markte zu tragen / wo die Skalps immer billiger werden« (*SM*, 60),
als »ein sich verweigernder Lastenträger / mit einem schweigend-
en Körper«, ein »Verdächtiger«. »Warum schweigt er«, heißt es
weiter, »man entfernt ihn / eine Wolke bleibt über seinem Platz
hängen / bis der Boden geschwärzt wird vom Schatten« (*SM*, 28).
Er weiß nicht nur, daß »die Marktschreier in Atemnot« geraten,
daß sie »jonglieren mit den Augen der Fische« (*SM*, 64), sondern

auch, daß »dieser Platz nachts / voll enthaupteter Märchenerzähler« (*SM*, 37) ist: daß, mit anderen Worten, das Märchener-
zählen, die Selbstexotisierung ihren Preis hat. Statt »auf Märkten
Gefühle gegen Erinnerungen« einzutauschen – »man beschmiert
sie mit Farben und verweigert ihnen die Erinnerungen« – ziehen
die wahren »Sprachschöpfer« es vor, »ihre Büchsen / an einem
geheimen Ort« zu verstauen (*SM*, 74, 26). Sie begnügen sich mit
»ausgemergelten Geschichten«, es macht ihnen nichts aus, ihre
»Klänge kentern« (*SM*, 43) zu lassen oder zuzusehen, wie »das
Meer rostet« (*FA*, 33).

Die Verlockung, mit exotistischem Material zu arbeiten, es zu
reflektieren oder bis zur Kenntlichkeit zu entstellen, ist in vielen
Texten spürbar. In den glücklichsten Fällen handelt es sich nicht
nur um kritische Gesten und Verkehrungen, sondern um den Versuch, mit der Sprache selbst über dem Abgrund, ja, dem Nichts zu
balancieren und der Fremderfahrung den falschen Boden, den die
Selbstexotisierung verheißt, zu entziehen. »Weder weiß ich wo
meine Beine bleiben / wenn ich schwimme«, beginnt eines der
schönsten Gedichte aus dem Band *Fernwehanstalten*, »noch wo
mein Kopf steht / unter meinen Armen / die Zunge ist fortgerissen
/ ihre Stelle taub [. . .]« (*FA*, 66). Nicht um orientalische Kulissen
und pittoreske Szenarien handelt es sich hier, nicht um die Rück-
kehr in die (falsche) Heimat des Exotismus, sondern darum, sich
mit der radikalsten europäischen Avantgarde, etwa Rimbaudscher
oder Celanscher Prägung, zu verbünden, die Entfremdungser-
fahrung der ästhetischen Moderne auf der Basis der eigenen, sehr
konkreten interkulturellen Fremderfahrung neu auszulegen und
zu radikalisieren:

> das ausgerissene Wild
> irrt in den Städten
> trägt seine nackte Haut durch die Nacht
> ich weiß nicht ob meine Stimme zählt
> wenn ich fortgeh wenn ich bleib
> in meinem einzigen zerrissenen Kleid (*FA*, 66)

Schon diese sporadischen Hinweise machen deutlich, daß Zafer
Şenocak seit Anfang der 90er Jahre sich der Verführung und den
Mechanismen des Exotismus noch unmißverständlicher entziehen
zu müssen glaubt als er es ohnehin schon in seinen früheren Gedichten versucht hatte. Ab Mitte der 90er Jahre wird diese Tendenz

vollends unverkennbar. In Şenocaks Arbeiten läßt sich immerhin eine konkrete Spur verfolgen, die von 1991 (Texten in dem Band *Atlas des tropischen Deutschland*) bis 1994 reicht (*War Hitler Araber?*) und dann in der zweiten Hälfte der 90er Jahre zu einer ganz neuen Schreibweise führt. Der Band mit dem provozierenden Titel *War Hitler Araber? IrreFührungen an den Rand Europas* enthält neben zahlreichen Essays zu deutsch-türkischen Themen auch einen Text mit dem Titel 'Das Leben ist eine Karawanserei', dessen Gattung von der der übrigen Texte absticht: er ist in Versen geschrieben, eine Tatsache, der der Untertitel Rechnung trägt: 'Ein Gedichtessay' (*Hitler*, 55–8). In dieser poetischen Reflexion wird auf den ersten Blick noch mit den Mitteln 'orientalischen' Bilderreichtums gearbeitet: Schon der Derwischspruch der Überschrift mit der 'Karawanserei'-Metapher scheint eine eindeutige Richtung zu weisen, ebenso Begriffe und Formulierungen wie »Wunderlampen«, »verlorene Zungen«, »Schattenreiche«, »das träge Sitzen in Teehäusern«, »Traumbilder«, »Märchen«, »Bauchtänzerin«, »heilige Stätten«, »Djallabija«, um nur einige zu nennen. Auch die Sequenz »ein Minarett bückt sich vor Durst in einen abwesenden Teich / die Kameltreiber haben sich Höhlen aus Schlaf gebaut / mit der Zeit von Spinnen« zeugt offenbar von 'asianischem Stil'. Aber bereits die erste aufmerksame Lektüre des gesamten Textes kann den Leser davon überzeugen, daß Şenocak das orientalistische Bilderarsenal einzig und allein zu dem Zweck verwendet, um es gegen sich selbst, gegen die zugrundeliegenden Ideologeme zu kehren, um, mit anderen Worten, Widerstand zu leisten gegen dasjenige, was wir mit Hijiya-Kirschnereit »Exotisierung« bzw. »Selbstexotisierung« genannt haben.

Wenn Şenocak seinen Gedichtessay mit dem Vers »wir berauschen euch« beginnen läßt, so ruft er ein weiteres Mal die dionysische Projektion des westlichen Orientalismus auf den Plan und schickt sich an, einen lyrisch-essayistischen Zweifrontenkrieg zu führen. Zunächst wird freilich nur eine Front sichtbar: als Gegner der poetischen Polemik erscheinen im folgenden vor allem jene westlichen Exotismusfans, die sich gern »berauschen« lassen, die es lieben, wenn die eingewanderten Dichter »Wunderlampen« auf ihren »Nachttischen« abstellen, wenn sie, »die auf ihre Sprache verzichtet haben«, »Märchen« in der fremden Sprache »erzählen« – denn »nur wenn wir Märchen erzählen sind wir glaubwürdig / nicht wenn ein Märchen uns erzählt und dabei bitter und bitter-böse wird«. Die fremden Dichter werden als Stellvertreter von »Phantasien« in Dienst genommen, die die Gastgeber selbst nicht zu äußern wagen, sie müssen die Vexier- und Spiegelbilder besetzen, den Ort des ganz anderen, nach dem das Abendland begehrt. Einige Varianten dieses reziproken Verhältnisses werden durchgespielt:

> eure Phantasie ist unsere Wirklichkeit
> unsere Wirklichkeit eure Phantasie
> so kommen wir ohne Phantasie aus
> in unserer Wirklichkeit von euch
> so haben wir ein Leben in euren Träumen
> [. . .]
> ein Leben ohne Zauber ohne Märchen ohne Tricks ist illegal
> nur eure Phantasie verleiht unserem Leben Legalität

Und Şenocak fährt fort mit einem die vermeintlichen kulturellen Identitäten verwirrenden Singular-Plural-Spiel, wie man es auch aus seiner bisherigen Lyrik kennt:

> wieviele Personen stellt jeder von uns dar
> wieviele Geschlechter jedes Traumbild
> die Fremde ist immer ein Zenne
> wieviele seid ihr
> seid ihr nur eines
> vereint zu einem
> [. . .]

Doch schon wenig später zeichnet die zweite Front sich ab, nämlich die Phalanx der fremden Dichter selbst, der Migranten, die die Etiketten des Exotismus akzeptieren und den westlichen Phantasmen willfährig entsprechen. Nachdem wir ein weiteres Mal den Refrain sowie die Überschrift in ihrer ausführlichen, sprichwortartigen Form gelesen haben, stoßen wir innerhalb des Gedichtessays auf eine andere literarische Gattung, die der Autor erprobt und – wie man sogleich bemerkt – parodiert: das exotische Märchen. In einer Art Einlage in dem ironisch-sarkastischen Monolog des Textes kehrt die Ich-Erzählerin offensichtlich in ihre orientalische Wüstenheimat, eine Karawanenszenerie, zurück. Sie fabuliert von ihrer Verkleidung (in einen Mann), davon, daß »finstere Gestalten« fremder Karawanen – »mit der Zeit haben sie eine Art Laserblick entwickelt« – die Verkleidung durchschauten und sie

der Reihe nach vergewaltigten; daß sie danach versucht habe, bei
den Frauen Trost zu finden – »denn die Frauen im Orient verstehen sich blind« –, aber stattdessen von diesen »Huren« bestohlen
worden sei. Schließlich habe sie der Karawanenführer, »der mir
versprochen hatte mich ins heilige Land zu führen«, hierher »zu
euch« gebracht – »nur Allah weiß wieviel der Schuft pro Kopf und
Einfall kassiert« – in »dieses kalte Land wo die Kamele sterben /
wo ich von Bürgersaal zu Bürgersaal / auf den Tagen des aus-
ländischen Mitbürgers / meine Kunst vorführen muß«: hier also
trete sie seither auf, »nur mit meinem / Märchen bekleidet [. . .]«
(*Hitler*, 56). Es bedarf kaum einer Erläuterung, daß all die zitierten
Parenthesen nur dazu dienen, orientalistische Klischees – wie Ver-
stellung, Sexualisierung, Archaisierung, Menschenhandel, blinde
Religiosität, Betrug und Gewalt – dingfest und kenntlich zu machen. Der Autor führt in satirischer Überspitzung vor, wie der
Mechanismus der Selbstexotisierung funktioniert, sobald »die
Bühne im Kopf aufgeht«, wie genau die von Edward Said heraus-
gearbeiteten Projektionsfelder auch auf jene Art von Literatur zu-
treffen, mit der 'Märchenerzähler' sich produzieren und
Aufmerksamkeit im 'Gastland' erregen.

Dieser die literarischen Gattungen hybrid vermischende Gedichtessay, der wie nebenbei ein Licht auf die künstlerische und
intellektuelle Spannbreite Zafer Şenocaks wirft (sie reicht vom
feinsinnigen Poeten bis zum gewandten Erzähler und scharfsinni-
gen Analytiker), mag in seiner Deutlichkeit, seiner drängenden, ja
polemischen Kraft für Überraschung sorgen – zumindest unter
denjenigen, die Şenocak als einen eher zurückhaltenden und nach-
denklichen, wenig auf direkte Konfrontation versessenen Schriftsteller kennen. So scheint es in diesem Fall nicht abwegig, einen
konkreten Anlaß für diesen Text zu vermuten. Der Band, der den
Gedichtessay enthält, ist 1994 erschienen. Am Ende des Textes
wird allerdings angemerkt, daß er bereits im August 1991 entstanden sei, in eben jenem Jahr, das als das dreißigste Jahr der Anwer-
bung von türkischen Gastarbeitern in Deutschland in die Annalen
einging, jenem Jahr auch, da erstmals eine türkisch-deutsche Autorin, Emine Sevgi Özdamar, den Ingeborg-Bachmann-Preis erhielt.
Das dreißigste Jahr im übrigen auch für unseren Autor selbst:
Zafer Şenocak wurde 1961 in Ankara geboren.

In dem 1992 erschienenen *Atlas des tropischen Deutschland* findet
sich ein Artikel, der bemerkenswerte Beziehungen zu dem soeben

diskutierten Gedichtessay aufweist. Bei genauerem Hinsehen läßt
sich sogar ein möglicherweise direkter Anlaß für diese poetische
Polemik erkennen. Am Anfang des Essays 'Wann ist der Fremde
zu Hause? Betrachtungen zur Kunst und Kultur von Minderheiten
in Deutschland' stellt Şenocak Überlegungen über die kulturelle
Situation der Migranten »im dreissigsten Jahr der Migration« an.
Er kommt zu dem wenig erfreulichen Schluß, daß im Land der
Gastgeber nicht so sehr ernsthafte literarische Bemühungen von
Migranten gefragt sind als vielmehr »Kebap und Bauchtanz«, oder
allenfalls Texte, die die »Bilder über den Fremden und seine Kultur, die in den Köpfen vorherrschen« bestätigen. Unter diesem
Stichwort fährt Şenocak fort: »Die Türkei beispielsweise ist ein
rückständiges, halbfeudales, muslimisches, also orientalisches
Land. Folglich müssen die türkischen Autoren der Gegenwart exotische Bilder von einer fremden, fernen Welt liefern: Romane, die
auf dem Land spielen, Reportagen über die Unterdrückung der
türkischen Frau, fremde Sitten und Gebräuche, folkloristische Re-
miniszenzen [. . .]« (*Atlas*, 69). Ein besonders exemplarischer Fall
scheint ihm die oben erwähnte Bachmann-Preisträgerin Emine
Sevgi Özdamar zu sein, da mit ihr – so die *Frankfurter Allgemeine
Zeitung* vom 2. Juli 1991 – der »hilflose Text einer deutsch schreibenden Türkin« nominiert worden sei, »der mit folkloristischen
Elementen aus der Märchentradition ihrer Heimat spielt, die von
den Juroren gutmütigerweise für Surrealismus gehalten wurden
[. . .]«. Auch folgenden Satz aus der *FAZ* zitiert Şenocak zustim-
mend: »vor dem Hintergrund zeitgenössischer türkischer Prosa,
die keineswegs naiv ist oder folkloristisch, ist die Wahl absurd, ja
beleidigend«. Şenocak kommentiert: »Wenn türkische Maler oder
Schriftsteller es wagen, Themen der Großstadt, des modernen Lebens, Sexualität und Rollenwechsel zwischen den Geschlechtern,
d.h. die Wirklichkeit in ihrer ganzen Komplexität auf experimen-
telle Art und Weise zu erfassen, fallen sie aus dem Blickwinkel
heraus« (*Atlas*, 69). Schon auf Grund dieser zeitlichen Konstellation
liegt es nahe, in der Bachmann-Preisverleihung (Juli 1991) an eine
Autorin, die ganz offensichtlich Selbstexotisierung betreibt, den
konkreten Anlaß für den polemischen Impetus in dem Gedichtessay (August 1991) zu vermuten. Als weiteres Indiz kann die
Feminisierung des lyrischen Ich angesehen werden. Jeden Zweifel
an diesem Zusammenhang räumt jedoch erst der Titel des Buches
aus, für den Özdamar den begehrten Preis erhielt. Er lautet: *Das*

Leben ist eine Karawanserei / hat zwei Türen / aus einer kam ich rein / aus der anderen ging ich raus.[5] Den gleichen Titel wählte Şenocak, wie wir gesehen haben, für seine poetische Polemik.

Wenn ich diesen Widerstand gegen die Verführung des Exotismus und der Selbstexotisierung so ausführlich kommentiert habe, so nicht nur, weil diese Spur sich auch in Zafer Şenocaks Werk über Jahre, ja ein ganzes Jahrzehnt hin beobachten läßt. Die jüngsten, fast durchweg prosaischen, als 'Roman' gekennzeichneten Werke Şenocaks, wie *Gefährliche Verwandtschaft* (1998) oder *Der Erottomane* (1999), belegen, wie ernst es ihm damit war und ist, moderne deutschsprachige Literatur zu schreiben, Literatur auf der Höhe der Zeit, im *Hic-et-nunc* einer mitteleuropäischen Großstadt – und sich nicht mit jenem schmalen anachronistischen Reservat zu begnügen, das die deutsche Kulturszene den Migranten, den 'Märchenerzählern', den fremden 'Eingeborenen' zugewiesen hat. Noch durch die letzten Seiten des Romans *Gefährliche Verwandtschaft* irrlichtern die 'Märchenerzähler', deren Treiben Şenocak virtuos karikiert:

> Einige arabische und türkische Kollegen hatten inzwischen die Erzählkunst ihrer Urväter entdeckt, die sie in Klassenzimmern in Volkshochschulen und anderen öffentlichen Orten ausübten. Märchen waren wieder erfolgreich. Wer Märchen erzählt, braucht Tiere, die ihn übersetzen. Die bevorzugten Tiere in diesen Texten waren neben Kamelen vor allem Esel. Da in Märchen die Tiere meistens schlauer sind als die Menschen, hatten die Esel immer einen weisen Spruch auf der Zunge. Man spürte, daß sie einen langen Weg zurückgelegt hatten, um zum deutschen Publikum zu sprechen. Ihre Trainer waren Meister ihres Berufs. Sie hatten ihre Tiere für den Besuch in Alamania bestens getrimmt. Die Esel sprachen alle Deutsch, wenn auch ein sonderbares Deutsch, weil sie das, was sie sprachen, nicht auf deutsch dachten. Deutsch ist eine Sprache, in der Esel nicht denken können. (*GV*, 130f.)

Die Tatsache, daß der Widerstand gegen die Märchenerzähler bei Zafer Şenocak so radikal ausfiel, ja nahezu zu einer Abwendung von der früheren Lyrik und ihrer unverwechselbaren Sprache führte, stellt den deutschen Kulturverantwortlichen, den Verlegern, Journalisten, Kulturbürokraten kein sehr rühmliches Zeugnis aus. Der Gattungswechsel von der Lyrik zur Prosa, der sich seit Mitte der 90er Jahre, gleichsam als Konsequenz über viele Jahre hin aufgebauten und aufgestauten Widerstands abzeichnet, impliziert auch einen grundsätzlichen, für manche Şenocak-Leser irritierenden Wechsel der Schreibweise. Die immer deutlicher werdende Verabschiedung der Metapher und die geradezu offensive Hinwendung zu einem schlichten, tagebuchartig-meditativen, möglichst unaufwendigen, unpretentiösen, unmanieristischen Erzählen von Geschichten erweckt mehr und mehr den Eindruck, daß wir es mit einem veränderten, auf neuen Wegen befindlichen Autor zu tun haben: einem Autor, der sich die Art und Weise, wie er seine Fremderfahrungen, Irritationen, Befremdlichkeiten artikuliert, von niemandem mehr vorschreiben lassen will. In einem Aufsatz über 'Literarische Übersetzung: Brücke oder Schwert?' hob Şenocak an einem Divandichter wie Nedim hervor, gerade »der lakonische Stil, die eigenwillige Bilderwelt und der präzise Umgang dieses Dichters mit der Sprache« seien »Charakteristika, die die Vorurteile der Orientalisten in Bezug auf den Stil der osmanisch-türkischen Dichtung widerlegen könnten« (*Hitler*, 52). Zafer Şenocak widerlegt sie auf seine Weise.

Anmerkungen

[1] Irmela Hijiya-Kirschnereit, *Das Ende der Exotik. Zur japanischen Kultur und Gesellschaft der Gegenwart* (Frankfurt am Main, Suhrkamp, 1988), 13–16.

[2] Edward W. Said, *Orientalism* (London, Routledge & Kegan Paul, 1978); *Orientalismus* (Frankfurt am Main; Berlin; Vienna, Ullstein, 1981).

[3] Yunus Emre, *Das Kummerrad / Dertli Dolap*. Aus dem Türkischen von Zafer Şenocak (Frankfurt am Main, Dagyeli, 1986).

[4] Ulrich Beil, 'Zafer Şenocaks ästhetische Subversion', in Irmgard Ackermann (hg.), *Fremde AugenBlicke. Mehrkulturelle Literatur in Deutsch-land* (Bonn, InterNationes, 1996), 141–3.

[5] Emine Sevgi Özdamar, *Das Leben ist eine Karawanserei / hat zwei Türen / aus einer kam ich rein / aus der anderen ging ich raus* (Cologne, Kiepenheuer und Witsch, 1992).

5

Writing Against the Grain:
Zafer Şenocak as Public Intellectual and Writer

MATTHIAS KONZETT

The role of the public intellectual, as Edward Said and Jürgen Habermas agree in otherwise divergent arguments, is strongly defined by the contradictory position of being both an outsider and insider to society.[1] The intellectual, while appealing 'to as wide a public as possible',[2] mimicking the *lingua franca* of society, chooses deliberately the path of 'dissent against the status quo'.[3] Intervening on behalf of public interests, the intellectual never caves in entirely to the demands of the political ideology of the day. 'For the intellectual', as Habermas writes, 'commits himself on behalf of public interests as a sideline . . . without being swallowed up by the organizational forms of political activity.'[4] The intellectual remains stubbornly in a position of what Said characterizes as 'exile and marginal, as amateur'.[5] In the past decade, Zafer Şenocak has occupied this position as one of the most innovative intellectuals and writers in Germany, inserting himself much more boldly than previous German-Turkish writers into the German public sphere, questioning boundaries that are all too neatly drawn between mainstream and minority writers.

However, as I will show in this essay, Şenocak's role as a public intellectual and writer cannot be entirely explained in the traditional mode of rational intervention in the public sphere. While this activity is largely reflected in his essays, it is limited to the role of pedagogy and enlightening an audience in present-day multicultural debates. As a literary author, Şenocak stresses instead the performative aspect of culture and presents a lifeworld that stands in stark contrast to his essays. The enlightenment ethos of the public intellectual is suspended in Şenocak's literary works and makes way for both the symptom formation of social life and the exhilaration of art converting this experience. Social pathology is no longer rationally corrected but is itself accepted as a lived experience, an intensified lifeworld requiring no superadded frameworks. Instead, the symptom, as Lacan would say, is enjoyed and indulged in as the only social reality that is verifiably a part of the author's experience. In doing so, Şenocak's essays and literary works stand in critical relation to one another, delimiting the sphere of practical politics from the aesthetics of cultural symbolization. The writing against the grain typical of the public intellectual is in turn challenged and countered by a literature going against the grain of the enlightened public sphere. Unlike so-called mainstream writers à la Günter Grass, the minority writer emerges immediately as a sociological phenomenon and thus cannot come to art without the burden of legitimating his art as part of a collective effort of recognition. Şenocak, as we will see, challenges this ethical imperative, creating a literature that refuses to provide a social justification for its mere artistic existence.

The rise of multiculturalism, which would appear to allow for a visible position for minorities in Germany, figures centrally in Şenocak's work as an ideological promise divided against itself. As Şenocak's work critically suggests, it is often no more than an invention in which the liberal-minded citizen congratulates him/herself for granting minority cultures their separate space. In reality, however, most Germans avoid any contaminating contact with minorities other than in the form of framing them in manageable terms of oppressed minorities requiring paternalistic care or of exotic and alternative lifestyles as a cure for their own cultural malaise of Western affluence. Şenocak's work counters the facile liberal rhetoric of multiculturalism with a consciously irreverent and satirical perspective, thereby avoiding the often cliché-ridden treatment and discussion of German-Turkish identity. As Leslie Adelson notes:

> Şenocak chastises both xenophobic animosity and xenophilic solidarity, to the extent that they allow only for an encounter (Begegnung) between Self and Other (das Eigene und das Fremde). This sense of facing each other across a firmly entrenched dividing line does not and cannot begin to accommodate the author's perception of a shared culture and history.[6]

Unlike an earlier generation of German-Turkish writers confronting mostly xenophobia in the conservative spectrum of society, Şenocak challenges the liberal camp as well with its complacent and politically correct management of migrant cultures and identities in Germany.

While Şenocak carries out the role of an intellectual writer in exemplary fashion by going against the grain of favourable public opinion, his success as a public intellectual is to a large extent determined by the public he attempts to reach. As Jean-Paul Sartre defines the codependence of writer and audience: 'All works of the mind contain within themselves the image of the reader for whom they are intended.'[7] This essay explores how Şenocak sizes up his audience, both as a critical observer of the German cultural public sphere and as an artist developing anticipatory strategies to force the audience to abandon convenient stereotypes pertaining to so-called minority writers. It will examine some of Şenocak's early prose work, mostly essays written for prominent German newspapers, which show him in the role of the intellectual critic, addressing such topics as the reception of German-Turkish authors as well as the changing cultural climate before and after unification. In this forum, Şenocak reaches a wide audience of newspaper readers but his role remains limited to arguments of enlightenment and is socially predetermined. W. E. B. DuBois's classic question 'How does it feel to be a problem?' lingers still over the corrective activities of the minority intellectual.[8]

The analysis by the author of his targeted sphere of reception in his essays provides the framework for understanding the literary strategies of identification and disassociation with which he subsequently stages the search for cultural identity in his literary prose. Şenocak's prose writings, as we will see, proceed with self-ironic distance. Narratives are never allowed to attain their *telos*, nor protagonists their desired realm of belonging. In this sense, the author not only exacts the intellectual rigour that Theodor Adorno demanded as the modern 'morality of not being at home in one's home'[9] but also gives voice to the inevitable displacement and dislocation that marks all attempts at social communication. The audience for literature, unfortunately, is much more limited and therefore undercuts the writer's appeal to a mainstream audience. This uneven balance between loss and gain in the forums of literature and public debate would seem to characterize the complex situation of the minority writer, having to manage the need for improved understanding and the need for achieving a live presence in the forms of social communication that are presently available. In spite of this dual thrust of Şenocak's work, the author's themes and concerns remain coherent and consistent with one another. The two genres offer merely different strategies of entering different communicative spheres and create a productive tension between corrective social intervention in public arenas and expression of the various symbolic distortions of social life as we come to know them before any corrective reflection can occur. It is particularly this latter aspect that characterizes the lived dimension of the work of art in which elective affiliation of life form prevails over social determination.

The Public Intellectual

Beginning with Şenocak's essays, I will consider how the author assesses his public and seeks to correct common stereotypes of and expectations placed upon minority writers. An immediate concern is the role of minority writing in Germany. Can this form of literature become mainstream currency in an already reduced public sphere of literary readers? Published in the aftermath of German unification, Şenocak's essay 'Wann ist der Fremde zu Hause?' (*Atlas*, 64–75) critically examines the reception of so-called foreign art and culture produced by residents of Turkish origin, the largest minority group in Germany. The general xenophobia in the political landscape, he notes, is curiously paralleled in the general lack of interest in the art of foreign residents:

> Doch betrachtet man die mangelhafte Rezeption der Kunst von Einwanderern durch deutsche Medien, dann fällt auf, daß die deutsche kulturelle Szene ein Spiegelbild der politischen ist, wenn es darum geht, die Anwesenheit von Einwanderern in Deutschland zu ignorieren. In dieser Szene haben sich Inseln gebildet, von denen aus manche, wenige Kulturvermittler quasi als Botschafter mit den ausländischen Künstlern, die sich am Rande der Kulturszene befinden, verkehren. Hier ein Professor, dort ein Kritiker, hier und da einige Kleinverleger, alle im schönen Gefühl, durch die Entdeckung multikulturellen Lebens etwas Avantgardistisches zu tun. (*Atlas*, 65–6)

Şenocak is wary not only of the arrogance with which a seemingly native culture celebrates itself but also of the facile conversion of German immigrant literatures into an area of specialization that no longer touches upon the entire public sphere. The jealously guarded and limited recognition of minorities, among an avant-garde of liberals, pushes them back into camps without wider public significance. As camps, they can be conveniently called upon if the nation needs to illustrate its multicultural standing, but can also be ignored when so-called German questions are at stake. Leslie Adelson alerts us to the fact that the politically correct and fashionable category of *Migrantenliteratur* 'perpetuates the notion that this body of literature is at best an expendable "enrichment" to "native" German literature'.[10] A social categorization guaranteeing the visibility of a minority, it appears, renders minority literature invisible due to its perceived special nature and interest.

Reviewing in similarly sceptical fashion the changing political and cultural climate of post-unification Germany, in 1992 Şenocak notes with early apprehension an increased deterioration of Germany's post-national culture that once drew its impulses from a variety of cultural backgrounds and allowed for a looser definition of German identity:

> Wer in den siebziger und achtziger Jahren in Deutschland aufwuchs, deutsche Schulen besuchte, konnte getrost auf Symbole verzichten. Kein Fahnenappell, wie in der Türkei heute noch üblich, kein National-gefühl, das sich ständig selbst zitieren muß. Auch die türkischen Symbole wurden von jedem von uns anders wahrgenommen, ergaben längst kein allen gemeines Gruppengefühl. Die türkische Minderheit ist auf dem langen Weg gewesen zur kosmopolitischen Gruppierung, und das in einem mitteleuropäischen Land, das sich einer übernation-alen Idee von einem vereinten Europa verschrieben hatte, mit starken pazifistischen Tendenzen. Nationale oder nationalistische Ziele wur-den nicht mehr von gesellschaftragenden Kräften verfolgt, sondern waren zu identitätsstiftenden Fiktionen von Randgruppen geworden. (*Atlas*, 21)

Turkish nationalism, as Şenocak observes critically, had no counterpart in the liberal political climate of West Germany that allowed instead for a higher degree of elective affiliation and thus for a cosmopolitan identity. Shortly after unification, however, Germany's once supranational climate suddenly has given way to rallying cries for new national standards of inclusion and exclusion. Contrary to the pervading euphoria over Germany's regained national territory, Şenocak notes with perplexity that even liberals are beginning to affirm a return to nationalism. 'Was ist in der Zwischenzeit, in der relative kurzen Zeitspanne seit der Maueröff-nung im November 1989 passiert,' he asks, 'daß ein Ex-Bundeskanzler dieser offenen, liberalen, kosmopolitischen orien-tierten Bundesrepublik [. . .] die linksliberalen Intellektuellen

bezichtigt, voreilig die vom Volk weiterhin geteilten Nationalge-
fühle über Bord geworfen zu haben' (*Atlas*, 21). Leading liberal
intellectuals and writers such as Helmut Schmidt, Martin Walser
and Botho Strauss have quickly abandoned their former post-
national positions to redefine German nationhood once again as a
sheltering identity of belonging, a category reserved for German
natives sharing the values of Western Christian culture. Şenocak
considers, for example, Helmut Schmidt's dubious statement
drawing a sharp line between Western and non-Western cultures:
'Die Türken als weitgehend muslimische Nation gehören einem
ganz anderen Kulturkreis an, der seine Heimat in Asien und Af-
rika hat, nicht aber in Europa'.[11] In an era of perceived crisis
marked by encroaching globalization, increased economic compe-
tition, erosion of cultural traditions, continued demands for Germany's historical accountability for the Holocaust, and
demographic changes in Germany's population, the once out-
moded term of nationhood is re-evaluated by conservatives and
liberals alike.

In his essay 'Nation, race, and immigration', Andreas Huyssen,
adopting a critical transatlantic perspective, attributes this resur-
gence of nationalism to a lack of concrete engagement with national identity prior to unification. He argues that Germany, by
insisting on its exceptionalism ('Sonderweg'), has displayed
merely a guilt-ridden 'postnational arrogance' rather than a true
cosmopolitan cultural climate. As a liberal, Huyssen too advocates
a reorientation towards nationhood, albeit in more pragmatic and
open terms of redefining citizenship: 'The nation state is still a fact
of life, and it will produce forms of belonging and identity needs
that cannot in all instances be satisfied by the abstract-universalist
principles of the constitution.'[12] Huyssen thinks in particular of the
long overdue reform of citizenship and immigration laws, never
embarked upon during Germany's divided post-war history.
Based on outdated concepts of biological nationhood, until recently citizenship laws remained highly restrictive and in themselves constituted a hidden national symbolism marking presumed
Germans from non-Germans. Contrary to Habermas's colour-blind
and neutral constitutional patriotism, ·Huyssen argues for civil
rights that 'involve cultural properties, traditions, memories, language'.[13] In Huyssen's analysis, extended citizenship along with an
enhanced immigration politics play a key role in the multicultural
reconfiguration of Germany. He calls on 'the democratic left to

reoccupy the discursive terrain of the nation',[14] and thereby move forward with the integration of Germany's migrant communities. With this pragmatic approach, informed by America's citizenship and immigration practices, Huyssen hopes to install and uphold a multicultural and Western democratic tradition from within Germany's political landscape. Trying to dispel the myth of Germany's exceptionalism, Huyssen asserts that 'Westernization and reconciliation in the broadest sense, while never complete, have functioned as powerful forces of "normalization" in Germany'.[15]

Although recent reforms of the citizenship laws are highly relevant in redefining and updating legal rights of residence, they cannot entirely assure a cultural recognition that is based for the most part on cognitive criteria beyond passports and documents. These criteria are often based on perceived differences between Western and non-Western cultures. Attributing a democratic deficit to countries outside the West (thereby concealing the West's own inability to meet these standards), these stereotypes place the non-Westerner under continual scrutiny in the West.[16] As Şenocak, a thoroughly acculturated German, soberly notes:

> Nach wie vor sehen die Deutschen jedweder Gesinnung in uns die Fremden. Selbst wenn man ihrer Sprache schreibt, bleibt man ein Exot, ein Eindringling, wird teils bewundernd, teils mißtrauisch inspiziert. Ein Türke liest den Koran, geht nicht in die Oper. Rassismus dieser Art braucht keine Keule, keine Nürnberger Gesetze, er wirkt intellektuell, über die Bilder im Kopf, durch unsichtbare und deshalb schier unüberwindliche Zäune. (*Atlas*, 22)

Due to deeply engrained habits of cultural perception, the reception of Turkish-German culture remains stuck in old stereotypes. Sympathetic calls for integration, such as Huyssen's, cannot surmount the invisible barriers that are already in place in such loaded terminology concerning the imagined differences between Western and non-Western cultures. Likewise, Turkish-German writers do not elicit the broader interest such as is granted, for instance, to British minority writers like Salman Rushdie, Hanif Kureishi or Zadie Smith who, in spite of controversy, benefit from a tradition (however problematic) of Commonwealth cosmopolitanism. In Germany, the slow path towards cosmopolitanism has come to an unexpected halt after unification, forcing Turkish-German writers to begin yet again from point zero. While literary criticism from abroad, particularly in the US and the United Kingdom, continues to sustain an interest in Turkish-German literature, it has yet to have a concrete impact on Germany's cultural sphere.[17]

The Writer

The sobering reality of Germany's cultural climate in the 1990s has found its way into Şenocak's recent literary prose, but it has not resulted in the popular accounts of victimization now so commonly found in conventional minority writings. Instead, the author has remained faithful to his intellectual stance by maintaining an ironic distance from all forms of sentimental identity politics. His literary prose can be seen as a synthesis of his earlier engagement with poetry and his expository essays for newspaper feuilletons. As a poet in the tradition of Ingeborg Bachmann and Günther Eich, Şenocak initially experimented in a lyrical and subjective mode. The phenomenon of cultural displacement is grasped in an existential, surreal-expressionist manner in volumes such as *Elektrisches Blau* (1983), *Flammentropfen* (1985), *Das senkrechte Meer* (1991) and *Fernwehanstalten* (1994). Alongside these works, Şenocak published a series of critical essays in various German dailies, challenging prevalent stereotypes pertaining to Turkish culture. *War Hitler Araber?* (1991), a collection of these essays, responds to the Gulf war and its xenophobic spectre of an anti-Western Islamic conspiracy. *Atlas des tropischen Deutschlands* (1993) attacks among other things the notion that Turks must forever remain a proletarian migrant culture in Germany, and attests to a growing critical awareness of the one-dimensionality of mainstream discourses on minorities.

More recently, Şenocak has found in his literary prose the perfect medium for the critical talent with which he challenges the sanctimonious expectations that are brought to so-called minority causes. These sometimes well-meant approaches quickly end up reifying the image of the Turkish resident in clichéd scenarios of cultural and linguistic illiteracy, socio-economic dependence and religious fundamentalism conflicting with Western secular values. As an alternative to these scenarios, Şenocak takes up the productive genre of the detective story, which other migrant writers like Aras Ören or, more recently, second-generation writers like Dilek Zaptçıoğlu and Hilal Sezgin have converted into a paradigmatic narrative depicting the search for ethnic and cultural identity.[18] In his story collection, *Der Mann im Unterhemd* (1995), Şenocak all but eliminates the sociological residues of his precursors to gain a fresh and unorthodox insight into the complexity of Turkish-German identity. The opening story 'Fliegen', for example, evokes the detective genre merely as a clichéd convention wherein a detective for 'multicultural' crimes enters into a futile search for criminal clues tarnished by cultural stereotypes. The search for a young woman, presumed abducted by Islamic fundamentalists, ends on a farcical and anticlimactic note when the detective discovers that she has faked her abduction in order to become an airline stewardess. The story parodies the predictable responses of German readers to Turkish culture. In keeping with the detective-story genre, it provides the reader with false clues based on stereotypical perceptions of Islamic conspiracy plots, only to end on another stereotype, that of the immigrant parvenu and economic opportunist.

A further target of Şenocak's black and subversive humour is the pious discourse of intercultural hermeneutics by which the 'foreign otherness' of an immigrant culture can be experienced through 'Betroffenheit', a form of empathetic intersubjectivity.[19] Şenocak questions this naive concept of intercultural empathy in his depiction of uncomfortable and problematic encounters with 'das Fremde' (the foreign, the other) in which the foreign resists domestication and instead disrupts the routine of German native habits. Şenocak's prose frequently launches into pornographic episodes that haunt the reader with his/her own stereotypes pertaining to the hypersexuality attributed to Mediterranean ('südländisch') or 'Oriental' cultures. The encounter with Turkish culture is far from easily accessible and is not served ready-made for intercultural consumption, but instead evokes viscerally xenophobic fears of threat, physical invasion and domination.

Die Prärie (1997) extends Şenocak's critical perspective in a more humorous fashion, parodying the author's own complicit role in a commodity culture that markets identity and multiculturalism. Sascha, the narrator, is a second-rate 'intercultural' writer rushing from one liaison to the next in which women serve him mainly for sexual gratification. In between these adventures, he takes up writing assignments for German journals and newspapers. Asked to write an essay about the fatwa against Salman Rushdie, as a presumed expert on Islam due to his Turkish background, Sascha copies the information from various handbooks and, in spite of many transcription errors, is able to satisfy an uncritical public demand for 'authentic' commentary on Islamic matters. This novel reflects a new stage in German ethnic literature, with its critique of its own commodity value on the literary market. Not surprisingly, the figure of Sascha eventually makes himself independent from the author's control and disappears into the Romantic myth of the American prairie. The novel ends with the author's apology for not being able to deliver to the reader the expected closures and redemptive images of his Turkish-German hero:

> Mir fehlt der Schluß. Sascha läßt sich irgendwie nicht beenden. Jetzt ist Marianne aufgetaucht, und alles droht wieder von vorne zu beginnen. Eine furchtbar langweilige Person, diese Marianne. Sie schneidet mich. Doch das ist mir letzten Endes egal. Wer interessiert sich schon für eine Frau, die sich Tag und Nacht mit Sprache beschäftigt. Die verwandelt jeden Menschen, der ihr begegnet, in Wörter. Selbstverständlich auch die Männer. Im Moment hat sie sich an Sascha herangemacht. Sie wird ihm weismachen wollen, wie wichtig korrektes Deutsch für den Sexgenuß ist. Vielleicht interessiert den deutschen Leser eine derartige Figur. Die Deutschen finden Leute, die sich wichtig machen, immer wichtiger als sie sind. Ohne Dünkel kommt man in Deutschland unter die Räder. (*P*, 102–3)

In comical distance to the German high seriousness represented by the German teacher Marianne, the author fears for his hero in case he should return to Germany. As in *Der Mann im Unterhemd*, Şenocak undercuts the heavy-handed enlightenment ethos that dominates the discussion of German minorities, turning it into a laughing matter. In Bakhtin's sense of carnivalization, Şenocak explodes the genre of minority writing and restores its openness and potential as a genre yet to be discovered. As one critic puts it: 'Das Subjekt, das sich mitteilt, ist sich selber eine fremde Person, die, wie es an einer Schlüsselstelle heißt, jemand anderen fragen müßte, sich dekodieren zu lassen.'[20]

In the novel *Gefährliche Verwandtschaft* (1999), Şenocak continues his enigmatic story about Sascha Muhteschem but pays greater attention to the hero's origins. Born to a German Jewish mother and a Turkish father, Sascha now exhibits a more crucial border position in the cultural negotiation of conflicting identities and legacies. After the sudden death of his parents in a car accident, Sascha inherits the diaries of his Turkish grandfather written between 1916 and 1936, an era that saw the demise of the Ottoman Empire and the emergence of modern Turkey. Since he cannot read the diaries of his grandfather, which are written in Arabic and

Cyrillic scripts, he sets out to reconstruct his family genealogy from memory and imagination in order to uncover the story behind his grandfather's mysterious suicide. This approach contrasts with that of his German girlfriend Marie, who is putting together a purely factual documentary film on Talat Pascha, the Turkish politician responsible for the deportation of hundreds of thousands of Armenians and their ensuing genocide, who was assassinated in Berlin in 1921.

The novel, moving freely between fact and fiction, shows the complexity of German–Turkish relations both past and present. Sascha's maternal Jewish grandfather, for example, finds asylum with his family in Turkey during the Nazi era. This individual story is complemented by historical accounts of friendly Muslim–Jewish relations during the Ottoman era and Turkey's former alliance with the German Empire. These multicultural configurations and legacies seem negated by the genocidal history of both countries and by their present uneasy relationship with one another. In the figure of Sascha's paternal grandfather, the novel also documents a thoroughly Western and secular Turkish tradition that is frequently denied to Turkey as a so-called 'Oriental' country, said to be outside the sphere of European culture. Sascha's own position within Germany as an assimilated part-Turkish resident throws further light on the limitations of liberalism and its multicultural categories that, while dismantling old stereotypes, erect new ones in their place. Sascha, for example, fails to benefit from his Jewish origins like other fellow writers in an era of philo-Semitism, while he is also not perceived as a genuine Turkish-German writer since he fails to reflect the proper class background as a migrant labourer. In an era marked by identity politics, his out-of-the-ordinary status of having a mixed lineage prevents him from gaining access to any of the ethnic camps, be they Jewish, Turkish or German.

This impasse in cross-cultural relations is underscored by the novel's ending. It appears that Sascha discovers the cause of his grandfather's suicide after having the diaries deciphered and translated by a multilingual expert. Sascha's grandfather ends his life just as he is about to accompany the Turkish team to the Olympic Games of 1936 in Berlin, upon receiving a letter from his former Armenian lover who escaped the genocide by going into exile. While it cannot be determined whether this is the 'true' cause of the suicide or Sascha's own invention, the symbolic significance of this act elucidates not only the private but also the political impasse surrounding the fate of the grandfather. As suggested by the text's complex figuration of setting, the grandfather appears to have internalized the fate of exile of the persecuted Armenian lover. Through his suicide he protests against Turkey's genocidal politics and rejects his national affiliation with Turkey as a competitor in the Olympic Games. He fails to arrive in Berlin, where another genocide is being prepared. Figuratively, the novel evokes two genocidal histories which mirror one another in the death of the grandfather. The novel, which ends on the stillbirth of a mutual critical encounter between German and Turkish history, spells out the legacy yet to be sorted out by the post-war generation. For Barbara Frischmuth, the novel amounts to a 'Forderung nach einer Auflösung der deutsch-jüdischen Dichotomie durch einen Trialog zwischen Deutschen, Juden und Türken'.[21] The call for the binary politics of German–Jewish or German–Turkish relations to be replaced with a multi-directional form of multiculturalism can be seen as an attempt to reverse the one-sided direction of majority–minority dialogue. It further provides a critical perspective for the realistic implementation of multiculturalism in Germany, one in which immigrant generations will have been superseded by thoroughly acculturated Turkish-German citizens demanding to be recognized as citizens first and not merely as representatives of a minority point of view.

Contrary to the normative and legal debates on citizenship which are beginning to dominate all discussions concerning cultural affiliation, Şenocak is, however, wary of liberal concepts like residence and successful acculturation. While these concepts are absolutely essential in guaranteeing a minimum of civil rights, they cannot summarize the aspirations of a migrant culture nor of a national culture for Şenocak, the writer:

> Selbst wenn sie hier Wurzeln schlagen und ihre Herkunft wie eine Pusteblume von sich blasen, müssen sie sich fragen, ob ihre Assimilation als Preis hoch genug ist, um die Reise nach Deutschland beenden zu dürfen, um das Haus am Ziel als das eigene zu bezeichnen. Vielleicht handelt es sich bei der Reise nach Deutschland nicht um eine Reise in ein Land [...] sondern um einen Gemütszustand, einen seelischen Raum, der unerreichbar bleibt. (*Atlas*, 23)

The act of refusing oneself the illusion of total residence and acculturation, of following Adorno's self-imposed imperative of 'not being at home in one's home', occupies the centre of Şenocak's work. It accounts for the split figuration of Şenocak's hero in his most recent novel *Der Erottomane* (1999), a hero who becomes involved in a mysterious murder case in Berlin, while simultaneously embarking on an imaginary eastward journey along the Silk Road. Indeed, the entire novel restores the enigma at the centre of migrant cultures and their representatives.

The story begins with the mysterious murder of R., as reconstructed by the unnamed German-Turkish narrator and his friend Tom (formerly known by his Turkish name Tayfun), the district attorney handling the case. In a maze of imaginary accounts, real and imaginary writings left by the victim, the story unfolds increasingly into an undecipherable mystery in which the case of R. was apparently invented by the DA for the sheer pleasure and pretext of writing. Upon this discovery, the narrator offers his own first speculative chapter on the case, ending the work in circular fashion on the mystery with which it began. Much of the story focuses on a possible sex crime and on an obsessive engagement with pornography which either made the victim vulnerable to the crime or led to his inviting it upon himself in an act of final ecstasy. In this speculative story where neither the crime nor its cause or motive can ever be truly identified, pornography becomes a cipher for the act of writing: 'Es interessierte ihn nicht, ob das alles gestellt war oder echt. Er hatte es längst aufgegeben, das Echte von der Fälschung zu unterscheiden. Alles im Leben erschien ihm echt wie auch gefälscht. Genau wie seine Geschichten' (*E*, 108).

This undecidability of fact and veracity is stressed by the text's frequent confusion of narrative voice. At the end of the section 'Texte aus dem Nachlaß von R.', for example, the reader is suddenly informed that these texts were not, as earlier indicated, those left behind by the victim, but had rather been invented by Tom, who has become a type of closet writer: 'Ein paar Tage später erhielt ich von Tom tatsächlich einige Texte aus dem Nachlaß von R., die ich für mich "Das Findelbuch des Erottomanen" nannte' (*E*, 14). We do not know whether the subsequent 'foundling book' section (where 'Findelbuch' also serves as subtitle for the whole novel) is actually by the victim or still by Tom, the aspiring writer. In addition, some sections on travelling clearly spell out the fantasies of the initial narrator: they may be his own writings, but possibly also written by Tom slipping into his role. The mystery is seemingly solved towards the end when the narrator writes:

Doch einige Details in Toms Prosa, die er mir als Nachlaß von R. zum
Lesen gab, hatten mich Verdacht schöpfen lassen. Meine Recherchen
bei der Polizei ergaben, daß der Tote ein Fernmeldetechniker gewesen
war, der einem brutalen Raubmord zum Opfer gefallen war. Tom war
in meinen Augen ein Schriftsteller, auch wenn er sich nicht zu seinen
Geschichten bekannte. (*E*, 106)

The emphasis on an imagined rather than inherited estate ulti-
mately stresses the autonomy of writing that prevails over identities of contingency and circumstance.

As Şenocak's most radical text so far, *Der Erottomane* entirely
does away with our conventional notions of minority writing and
appears to have moved towards a first avant-garde treatment of
ethnicity, refusing to accept assigned social and cultural identities
but instead subjecting them to a process of aesthetic play and
variation. Indeed, ethnicity is barely touched upon, but is presented along with other destabilized identities of sexuality and
nationhood in an exploration of uncharted territories of identity
across settings in the former Soviet Union, Paris and Berlin (reminiscent of Joseph Roth's diaspora novel *Flucht ohne Ende*). In contrast to the traditional avant-garde that demands a politicization of
aesthetic values and institutions, Şenocak's ethnic avant-garde
aims towards a depoliticization of a politically over-determined
identity. The pathological qualities of cultural displacement are
acknowledged through the stress on pornography as the correl-
ative of the invasive and voyeuristic close-up examination of the
foreigner. At the same time, this pathology is embraced, treated as
a potential aesthetic framework for the testing and rehearsal of
unstable identities. What appears as an over-determining sociological and political situation makes way for the author's *jouissance*
that reconverts cultural stereotypes into productive forms of intensified aesthetic pleasure/unpleasure.

The Intellectual Writer
Şenocak's work as an intellectual and writer calls for a rethinking
of the concept of citizenship beyond its legal implications as an
ongoing and developing social and civic partnership. It has often
been pointed out that Germany's concept of citizenship is prob-
lematically rooted in organic and biological notions of blood lineage. A recent shift towards an American-style concept of *jus soli*, in
which territory rather than birth is the defining characteristic of
citizenship, is supposed to remedy the situation. However, even

here, the biological act of being born not unto a biological people but unto a territory emphasizes inheritance rather than social action based upon assumed responsibility. In this legal configuration of citizenship, the migrant is still seen as the latecomer to a national territory, whereas the native-born readily takes his citizenship for granted. National life, as Benedict Anderson has compellingly argued, cannot be reduced to legal codes but is built on complex forms of elective imaginings defining social, moral and existential affiliation.[22] Concepts of coexistence must be based on forms of civic hospitality that meet the migrant halfway rather than merely condescend to acts of tolerance.

In a recent study, Yasemin Soysal has shown that the scope of citizenship and cultural affiliation in European nation states depends largely on national models of social organization. These models range from self-management corporatist (Sweden, the Netherlands), to liberal (Switzerland, United Kingdom) and statist paradigms (France).[23] Germany, she argues, is socially the most cohesively organized country, and it handles the question of acculturation through strong collective intervention on the level of both corporate and state regulation.[24] It is not surprising, then, that collective attitudes towards migrant communities flourish particularly in Germany, where the state demonstrates such attitudes through its own example. Unlike the liberal model, which places the entire burden of acculturation on the success or failure of the individual, the statist-corporatist model of managing acculturation involves strong interventions on behalf of migrant groups through public institutions (such as 'Ausländerbehörden') and encouragements to self-organize in nationally or religiously specific migrant associations. Compared with other models, this approach may guarantee a higher degree of regulation of immigration flow along with efficient provision of social welfare benefits. But this is bought at the cost of achieving a form of individual acculturation which proceeds at one's own pace. It confines the immigrant to the position of a state-monitored minority. For the intellectual, who wishes to dissolve any inherited identity so as to choose his or her particular cultural affiliations freely, this type of collective framing poses a serious problem.

For an intellectual, it is not sufficient to critique society from a position of ideology, claiming to possess the correct political truth as opposed to one's adversaries. Şenocak rejects such a privileged point of view and remains an uncomfortable observer of all parties involved. In his case, as we have seen, it becomes necessary to remain unpredictable as a Turkish-German citizen in order to ensure that he is perceived first of all as an individual in the face of the predictable identities that society obliges him to assume. In this respect, his work rejects the sentimental myths of oppressed and model minorities, and of all collective identities other than those chosen deliberately by the author. And yet Şenocak's critical manoeuvres aiming to defend the integrity of his individuality remain incomplete unless they are reciprocated on the level of public reception in a critical spirit of poetic renewal. This is what Şenocak's work calls for, and his strength lies in his vision of a radically democratic Germany where Germans and Turkish Germans encounter one another on an equal economic, social and cultural footing. Will mainstream German society be able to accept the Turkish-German citizen competing with 'white' Germans at all levels? Will it have space for assimilated and well-educated Turks who break with cultural stereotypes of the migrant labourer ('Ein Türke geht nicht in die Oper', a stereotype exposed in the essay of the same title, *Atlas*, 20–30), speak standard German and display an intimate knowledge of German culture? Will citizenship be understood as the active formation of social and civic affiliations beyond the legal minimum of mere tolerance and have its roots in aesthetically shared and mediated forms of culture? And will these aesthetic negotiations be conducted in new forms of discursive and institutional practices that include participants as individual voices and not merely as representatives of collective groups?

Şenocak, as this essay has attempted to show, balances the needs of pedagogy and cultural performance in two complementary writing roles, namely that of the cultural intellectual/critic and that of the imaginative writer. These two activities stand in a dialectic relation to one another and secure Şenocak the position of a complex intellectual writer, defying the stereotypical genres and categories of migrant writing. He resembles instead the complex profiles of Viennese Jewish writers at the turn of the last century, with their sophisticated interventions in the cultural public sphere as a group between migration and assimilation. Unfortunately, Şenocak's unique stance has yet to be fully recognized as reflecting not only the point of view of a minority but also much more broadly, that of the new multicultural Germany. For multiculturalism is more than a paradigm for accommodating the increasing range of migrant cultures across the European continent; it seeks also to disrupt the myths of indigenous, native or anterior cultures.

Notes

[1] Edward W. Said, *Representations of the Intellectual* (New York, Vintage, 1996); Jürgen Habermas, 'Heinrich Heine and the role of the intellectual in Germany', *The New Conservatism: Cultural Criticism and the Historians' Debate*, ed. and trans. Shierry Weber Nicholsen (Cambridge, MA, MIT Press, 1992).

[2] Said, xiii.

[3] Ibid., xvii.

[4] Habermas, 87.

[5] Said, xvi.

[6] Leslie Adelson, 'Coordinates of orientation: an introduction', *ATG*, xi-xxxvii (xxix).

[7] Jean-Paul Sartre, *What is Literature? and Other Essays* (Cambridge, MA., Harvard University Press, 1988), 73.

[8] W. E. B. DuBois, *The Souls of Black Folk* (New York, Vintage, 1990), 7.

[9] Theodor Adorno, *Minima Moralia: Reflections from Damaged Life*, trans. E. F. N. Jephcott (London, Verso, 1999), 39.

[10] Leslie Adelson, 'Opposing oppositions', *German Studies Review* 17, 2 (1994), 305–30 (305).

[11] Helmut Schmidt, quoted in *Hitler*, 5.

[12] Andreas Huyssen, 'Nation, race and immigration: German identities after unification', *Twilight Memories* (New York, Routledge, 1995), 77.

[13] Ibid., 83.

[14] Ibid., 84.

[15] Ibid., 71.

[16] Jürgen Habermas locates the democratic deficit in Germany more specifically than Huyssen with the former East Germany, thereby refraining from using the term Western democracy in a broader and discriminatory fashion. See Jürgen Habermas, 'The normative deficits of unification', *The Past as Future*, trans. Max Pensky (Lincoln and London, University of Nebraska Press, 1994), 33–54.

[17] This statement is not meant as a criticism of the important work done by American and British scholars on German-Turkish literature. It merely aims to note its as yet limited reach into German culture.

[18] See Aras Ören, *Bitte nix Polizei* (Düsseldorf, Claassen, 1981; repr. Berlin, Fischer, 1983) and the 'sequel' *Berlin Savignyplatz* (Berlin, Espresso,

1995); Hilal Sezgin, *Der Tod des Massschneiders* (Hamburg, Hoffmann und Campe, 1999); Dilek Zaptçıoğlu, *Der Mond frisst die Sterne auf* (Stuttgart, Thienemann, 1999). The type of the Turkish private eye was established by the non-Turkish writer Jakob Arjouni in *Happy Birthday, Türke* (Zürich, Diogenes, 1987) and several subsequent 'Kayankaya' novels.

[19] The debate between intercultural hermeneutics and a more sober cultural studies approach to German-Turkish culture has led to an interesting critical exchange between Ülker Gökberk and Leslie Adelson in the American reception of German-Turkish literature. See Gökberk, 'Culture Studies und die Türken', *The German Quarterly* 70, 2 (1997), 97–122; Adelson's response in 'Forum', *The German Quarterly* 70, 3 (1997), 277–82.

[20] Hans-Jürgen Heise, 'Mit kalkuliertem Unschuldsblick', *Süddeutsche Zeitung*, 23 October, 1997.

[21] Barbara Frischmuth, 'Der Blick des Randgängers. Ein Roman von Zafer Şenocak', *Neue Zürcher Zeitung*, 7 April, 1999.

[22] Benedict Anderson, *Imagined Communities* (London, Verso, 1991). See particularly Anderson's discussion of what motivates sacrifice in war. According to Anderson, willingness to die for one's country derives from quasi-religious national imaginings rather than concrete political ideologies ('Cultural roots', 9–12).

[23] Yasemin Nuhoğlu Soysal, *Limits of Citzenship: Migrants and Postnational Membership in Europe* (Chicago, University of Chicago Press, 1994), 36–41.

[24] Ibid., 77-8.

6

Odysseus on the Ottoman, or 'The Man in Skirts': Exploratory Masculinities in the Prose Texts of Zafer Şenocak

MORAY McGOWAN

The *Odyssey*, that formative European text, already displays tensions between purpose and aimlessness, order and chaos, the charted and the chartless, the linear and the amorphous, tensions resolved to the advantage of the former. European culture's subsequent polarization, in all its countless modulations, of Europe and Asia, Occident and Orient, is prefigured here, if not as schematically as this brief summary suggests. In the *Odyssey*, *telos* finally triumphs over indirection. Odysseus loses his way, but not his goal; he finds his way home, routs the indolent suitors and reasserts himself as the man of the house, as an 'Europäer',[1] by firing an arrow die-straight through twelve axeheads.

Three millennia later, post-colonial cultural perspectives are insistently questioning a European Enlightenment which all too often interwove cartography, gender and nationalism into fabrics of dominance. Meanwhile, the Turkish diaspora has placed the German Turk Zafer Şenocak in the 'kaltes Europa' of Berlin (*E*, 125), where, unmapping as he unmans, he writes texts which insistently destabilize the boundaries of the narrating and narrated self and apparently fixed constructions of gender, sexual, national and ethnic identity. At the turn of the twentieth to the twenty-first century, Şenocak is writing in a world of 'leaky bodies and boundaries'[2] in a multiple sense. Both the theoretical abstractions of post-modernism and post-structuralism and the material realities of international migration and communication, of prosthetic surgery, genetic engineering and new reproductive technologies, have come to challenge the once stable taxonomies of the patriarchal Enlightenment. They challenge too the drive for epistemological control via charts and classifications, and the closely related, gendered oppositions of inferior female chaos and superior male order, amorphousness and pattern, anarchy and discipline, the rhizome and the linear form.

Leaky Bodies and Boundaries is the title of a recent study by Margot Shildrick of the relationship between gender-related discourses of power and the implications of new reproductive technologies. As her subtitle *Feminism, Postmodernism and Bio-ethics* suggests, Shildrick's is a feminist project. In a time of crisis for masculinity,[3] a world of 'Herrscher, die ihre Herrschaftsgebiete verloren hatten. Lauter enttäuschte Tamerlans, die sich in winzige Appartements zurückgezogen hatten' (*E*, 65–6), Şenocak's reappropriation for his male characters of the fluidities and flexibilities which feminism has laboriously identified, relegitimated and rendered available to the post-modern self, is complex and indeed ambivalent.

Firstly, precisely in its flux, gender functions in his work as a metaphorical site for the questioning of ethnic identity, of the fixed simplifications of the relationship of the German and the Turk.[4] These were always rendered doubtful, in fact, by Turkey's own multiple ambivalences: European and Asian, grounded in Islamic culture yet constitutionally secular, heir to numerous ancient indigenous cultures yet also product of complex historical migrations, semi-feudal over much of its vast rural regions yet the world's thirteenth largest economy. Turkey is, in a sense, a microcosm of larger apparent oppositions which are in fact complex interminglings. As Şenocak's poem 'Archivare in Istanbul' observes, 'Europa ist eine Abart Asiens / Asien eine Abart Europas' (*SM*, 9).

Since the beginning of the numerically significant migration of Turks to Germany in the 1960s, new levels of complexity have been added. 'Germany's resident Turks' are not simply Turks transplanted, but a constantly developing, internally differentiated population in their own right, an important and dynamically changing factor in the still unsettled cultural contours of unified Germany.[5] Where Turkish intellectuals in Turkey display, in the ambivalence of their relationship to Europe, what Şenocak has called a 'gebrochener Blick nach Westen',[6] Şenocak typifies those Turkish intellectuals in Germany who engage fully in German cultural debate and refuse any kind of ghettoization. He feels himself, as the figure R. in his text *Der Erottomane* puts it, 'als halber Asiate, als ganzer Europäer. [. . .] Ich bin in allen Metropolen Europas zu Hause, bin hier unter Meinesgleichen' (*E*, 16). This self-positioning of many Turkish intellectuals leads also to what one can call a 'fractured gaze *from* the West', an at least partly sceptical gaze towards Turkey and its culture.[7] Taken together, these perspectives generate and accentuate a critical doubting of all constructions of national, ethnic or cultural identity. For Şenocak, the consequence is not, emphatically, some woolly multiculturalism, but an encouragement of the heterogeneous in order to frustrate the simple oppositions which lead, almost inevitably, to hierarchies of difference. The shifting, multifaceted character of his male figures' masculinity, a sense of male selves in flux, relates to his pursuit, in his essays, of a new consciousness of 'what it means to be German [an identity which for Şenocak clearly includes German Turks like himself] in an ethnically and culturally heterogeneous German society'.[8]

Şenocak's literary struggle against crude binary polarizations is prominent in his collection of essays *Atlas des tropischen Deutschland*, in which he plays with psychoanalytic categories such as temperate male orderliness versus tropical female disorder. The opening quotation from Elias Canetti declares that the German national symbol was the army, 'der marschierende Wald': German love of the forest was not simply love of nature, but of the pine forest with its rule-bound, rigid, parallel, upright trees in orderly separation one from another (the uniformed, helmeted lines of the Nuremburg rallies), in contrast to the chaos of a tropical forest (*Atlas*, 5). Şenocak does not, though, simplistically perpetuate the 'us and them' polarity of much migrant critique of German orderliness and discipline. Rather, positioning his work within contemporary German intellectual debate, he explores real and putative tropical disorderliness within German culture itself.

The second area of complexity in the role of masculinity in Şenocak's texts lies in its link to the treatment of this theme in other Turkish writing in Germany.[9] This link is palpable, but hardly straightforward. Though of course Turkish writing in Germany is far more than 'Gastarbeiterliteratur', manual labour remains a central theme. Moreover, 'work defines men'.[10] However, while manual work in particular may confirm traditional masculine identity, it may also undermine this identity through low status

and exclusion from discursive power, a feminization exacerbated
in the first years of Turkish labour migration to Germany by the
attitudes of German foremen, management, government and other
agencies.[11] The anxieties this can generate within traditional conceptions of masculinity are addressed in Güney Dal's novel *Wenn
Ali die Glocken läuten hört*. Turkish laboratory assistant Kadir Derya
is literally unmanned and metaphorically regendered by the in-
dignities of migrant labour. Herr Hartmann (*sic*), his German su-
pervisor, has given him hormone pills as a placebo for his stomach
ulcers. Kadir watches in alarm as his breasts grow as big as water-
melons and his nipples as swollen as ripe blackberries, and fears
that his penis may drop off.[12] Ashamed of his lost manhood, he
plans to squeeze his breasts back into his body by squashing them
under a massive wardrobe. But this would require male assistance,
and with it the risk of shameful sexual advances (*Ali*, 36). Eventually, desperate, Kadir tries to restore his masculinity by amputat-
ing his right breast with a kitchen knife (*Ali*, 150–3). Migrant
labour's psychological scarrings take literal form in this image,
which strikingly genders the dependency of the migrant on his
German hosts, but also mocks the panic with which a rigid heterosexual masculinity responds to the blurring of its boundaries.

In contrast, Zafer Şenocak's texts offer an experientially liberat-
ing journey through fluid ethnicities and sexual orientations, more
reminiscent of the games of gender performance in Thomas
Meinecke's *Tomboy*,[13] with its explicit quotation from Lacan and
Judith Butler. Şenocak's Turkish-German man is post-modern,
polymorphous, sometimes indeed androgynous, affirming and
exploring the dissolution of boundaries which led Dal's Kadir to
self-destructive panic. While 'wir nach Angstschweiß riechenden
Männer / beißen in rohe Zwiebeln', the androgynous, bisexual
hero/ine of the poem 'Lu', a man with the snakes and a woman
with the bears, is fiercely insistent on his/her identity only when
others seek to categorize her/him (*FA*, 25–7).

Moreover, though the male body plays a central role in Şenocak's subversion of gender stereotypes, it is not the male body as
casualty of production familiar from much literature of Turkish
migrant labour experience.[14] Remembering that 'work defines
men', we should note that, for the majority of his male narrators or
focalizer figures, work is either thematically absent, peripheral or,
typically, that of the writer. As a homeworker, the writer is argu-

ably in some ways feminized, though his experience differs crucially, of course, from that of the labourer. Above all, the writer is in much stronger control of the instruments of the male *logos* than the migrant labourer. As a result, Şenocak's texts show that unsettling the fixed certainties of gender positions does not necessarily imply uncertainty in a negative sense. The migrant labourer's muzzled tongue becomes the exploratory organ of a masculinity liberated and sexualized by its migrant ambivalence.

While Şenocak rejects the self-image of the migrant as victim, traces of it can be found in the ambiguous gendering of his male figures' encounters with German women, and in the provocative way he positively reintroduces characteristics often associated with an 'effeminate' Orient into the representation of his narrators and central figures. Şenocak is an intellectual at home in a Western metropolis, but also one who knows that 'the Turk', the man in skirts, is charged with erotic ambiguity in the Western imagination.[15] Though sometimes with mixed feelings, his male figures enjoy the fruits of the exotic allure this ambiguity nurtures.

This polyvalence relates to the third ambivalence in Şenocak's reappropriation for his male figures of the feminist concept of gender fluidity. Eve Kosofsky Sedgwick has suggested that masculinity and femininity may in fact not be opposites at either end of a linear spectrum, but may perhaps be orthogonal, existing on separate, non-intersecting planes, so that any individual may have a lot, or a little, or none, of either, or of both.[16] Certainly, Şenocak's texts do much more than simply invert gender characteristics along an otherwise unchanged linear spectrum: many of his male figures display a high degree of femininity as well as masculinity, in terms both of sexuality and of other gender characteristics. Despite this, and of course because of it, they remain highly male in focus: many are self-confident venturers, even if the worlds they explore are as yet trackless and tentative. In contrast, Şenocak's women figures may sometimes be positioned as dominant but remain, almost without exception, shadowy bit-players to the male principals. Thus, though the narrator of 'Fridaynightfever' in *Der Erottomane* claims that some of the women who work in brothels experience self-fulfilment, this is unconvincing compared with the brothel's function for male self-confirmation as well as physical gratification. Hardly surprisingly, it is not a sex worker but a customer who declares: 'Ich bin nirgendwo so sehr ich selbst wie in einem

Bordell' (*E*, 71). Equally, 'Mitra' (*E*, 74–81) has barely introduced
its eponymous female focalizer when she is driven off-stage by an
exploration of further possibilities of polymorphous male sexual
experience.

Şenocak does not refer explicitly to the man in skirts. However,
the title of his volume *Der Mann im Unterhemd* (1995) alludes ironically to Ernest Hemingway, that leading member of what Peter
Schwenger calls 'the virility school' of American writing.[17] Two
stories in *Der Mann im Unterhemd* illustrate particularly strikingly
Şenocak's exploration of gender possibilities. 'Die unterirdische
Stadt' takes a male fantasy to its nightmarish conclusion: a subter-
ranean city run by dominatrices devoted to eradicating men by
killing them off through ceaseless and uninterrupted sexual activity (*MiU*, 93–103).[18] Here, as elsewhere, Şenocak plays with pornographic language and images. In 'Rolling Stones' a man allows a
woman to remove his pubic hair, oil his body and write poetry on
his shaven skin, which thus, inverting conventional gendering,
becomes her text. With the exchange of activity for passivity comes
a loss of corporeal identity: 'Mein Körper hatte keine festen Konturen mehr' (*MiU*, 114). Allowing himself to be treated like a
helpless baby evokes images from his past which read like a psy-
choanalytical sketch of male heterosexual development seen as a
process of repression:

> Ich bestieg eine weiße Stute. Das Pferd trat auf der Stelle. Ich wachte
> wieder auf. Wellen peitschten mir ins Gesicht und mein Schwanz
> wuchs. Mutters Körper in einem durchsichtigen Nachthemd tauchte
> nachts aus dem Dunkel auf. Irgendwann lernt man die Mutter von an-
> deren Frauen zu unterscheiden. Irgendwann zieht die Tante [who in
> an earlier scene had lain beside him, caressing his penis] ihre Hand
> zurück. Irgendwann ist man mutterseelenallein. (*MiU*, 116)

Here, primal harmony with the mother is lost in the process of
male identity formation.[19] When Güney Dal's Kadir experiences his
loss of masculinity, his terror erupts in a hallucination in which
Kadir switches from being the rider to being the horse (*Ali*, 63).[20]
Şenocak's narrator in 'Rolling Stones', in contrast, is untroubled by,
indeed celebrates, his own polymorphousness. He paradoxically
remains, at this specific moment of sexual and gender fantasy, in
the saddle.

Şenocak's *Die Prärie* (1997) is again a text of male and narratorial as much as migrant self-exploration: the two are ironically interwoven in the experience its Turkish-German writer-narrator has on a writer-in-residence stay at a US college, namely of losing 'die Orientierung' (*P*, 69), the themes echoed in genre-crossing form and multiple narrative perspectives. 'Heute schreibt jeder über sein eigenes Geschlecht, als handelte es sich dabei um das Vaterland, dessen Verteidigung ansteht. Ein obskurer Geschlechtspatriotismus macht sich breit' (*P*, 9). Here, the writer Sascha is more interested in sex and sexuality than in his Islamic roots. His father, insistently secular in revolt against his pious grandfather, is largely ignorant about Islam. Thus when Sascha is commissioned to write a piece on the fatwa and literature, he is forced to immerse himself in reference books; Islam 'verdrängt sogar den Sex', he notes ruefully. The 'Nachkommen prüder Protestanten' in the editorial offices would 'lieber den Islam zum Thema machen [. . .] als die interkulturelle Geilheit. Nicht einmal mit dem zugefügten Adjektiv interkulturell konnte ich bisher die Aufmerksamkeit für meine Passion erregen. Ansonsten zieht das immer, wenn man ein abgestandenes Thema an den Mann bringen will' (*P*, 40–2).

In *Die Prärie*, the narrator reflects that, whereas women are transparent (in the sense of being open, without rigid outer boundaries), 'die Männer haben mindestens zwei Häute, manche stecken sogar in Kapseln' (*P*, 7). As Kafka's *Die Verwandlung* suggests, men's own fluidity beneath their armoured carapace may be a source of terror. Şenocak's narrator, however, positively seeks out this fluidity. Accosted by a woman with glances 'wie Pfeile' on an empty subway train, he allows himself to become the hunter's 'Beute', admitting a passive role conventionally figured as feminine into the polymorphous cast of the complex masculinity his text performs (*P*, 17). He explores the relationship between certain kinds of writing and sexuality: the disintegration of boundaries and fixed categories, and the writer's experience of prefiguring and preforming lived experience in texts. It is not only women who 'wissen, daß sie nur als Bilder im Spiegel eines Mannes existieren', a familiar point in the constitutive dominance of the male gaze (*P*, 6). In his relationship with the call-girl Veronika, his ironic muse, who inspires him to write as many sentences a day as she has clients, the narrator experiences this indeterminacy as mutual. Gender, text, nation and origin begin to dissolve (*P*, 13).

Die Prärie plays self-mockingly with clichés of male sexuality: obsession with sex, discussion of seduction techniques, sexual pursuit as a form of hunting (*P*, 84), woman as mysterious Other whom it is the man's role to 'entschlüsseln' (*P*, 49–51). Men 'drehen ein Leben lang den Schlüssel zu einer Frau im Schlüsselloch herum. Vergeblich. Vielleicht ist da, wo das Schloß steckt, auch gar keine Tür' (*P*, 47). There are several nuances here, from infantile schoolboy humour through misogynist objectification to a critique of men's imprisonment in constructions of the male self which, by causing them to see the penis as organ not only of gratification and procreation, but also of revelation, ensure their endless puzzlement and isolation. Hence their imagined longing to lay down their self-styled hero role. 'Der eigentliche männliche Traum unserer Zeit ist nicht der Traum von der Macht, sondern der Traum von der Machtlosigkeit' (*P*, 64). So long as it remains a dream, though, the sleeping man used by a sexually voracious woman is a male projection, not the promise of abandonment of patriarchal power in the waking, empirical world.

Şenocak's *Der Erottomane* (1999) explores masculinities and the male body and its cultural, psychological, sexual, signifying possibilities to an extent rare in German literature. The text is a mosaic of thematically linked but self-contained fragments, a complex maze of shifting identities, to unravel which is to risk imputing to this studiedly counter-hermeneutic writing the very linearity and rationality it resists.[21] The title, punning 'erotomaniac' and 'He-Ottoman', ironically blends Şenocak's gender awareness and the orientalist image of the sensual Turk. The subtitle, *Ein Findelbuch*, playing on 'Findelkind', the abandoned child of unknown parents, reflects the text's complex games with authorship and narratorial position: firstly, the main narrator, whose texts are italicized; secondly, his *Staatsanwalt* friend Tom, who was previously the Turk Tayfun before undergoing the 'kosmetische Operation' (*E*, 8) of acquiring German citizenship (ironically, the unnatural undertaken in order to become naturalized), in order to become a government employee; thirdly, the texts of the writer R. (Robert), whose murder it is Tom's task as *Staatsanwalt* to investigate. As we follow the merging and diverging streams of an identity in constant flux (this, rather than any linear plot, providing the text's continuity), it becomes increasingly probable that the narrator, Tom and Robert are all one person. In the key central section entitled 'Tom und Robert'

(*E*, 55–68), the two eponymous figures are clearly distinguishable, indeed sharply contrasted, but as Jekyll and Hyde twins 'im gleichen Körper' (*E*, 55). The narrator now admits: 'Ich habe zwei Namen. Tom und Robert [who are] ein und dieselbe Person' (*E*, 71). Later, the narrator claims to have sensed from the beginning 'daß Tom Robert war, und daß es Robert nie gegeben hatte' (*E*, 106). Instead, Tom had used a newspaper report of a murder to lay a false trail, both to express his fantasies through the figure of Robert and simultaneously to deny his authorship of them. For the narrator, this is unproblematic, simply confirming that Tom is 'ein Schriftsteller'. But Tom also experiences, stigmata-like, the 'rote Einstichstellen, dunkelblaue Blutergüsse' inflicted on the murdered Robert (*E*, 119).[22] The narrator closes his narratological reflections with the comment: 'Endlich konnte ich meine große Reise antreten' (*E*, 106), a journey which has been made already by Robert. The first chapter of his new novel, entitled 'R.', then forms the final section of *Der Erottomane* (*E*, 107–26). However, since this final section refers to both Tom and Robert in the third person, but is not italicized, it may even introduce an additional narrator. The performed and constructed fictionality of the multiple narratives, the various fictional authorial positions of the texts within the text, the exchanges of identities, of bodily fluids, of wounds, emphasize the performedness and constructedness of the masculinities they exemplify and explore.

The text is itself a journey, a reverse Odyssey, a journey away from Europe or perhaps more precisely into a labyrinthine, sensual – tropical – underworld beneath the 'kaltes Europa' in which it draws to a close (*E*, 125). Just as its narrators lose their sense of purpose, so too the text loses its way and can thus be seen as an unpicking of goal-directed masculinity. Its languid sensuality, though undercut by moments of often crude humour, risks confirming stereotypes, as at least one review seems to confirm: the novel 'nous convie à une expérience perverse de la langue, lente et asphyxiante comme un bain turc, un bondage ou encore un coup de "fouet à sept langues"', the last image, as the review acknowledges, drawn from the text itself.[23] There are numerous echoes of the tradition, reaching back to de Sade, of textual exploration of the symbolic practices of power as they manifest themselves in sex.

At the outset, the narrator announces his imminent journey into Asia along the Silk Road: Konstanza, Istanbul, the Black Sea coast,

Trebizon, Odessa, 'Baku, Aschabad, Taschkent, Buchara, Samar-
kand, Mongolei, Chinesische Mauer, Peking, Schanghai'. He
would, explicitly, not follow 'den Spuren Marco Polos', but 'meine
eigene Seidenstraße konstruieren', to realize a dream 'vom Weg-
kommen, vom Sichselbstverlieren, vom Verwischen der eigenen
Spuren'. Travel guides and maps pile up on his desk, but 'aus der
Reise wird nichts' (*E*, 7). First he must engage with the puzzling,
amorphous figure of the dead R. who, if he ever existed at all, is
now visible only through texts which may be R.'s, Tom's or indeed
the narrator's own.

In the narrative purportedly by R., again the narrator under-
takes journeys which challenge linear purposefulness and the discrete self: he has 'keine Ziele' and plans his itinerary only at the
last minute, using a fifty-year-old map whose once-important
routes are now scarcely used; he takes little luggage, changing his
clothing in each new city, discarding 'was mich davor begleitet
und bekleidet hatte' (*E*, 17).[24] The link between travel and gender,
which, as I suggested, can be traced back to the *Odyssey*, is made
explicit in *Der Erottomane* in a passage where the prosecutor Tom
describes R.'s sexual activity as characterized by involuntariness,
indifference and a dissociation between 'Trieb' and 'Geschlecht':
'Seine Triebe schrieben ihm vor, sich Frauen hinzugeben ohne sein
Geschlecht zu fühlen'. In this masculinity, 'Triebe' and 'Geschlecht'
are asynchronous, the former involuntary reflexes, the latter 'ein
lauernder, verschwiegener Forscher'. The ambiguity here of
'Geschlecht' as both 'sex' ('male', 'female' or whatever) and 'sexual
organ' or 'member' is only partly clarified by Tom's statement that
'Das Geschlecht des Mannes ist längst nicht mehr eine Ver-
längerung seines Körpers, sondern ein Reisender, der unbekannte
Orte aufsucht. An diesen Orten hinterläßt er keine Spuren' (*E*, 9–
11). Understood empirically, this seems a spurious claim (and one
which indirectly justifies sexual irresponsibility), since the traces
left by the penis are manifold and manifest. But 'das Geschlecht
des Mannes', understood symbolically as the phallus, the 'signifier
of signifiers',[25] can indeed take on an existence separate from the
instinctual sexual drives. *Der Erottomane* as a whole can be seen as
a journey both into masculinity and of masculinity, the phallus
exploring itself, its limits and its possibilities.

For Tom, R.'s attitude to his own body and its activity is more
bemused than celebratory. He is a 'typischer Vertreter seiner

Generation', largely free of family ties, with neither ideals nor ambition to understand or change his life: 'Den anarchischen Zustand seines Körpers hatte er als miniaturhafte Abbildung des anarchischen Zustandes der Gesellschaft wahrgenommen, ohne daß ihm dabei das Wort Freiheit in den Sinn gekommen wäre. Wo es keine Ordnung mehr gibt, verliert auch die Freiheit jegliche Bedeutung' (*E*, 9–10). 'In Anlehnung an seine unabschüttelbare Herkunft und sein verwegenes Schicksal nannte er sich einen Erottomanen' (*E*, 10–11).

This self-conscious name he gives himself (in another passage it is given to R. by a dominatrix with whom he engages in transsexual experiments, *E*, 63) emphasizes the fact that the body which R. inhabits is partly constructed from the projections of others. That this is often seen as a female experience adds further fluidity to his masculine identity, especially since it is, in fact, a source of discomfort as well as sexual gratification.[26] The narrator recalls a relationship with a woman for whom he was the exotic stranger offering not only erotic attraction, but even the 'Geborgenheit' possible only where not everything is familiar, revealed. 'Etwas in mir erinnerte sie an Asien. Ein deutscher Mann in meiner Lage hätte sich geschmeichelt gefühlt. Ich dagegen fühlte mich deplaziert, unverstanden, irgendwie ins falsche Fach gelegt' (*E*, 15–6).

As in *Die Prärie* or *Der Mann im Unterhemd*, the masculinities in *Der Erottomane* include relatively conventional aspects. For example, after he has taken over a second-hand bookshop in an unnamed and mysteriously timeless oriental city, R.'s project of reestablishing rational order and the invulnerability of the male who is armoured with privileged knowledge – 'die Geheimpläne dieser Stadt enträtseln und unverwundbar werden' (*E*, 35) – is diverted and eroded by an erotic encounter. The woman who reawakens R.'s long-passive sexuality is described as 'die schwarze Krake' who is imprisoning and devouring R., a conventional projection of male fears (*E*, 39). At the same time, however, R.'s narrative suggests counter-currents to conventional sexual patterns. Each time, for example, he refuses to sell her a book, 'spürte ich einen Messerstich in meinem Rücken, dessen Schmerz bis in meine Brust hineinreichte und, nachdem die Frau den Laden verlassen hatte, in eine wohltuende Wärme überging' (*E*, 34). After penetration by a phallic woman (she is 'eine große, athletische Frau') comes her detumescent withdrawal from the shop – enclosed spaces stand, in psychoanalytic terms, for receptive, conventionally female, sexual organs – and then, post-coital warmth.

However, the description of the woman as 'die schwarze Krake' stems from the city's white-uniformed 'Kommandant', who also sneers at R.'s masculinity, mocking 'deinen kümmerlichen Stachel' as useless unless he intends to penetrate himself like a cornered scorpion (*E*, 40). The 'Kommandant' orders him to leave on a ship the following morning. 'Warum man auf dem Meer weiße Uniformen trägt?' ponders R., and repeats the Kommandant's description of the woman: the ship will carry him so far away, 'daß die schwarze Krake mit ihren langen Armen mich nicht einmal in meinen Träumen greifen kann' (*E*, 40). In panic, he represses his much more ambivalent earlier reaction to the woman, seeking to exorcize the dark chaos of an encounter with assertive femininity by means of whiteness and the male-dominated clarity of the ship at sea.

'Durst' (*E*, 49–54) describes a heterosexual relationship charged both with conventional romantic elements and with those of a radical sexuality: a chance meeting; the fact that no word is spoken and nothing eaten or drunk except what they take from each other's bodies; an abiding strangeness which survives and heightens the erotic encounter; an intensity such that the narrator claims not to have slept with, nor even desired any other woman since; the motif of thirst as metaphor for, as well as memory and consequence of, the extreme physical intensity of their coupling. Rather than taking the phallic initiative, the narrator is reserved and cautious, and this encounter too contains elements of gender reversal: 'Sie trug Handschuhe. Ich roch und schmeckte das Leder, als sie ihre Finger in meinen Mund steckte. [. . .] Eine Frau hat kein Glied, dafür aber zehn Finger, die kein männliches Glied ersetzen kann' (*E*, 51). Such passages make it clear that Şenocak is exploring differences between gender and sexual physiology: a woman practises penetrative sex on a man, though she has no penis; and this penetrative sexual act does not, in fact, alter their respective maleness and femaleness, just its manifestations. Her performance of maleness through a penetrative act is a female performance.

The reverse, namely male performance of gender attributes conventionally figured as feminine, is exemplified in 'Zenne' (*E*, 45–8; a 'Zenne' being a male actor who plays female roles). Performativity, understood, with Judith Butler, as 'the reiterative and citational practice by which discourse produces the effects that it names', does not, Butler stresses, imply free choice; but it emphasizes identities as constructed and therefore as susceptible to intervention.[27] The 'Zenne' barely remembers 'mein eigenes Geschlecht', and is content 'daß meine Männlichkeit ein verlorener Teil von mir ist' (*E*, 45). He cannot imagine living 'ohne auf der Bühne eine Frau zu sein. Ich sage das nur, weil ich weiß, daß ich kein Geschlecht habe' (*E*, 48). His identity – as someone who plays and is known to be playing a woman – is constituted wholly in performance. But although he has 'kein Geschlecht' in the sense of organs which function as male sexual organs, he himself argues that he must be a man, or he would not have been put on stage as a 'Zenne'. Thus, though it challenges heterosexual conceptions of the masculine, this particular subject position from which feminity is performed is, by definition, male (*E*, 45).

The same is true of Robert's submission, in the section 'Tom und Robert', to a series of feminizations by a 'Gebieterin', which quite literally widen the scope of his masculinity. She blindfolds him and shaves his body. 'Ihre erste Erektion war für Robert sehr schmerzhaft.' As a 'Jungmann', his body is unprepared for 'die Verfremdung ihres Geschlechts'. This act of female–male penetration is described as her conquest of 'die Festung des Erottomanen' (*E*, 64–5). Şenocak plays here with a structurally similar gender reversal to that found in the metaphysical poetry of John Donne and others, where the courtly love conceit of the worshipped lady as fortress is transferred to the religious sphere and where the male poetic subject adopts a female position as a fortress vis-à-vis a phallic God.

This link was suggested by Şenocak's own argument that sexuality is where religion's possibility for metaphysical experience is reconnected with the body, and that his texts' explorations of sexuality seek to restore the union of religion and the body, which Islam represented in its early phase but has subsequently lost.[28] Do they succeed, or are they clever semi-pornographic games? With regard to this question, the section 'Fridaynightfever' in *Der Erottomane* (*E*, 69–73), explicitly linking religion and sexuality, demonstrates the ambivalence we have seen to be typical of Şenocak's work. Its title provocatively merges Travolta and the Muslim holy day; the text takes blasphemous sideswipes at Muslim sexual practices, including those of the religion's founder, and celebrates the tension between arousal and control generated by walking the streets with no undergarments (in both men's and women's sexual fantasies, a practice more commonly attributed to women). While this latter element could be read on the same level as schoolboy stories about pocket billiards, the section closes with a quest to transcend the mundane experience of 'den kleinen Sex', 'den romantischen Sex', through the 'Ausschweifungen' of group sex, rejecting the idea of sexual coupling as 'ein Fest der Zweisamkeit' (*E*, 72). In the couple, R. argues, 'definiert sich die Eine durch die Kontrolle über den Anderen. Bei der Gruppe dagegen konzentriert sich alles auf ein Zentrum, das variieren kann' (*E*, 72). While the couple necessitates a process of domination which is only confirmed by its inversion (whether in homosexual relations or in heterosexual ones where the power gradient is simply reversed), group sex, the text suggests, offers a challenge to hegemony through a decentring praxis. Read in the AIDS age as justifying real practices, this would be highly problematic. But it is of course a text, and its image of the roving centre, as a means to avoid the one-way domination which lurks in most binary pairings, is a provocative metaphor for the process of deconstruction.[29]

'Tom und Robert' (*E*, 55–68) is literally the central and arguably the crucial section of the text. It contrasts the two very different, yet symbiotic identities within the narrator's person and examines his uncertainty as to which is 'really' him. His delegation of the answer questions the myth of male decisiveness: 'Irgendwann wird es eine Frau geben, die diese Frage für mich beantworten wird' (*E*, 55). This in itself conventional idea is rendered much more original by the complex gender practices described; not only taken together, but even seen individually, Tom and Robert display multiple gender behaviours which a conventional view of gender would find mutually incompatible.

Tom is a 'Holzfäller' and exhibits many traditionally masculine characteristics. He is almost permanently aroused, 'aber mit seinem Lustorgan geht er sparsam um. Er organisiert sein Liebesleben wie eine Arbeit' (*E*, 55), practising a disciplined, essentially misogynist sexual routine for its own sake and without reference to his partners' possible needs. An aggressive male, his relationships are rapidly initiated and shortlived; at night 'schreibt er sich den Tag vom Leib'. Moreover, he 'trägt Kriegsbemalung auf seinem Hoden' (*E*, 56–7). Thus, although his sexual body does, unusually for representations of male sexuality, extend to include his testicles, this is not 'the testicular and testerical aspect of male sexual anatomy and physiology', which, in a provocative essay on 'The male body and literary metaphors for masculinity', Arthur Flannigan Saint-Aubin suggests would promote 'an entirely different metaphoricity [. . .] passive, receptive, enclosing, stable, cyclic, among others – qualities that are lost when male equals penis', when masculinity's psychological and cultural meanings are 'assumed to be the homologue of the phallic genitality of the male with, at the very least, metaphoric connections to it – in part, aggressive, violent, penetrating, goal-directed, linear'.[30] In fact, these last, conventionally masculine, qualities are very much those displayed by Tom. But Şenocak again frustrates easy gender polarization by having his narrator note that 'Tom teilt seine Gefühle zwischen den Geschlechtern auf, läßt sich von einem Geschlecht zum anderen treiben' (*E*, 56).

Robert, in contrast, is consistently heterosexual. But his masculinity too takes highly ambivalent forms. He is a life-affirming dandy, attractive to women, but arousing not their femininity but 'ihre Männlichkeit'. Though his obsession with women is 'epidemisch', he does not seek a Don Juan role, but rather subordinates himself. He plans to write the romantic novel of the millennium, in which all men will disappear. But the result will be a fictional world not of women as such, but one where all the figures will be 'weibisch [. . .] irgendwie eine Kopie der Weiblichkeit' (*E*, 57). This too is an act of mimicry where the feminine is performed as a constitutive part of the masculine. In contrast to the narrator of *Die Prärie*, for Robert the woman rather than the penis is the instrument of revelation (though it is, of course, a woman whose physical contact with him is partly phallic). Yet his relationships with women serve his own internal goals: 'Er lebt nicht nach seinem Gefühl. Er lebte nach den Konstruktionen in seinem Kopf. Frauen waren für ihn wie Schlüssel zu einem Haus, das er sich im Kopf erbaut hatte' (*E*, 60).

Then, however, he enters a relationship with a woman whom he imagines as a 'starkes Wesen' and who embodies both motherliness – she is larger than he and with a comforting voice – and phallic maleness: 'im Innern war sie beinhart. Eine Frau ohne Härte wäre nichts für ihn. Manchmal wollte er ihr ganzes Gewicht auf sich spüren. Auf seiner Zungenspitze' (*E*, 57–8). The subjection of the male body to the female gaze and to female signification has parallels in the 'Rolling Stones' section of *Der Mann im Unterhemd*. Robert too must keep his body shaved, for 'Sie schrieb ihre Gedanken auf seinen Körper' and 'nur glatte Körper können tiefe Gedanken behalten' (*E*, 63–4). The intensification of the masochistic element is accompanied firstly by transformations in his use of language – stories, parables and shifting meanings of everyday words change his perception of the normal world – and secondly by a religious experience which emanates from the act of submission, a 'Bestimmung' which he had long been prevented from acknowledging by Tom, 'dieser Aufsässige, dieser Höllenhund' (*E*, 63). But this possibly plausible religious experience is immediately related back to 'die gute Seite seiner Gebieterin [. . .] die siebenzüngige Peitsche', to pain and its erotic anticipation (*E*, 63). Whilst in many religions spirituality is indeed achieved through radical self-punishment, from fasting via flagellation to self-mutilation, its purpose is the freeing of the self from the demands of the body, not the experience of pain as the sensual pleasure of 'einen Schwebezustand zwischen Schlaf und Tod' (*E*, 65). A condition of the self where 'Fühlen' is only possible through pain is surely a sickness not a liberation.

The very ease with which Şenocak's prose, and *Der Erottomane* above all, can slip from the transgressive to the merely pornographic risks leaving uneasy precisely those readers who are willing to engage with his provocative forays into gender and ethnic fluidity. At the same time, Şenocak's work is one of the most strikingly original examples of a dialectic whereby, out of a process set in train by Turkish migration to Germany, writing is emerging which has long left these origins behind it. This work's contribution to a developing post-national culture in Europe is crucially interwoven with its explorations of lived and imagined masculinities. As we have seen, Şenocak's texts suggest a poetic consciousness almost wholly free of the material forces which have determined other Turkish-German masculinities. Yet his texts are none the less focused – with an intensity that the cool playfulness of the style tends to obscure – on the question of masculinity in a time of its crisis. And these texts, in their literary form, in their fluid treatment of time, place, plot and character, and in the shifting positions from which gender is performed, can be read as the products of a migrant consciousness, a new Odysseus, a post-European European.

Notes

[1] Heiner Müller, *Herzstück* (Berlin, Rotbuch, 1983), 104; Müller here paraphrases the somewhat more complex engagement with the *Odyssey* in Horkheimer's and Adorno's *Dialektik der Aufklärung*.

[2] Margot Shildrick, *Leaky Bodies and Boundaries: Feminism, Postmodernism and Bio-ethics* (London and New York, Routledge, 1997).

[3] From the very extensive recent literature on masculinity and its crises, in addition to texts cited in the course of the essay, I have drawn on: Peter Middleton, *The Inward Gaze: Masculinity and Subjectivity in Modern Culture* (New York, Routledge, 1992); D. H. J. Morgan, *Discovering Men* (London, Routledge, 1992); Anthony Rowland (ed.), *Signs of Masculinity: Men in Literature 1700 to the Present* (Atlanta, Rodopi, 1998); Lynne Segal, *Slow Motion: Changing Masculinities, Changing Men* (London, Virago, 1990).

[4] See Leslie Adelson, 'Coordinates of orientation: an introduction', *ATG*, xi–xxxviii. *Gefährliche Verwandtschaft* (Berlin, Babel, 1998) explores a further dimension of hybridity, a Turkish-German-Jewish triangle.

[5] Adelson, in *ATG*, xii and xxiv.

[6] Zafer Şenocak (ed.), *Der gebrochene Blick nach Westen. Zu Positionen und Perspektiven türkischer Kultur* (Berlin, Babel, 1994).

[7] See Moray McGowan, '"The Bridge of the Golden Horn": Istanbul, Europe and the "Fractured Gaze from the West" in Turkish writing in Germany', in Andy Hollis (ed.), *Beyond Boundaries: Textual Representations of European Identity* (Amsterdam and Atlanta, Rodopi, 2000), 53–69.

[8] 'To my readers in the United States', in *ATG*, xxxix–xli (xl–xli).

[9] See Moray McGowan, 'Multiple masculinities in Turkish-German men's writing', in Roy Jerome (ed.), *Conceptions of Post-War German Masculinity* (Albany, State University of New York Press, 2001), 289–312.

[10] Ian M. Harris, *Messages Men Hear: Constructing Masculinities* (London, Taylor and Francis, 1995), 23.

[11] Migrant labourers are feminized both as migrants and as labourers: see Arthur Brittan, *Masculinity and Power* (London, Blackwell, 1989).

[12] Güney Dal, *Wenn Ali die Glocken läuten hört* (Berlin, edition der 2, 1979), 59 and 26. Future references identified by *Ali* and page number in the text. Leslie Adelson offers an illuminating reading of this novel: 'Migrants and muses', in David E. Wellbery (ed.), *The New History of German Literature* (Cambridge, Harvard University Press, forthcoming 2003/4).

[13] Frankfurt am Main, Suhrkamp, 1998.

[14] For examples of this motif see my 'Multiple masculinities', 297.

[15] For a more in-depth discussion on the 'man in skirts,' see Graham Dawson, 'The blond Bedouin: Lawrence of Arabia, imperial adventure and the imaging of English-British masculinity', in Michael Roper and John Tosh (eds), *Manful Assertions: Masculinities in Britain Since 1800* (New York, Routledge, 1991), 113–44.

[16] Eve Kosofsky Sedgwick, 'Gosh, Boy George. You must be awfully secure in your masculinity', in Maurice Berger, Brian Wallis and Simon Watson (eds), *Constructing Masculinity* (New York and London, Routledge, 1995), 11–20 (15–16).

[17] Peter Schwenger, *Phallic Critiques: Masculinity and Twentieth-century Literature* (New York, Routledge, 1984), 13.

[18] Akif Pirinçci's *Yin* (Munich, Goldmann, 1997) develops this motif still further: a man-killing virus has left an all-female world.

[19] See David D. Gilmore, *Manhood in the Making: Cultural Concepts of Masculinity* (New Haven, Yale University Press, 1990), 27–8.

[20] The migrant labourer narrator of Aras Ören's poem 'Grunewald' also imagines himself the steed of a sleek white rider: Ören, *Texte. Anhang: Texte aus dem Revier*, translated from Turkish by Alp Otman [= *Asphalt 6: Zeitschrift für kritische Literatur und bildende Kunst*] (Wanne-Eickel, Proletenpresse, 1971), 10.

[21] The term 'counter-hermeneutic' is Şenocak's own, taken from an interview which, ironically, offers highly revealing insights into the 'meanings' of his work: Frédéric Ciriez, 'L'Erottoman ou la langue comme puissance et impuissance sexuelle', fnac café litteraire online, 18 March 2001, at www.fnac.net/le_café_litteraire_2001/html/zafer_senocak_interview.html [and www.swan.ac.uk/german/cheesman/senocak/fnacinterv.html] (both accessed September 2002).

[22] The word 'stechen', connoting sexual penetration, occurs frequently in the text; 'Ergüsse' too cannot, in Şenocak's sexualized prose, be free of associations with the male orgasm.

[23] Ciriez, 'L'Erottoman ou la langue' (see note 21).

[24] R.'s narrative, especially in the section 'Der Antiquar', contains not only 'der Traum eines jeden Reisenden [. . .] nicht nur die Orte, sondern auch die Zeiten zu wechseln', but also the seemingly contradictory desire 'Ordnung in die Zeiten [zu] bringen' (*E*, 18, 23). Not every impulse he pursues leads to dissolution of patriarchal linearity; but this too is part of the overall effect of a labyrinthine narrative puzzle under the prose's limpid surface.

[25] Jacques Lacan, quoted in Anthony Clare, *On Men: Masculinity in Crisis* (London, Chatto and Windus, 2000), 9.

²⁶ The disconcerting experience of Turks in Germany as the erotic objects of Western women's projections of cultural otherness is a common theme of the Turkish-language 'Germany literature' published in Turkey in the early years of the labour migrations. See, for example, the texts by Bekir Yıldız or Fethi Savaşçı quoted in Wolfgang Riemann, *Das Deutschlandbild in der modernen türkischen Literatur* (Wiesbaden, Harrasowitz, 1983), 72–5 and 103. Cf. Savaşçı's *München im Frühlingsregen*, trans. Zafer Şenocak (Frankfurt am Main, Dağyeli, 1987).

²⁷ *Bodies that Matter: On the Discursive Limits of 'Sex'* (New York and London, Routledge, 1993), 2.

²⁸ Ciriez, 'L'Erottoman ou la langue' (see note 21).

²⁹ By contrast, 'Das Haus im Süden' (*E*, 82–94), with its images of paedophilia, torture, mutilation and necrophilia presented with no marked variation in Şenocak's quietly sensual language, as if these too are simply part of the polymorphous panorama, remains an intransigently problematic text.

³⁰ In Harry Brod and Michael Kaufman (eds), *Theorizing Masculinities* (Thousand Oaks, London and New Delhi, Sage, 1994), 239–58 (239).

7

Der Erottomane:
Ein Vexierspiel mit der Identität

MONIKA CARBE

Eine Annäherung

Der Titel *Der Erottomane* macht neugierig, wird hier doch ein facettenreiches Spiel mit der Etymologie getrieben. Als Personen existieren 'Ottomanen' nur in den Köpfen nostalgischer Orientreisender, denn es handelt sich um eine verballhornte Übersetzung, die sich – über das Englische – seit dem 19. Jahrhundert von Generation zu Generation schleppt; gemeint sind die Osmanen. Das aber weiß der Erfinder des Titels und setzt noch ein 'Er-' davor, das maskuline Personalpronomen im Deutschen, im Türkischen aber den Begriff für den militanten, offensiven Mann. Nicht zu vergessen ein weiteres Wortspiel, das sich darin verbirgt: das manische Element einer ungezügelten Geilheit. Und natürlich das Sofa, auf dem sich herrlich koitieren lässt.

In scheinbar vertrauter Umgebung beginnt der Roman, oder, um den Untertitel zu zitieren, das 'Findelbuch'. Der Ich-Erzähler, ein Schriftsteller, zieht aus einer Berliner Wohngemeinschaft aus, da er seinen beiden Mitbewohnerinnen zu anstrengend wird, schließt zuvor jedoch seine 'Moabiter Trilogie' ab. Mit der Anspielung auf dieses (fiktive) Werk wird zum einen angedeutet, dass er nicht etwa ein Möchtegern-Schreiber, sondern ein ernst zu nehmender, arrivierter Autor ist, zum anderen, dass Berlin sein Thema ist, das Berlin von heute mit seiner nationalsozialistischen Vergangenheit, mit Moabit als Sitz des NS-Volksgerichtshofs, Berlin als »Ort der Geschichte und als Ort der Schuld«.[1]

Er findet sich in einem winzigen Appartement wieder und stößt auf eine Zeitungsmeldung über einen Mord. Von einem Freund aus Studientagen, dem Staatsanwalt Tom, wird er gebeten, sich auf diesen Mordfall einzulassen, dem der Staatsanwalt sich selbst schon, wenn auch etwas unbeholfen, literarisch genähert hat. Mit

Skepsis geht der Autor an diese Aufgabe, die ihm mehr und mehr als Sisyphusarbeit erscheint. Da gibt es vieles, allzu vieles zu sortieren: Die Aufzeichnungen Toms, die nachgelassenen Schriften des Mordopfers R. – und Texte des Ich-Erzählers selbst, Träume, unter anderem, von Reisen in Städte, deren Namen zwar auf dem Atlas verzeichnet sind, die aber imaginären Charakter haben.

Von dem Moment an, als Tom dem Erzähler Texte aus dem Nachlass des Mordopfers R. übergibt, beginnt – und das macht etwa zwei Drittel des Buchs aus – ein Vexierspiel mit Individuen, die auf der Suche nach ihrer Identität sind. Die Leiche von R., eines erfolglos Schreibenden, der so geringe Einkünfte hatte, dass selbst die Finanzbeamten mit einem mitleidigen Achselzucken von einer steuerlichen Veranlagung absahen, muss ein Sadomasochist osmanischer Herkunft gewesen sein. So jedenfalls stellt es sich nicht nur dem Freund des Staatsanwalts dar, dem Erzähler der Rahmenhandlung, sondern auch allen weiteren Personen, die mit der Aufklärung des Mordfalls befasst sind.

Trotz der eingestreuten Kommentare des Erzählers der Rahmenhandlung fühlt man sich irregeleitet. Wollte er nicht selbst – realiter oder in Gedanken – nach Konstanza, Odessa, Batumi und Baku reisen? Wieso finden sich die Prosastücke nun als »Berichte von einer imaginären Reise« unter dem Nachlass des Mordopfers? Und Tom, der Staatsanwalt, verschmilzt mit einem fiktiven Robert, der vielleicht mit der Leiche des R. identisch ist.

Von Kapitel zu Kapitel wird es schwieriger zu unterscheiden, von wem diese Texte stammen, vom Staatsanwalt oder vom Schriftsteller, die sich beide mit dem Fall befassen – oder vom Opfer des Ritualmords, das, wie sich herausstellt, seinen Tod bewusst gesucht und herbeigeführt hat. Das erzählende Ich bewegt sich in einer nur scheinbar realen Welt; je mehr es sich auf die Einzelheiten seiner Umgebung einlässt, desto stärker verschwimmen die Konturen der Gegenwart und dessen, was man gemeinhin Wirklichkeit nennt. »Auf der Suche nach der eigentlichen Geschichte« (*E*, 86) werden Geschichten in Andeutungen erzählt, Wahrnehmungssplitter, die nur ansatzweise zu einem Erzählgewebe verdichtet sind. Für den Leser ergibt sich ein Puzzle aus gestochen scharfen Prosa-Elementen, die sich nur mit Geduld zu einem Ganzen zusammenfügen lassen.

'Der Antiquar' (*E*, 17–40) zum Beispiel hat surreale Züge; in einer Stadt mit geisterhaften Umrissen beschließt das Ich als Durchreisender, die einzige Buchhandlung am Ort, das Antiquariat, zu

übernehmen, besessen von der Idee, mit den Büchern auch »die
Zeiten zu ordnen«, Vergangenes in ordentlichen Epochen auf den
Regalen sichtbar werden zu lassen. In 'Fridaynightfever' (*E*, 69–73)
macht sich der Erzähler auf den Weg ins Bordell, nicht ohne ein
paar blasphemisch anmutende Seitenhiebe auf den Propheten Mohammed, den Gründer einer Religion loszulassen, der er sich nicht
mehr zugehörig fühlt – eine versteckte Solidaritätserklärung für
Salman Rushdie.[2] Tom, der Staatsanwalt, das Mordopfer R. und
der Ich-Erzähler verschmelzen mehr und mehr zu einer einzigen
Figur; ihre Wahrnehmungen sind kaum voneinander zu unterscheiden.

Manchmal gewinnt man den Eindruck, derjenige, der den Auf-
trag angenommen hat, Licht in die mysteriöse Angelegenheit zu
bringen, versucht, sich durch die verschiedenen Bewusstseins-
schichten der Figuren, die doch nur Facetten seiner selbst sind,
durchzuarbeiten, ihre Gedanken und Gefühle zu beschreiben, ohne
sie zu werten, vor allem, wenn es um jene sexuellen Praktiken
geht, die von der Lüsternheit eines Mannes zeugen, der die Fol-
terung durch dominante Frauen herausfordert. Nachdem er sich
als behutsam lesender und schreibender Autor auf die verschiedenen Aspekte der Personen – des eigenen Ich, des ermittelnden
Staatsanwalts und des Mordopfers – bis an die Grenzen der eigenen Miterlebensfähigkeit eingelassen hat, beschließt er, seine
Reise in jene fernen Orte – Konstanza, Odessa, Batumi, Baku –
anzutreten, von denen er bisher nur träumte. Ergebnis seiner
Nachforschungen im Seelen- und Hormonhaushalt der Figuren
des mörderischen Mosaiks aber ist das erste Kapitel eines Romans,
das er über diesen Fall schreiben wird. Es steht am Schluss des
Buchs.

Erzähltechnisch verfährt Zafer Şenocak nach einem raffinierten
Schachtelsystem. Der Reiz dieses 'Findelbuchs' liegt in dem Spiel
des Autors mit den Erwartungen seiner Leser, die zwar in keiner
Weise enttäuscht werden, wenn es um gekonnt beschriebene
sexuelle Praktiken geht, wohl aber in Fragen der Handlungsfäden.
Stilistische Kabinettstücke sind die einzelnen Texte allemal, aber
die Verknüpfung mit der allgemeinen Handlung ist zu vage, um
sich auf das orientalische Prinzip der Geschichten in der
Geschichte zu berufen. Auch das ist offensichtlich Strategie. Dieser
Autor ist nicht bereit, das Vorurteil zu bedienen, dass er als
Dichter aus dem Morgenland, der deutsch schreibt, Literatur nach
dem Muster von Tausendundeiner Nacht produzieren müsse.

Stattdessen spielt er mit Bewusstseinsebenen, die so ineinander übergehen, dass die einzelnen Personen nicht mehr trennscharf voneinander zu unterscheiden sind. Vom Vordergründigen dringt er immer tiefer in die psychischen Schichten seiner Figuren ein, die ein Erschrecken über deren inneres Grauen hervorrufen. Sexualität und Todesnähe, die Suche nach der Auflösung des Ich im Rausch der Sinne, die kein liebendes oder geliebtes Du kennt, stehen als Grundgedanken hinter diesem Puzzle-Spiel.

Gespaltene Persönlichkeiten

Bei einer genaueren Untersuchung der einzelnen Teile und Splitter dieses Puzzles, die sich keineswegs immer passgenau ineinander fügen lassen, sollte man die grundsätzlich ironische Erzählhaltung nicht aus den Augen verlieren. Jede einzelne Romanfigur ist in sich gespalten, und dennoch griffe eine allein vom Tiefenpsychologischen ausgehende Betrachtungsweise zu kurz. Denn die Spaltung hat viele Ursachen, die weder mit dem konventionellen noch einem wie auch immer gearteten unkonventionellen Instrumentarium der Psychoanalyse zu fassen sind. Ist der Riss doch ein interkultureller, der etwa durch die Person des Staatsanwalts wie durch jene des Mordopfers geht. Selbst jene tragenden Figuren des Romans, die überwiegend in deutschen Landen sozialisiert wurden, haben ihre Wurzeln in einer anderen Region, zum größten Teil in der Türkei, und sei es nur durch vage Erinnerungen der vorangehenden Generation vermittelt. Außerdem beherrscht Zafer Şenocak, wie gesagt, die Kunst des uneigentlichen Sprechens, die Ironie, so perfekt wie kaum ein anderer, der die literarische Tradition der Deutschen studiert hat.

> *Tom hieß nicht immer Tom. Um in den Staatsdienst aufgenommen zu werden, musste sich der gebürtige Türke einer »kosmetischen Operation«, wie er es nannte, unterziehen. Er nahm die deutsche Staatsbürgerschaft an. Da er keine halben Sachen mochte, änderte er bei dieser Gelegenheit auch seinen Namen. So heißt er jetzt nicht mehr Tayfun, sondern Tom. (E, 8)*

Was unter einer anderen, offensiveren Perspektive als opportunistische Überanpassung gewertet werden könnte, nimmt der Ich-Erzähler seinem Freund nicht krumm; er merkt nur kurz an, welchem Identitätswechsel er sich unterzogen hat, Tom, der ihm einer der liebsten Gesprächspartner ist. Denn er provoziert und er evoziert neue Ideen bei seinem Gegenüber. Die Tatsache aber, dass der – in diesem Stadium des Findelbuchs noch – fast auktoriale Erzähler Toms Identitätswandel an dieser Stelle kaum wertet, zeigt, dass er gegen jedweden Nationalismus gefeit ist. Er wirft ihm nicht etwa vor, er habe sein 'Türkentum' damit verraten, sondern zwischen den Zeilen ist eine eher pragmatische Haltung herauszulesen: Ein Mensch nimmt die Staatsbürgerschaft des Landes an, in dem er vielleicht schon seit seiner Geburt lebt, in dem er zur Schule gegangen ist und studiert hat. Um Beamter zu werden, braucht man den entsprechenden Pass. Den Namen hätte 'Tayfun' nicht wechseln müssen, aber er wollte sich diesem Staat mit Haut und Haaren verschreiben. Ob dies nur 'kosmetisch' ist, sei dahingestellt. Gegen Ende des Buchs, im Schlussteil, dem – wie der Verfasser erklärt – ersten Kapitel eines zu schreibenden Romans, wird dieser Aspekt wieder aufgegriffen:

> Der Staatsanwalt bekommt einen Anruf vom Standesamt. Das Opfer hat sich mit achtzehn Jahren einbürgern lassen. Bei dieser Gelegenheit hat er sich auch einen anderen Namen geben lassen. [. . .] Das war vor zwanzig Jahren. Es steckten also in dem Mann zwei Personen. Wenn die eine Person gestorben ist, lebt dann die andere weiter? (*E*, 117)

Auch hier wird nicht direkt gewertet, und doch zeigt diese rhetorische Frage, dass Identitätswechsel tödliche Folgen haben kann – für das erste, ursprüngliche Ich. Die Authentizität der Person geht verloren.

Viel drastischer wird der Identitätswechsel am Beispiel der 'Zenne' (*E*, 45-8), eines – vermutlich – entmannten Schauspielers, aus dessen Andeutungen hervorgeht, dass er Türke ist. Wie beim 'Antiquar' und 'Fridaynightfever' handelt es sich hier um einen eingeschobenen Text, der wohl aus dem Nachlass des Mordopfers stammt. Für die 'Zenne', einem Eunuchen vergleichbar, ist alles in Frage gestellt, nicht nur die eigene Männlichkeit, an die sie sich nur noch verschwommen erinnert. In Zweifel gezogen ist vor allem auch der Bereich der Religion, in der dieses Neutrum ohne Geschlecht – noch nicht einmal eine Frau – aufgewachsen ist:

> Ich habe kein Geschlecht. [. . .] Ich lese keine Bücher. Also lese ich auch nicht den Koran. [. . .] Überhaupt soll das Buch gar keinen Autor gehabt haben. Ich glaube nicht an so etwas wie an ein Buch ohne Autor. Während es selbstverständlich viele Autoren ohne Bücher gibt. Ich bin mir sicher, dass der Autor des Koran eine Zenne war. (*E*, 47)

Wieder eine Blasphemie, ähnlich wie im 'Fridaynightfever', eine Beleidigung des Propheten, zugleich aber auch ein Rütteln an den Grundfesten des Islam, der davon ausgeht, dass der Koran kein von Menschen geschaffenes Buch ist, sondern dem Propheten durch Vermittlung des Erzengels Gabriel – von Gott – eingegeben wurde. Dieser 'Zenne' ist jede Identität verloren gegangen; das Sich-Eins-Fühlen mit der Religion, in der er/sie/es offensichtlich aufgewachsen ist, und die Heimat im eigenen Geschlecht. Was bleibt, ist – zum Glück – das Theater, eine andere Welt, die die Welt auf irreale Weise darstellt und daher nicht mit den moralischen Maßstäben einer religiösen oder einer sexuellen Alltagsideologie zu messen ist.

Der Identitätswandel, der nur zum Teil bewusste Wechsel der Identität, wird bei allen Figuren des Buchs durch die Migration ausgelöst. So auch bei 'Mitra', einer jungen Frau aus einem ungenannten Land, das Persien sein könnte (*E*, 74–81). Zwischen den Büchern ihres Großvaters aufgewachsen, lässt sie sich von Marie, einer Berlinerin französischer Herkunft, zum Mitreisen und zur Liebe verführen, um ihr Geld schließlich als Domina in einem sadomasochistischen Kabinett zu verdienen. Auch für sie, wie für die männlichen Figuren, scheint die Endstation Prostitution zu sein. In dieser Reduzierung des männlichen wie des weiblichen Menschen auf das Geschlecht liegt ein extrem destruktiver Zug, vielleicht auch, weil die Zeugungsorgane so ganz und gar nicht mehr zur Fortpflanzung gedacht zu sein scheinen. Mit einer Ausnahme: In dem Text 'Der Fremdenführer' (E, 95–100) kommt eine Frau auf eine Insel, die ein wenig an die Stadt im Nirgendwo erinnert, in der 'Der Antiquar' angesiedelt ist, um in aller Anonymität ein Kind zu empfangen.

Orientierung im Erzählgefüge

Es ist wahrhaftig nicht leicht, sich als unvoreingenommene Leserin oder als an Zafer Şenocaks guten Stil gewöhnter Leser in dem Buch zurechtzufinden, da der Begriff des 'Gefüges' einer eher traditionellen Erzählweise verpflichtet ist. Das erste Kapitel des zu schreibenden Romans steht am Schluss, wie gesagt, und kurz davor zeigt der Erzähler Erbarmen mit dem zeitweise ein wenig hilflos im 'Findelbuch' verlorenen Leser, der nach dem roten Faden suchenden Leserin. »Zafer Şenocak erzählt nicht nur die kriminalistische Geschichte einer Reise, er erzählt auch den Krimi einer Fiktion, und dies mit gekonnter Lakonie«,[3] so kommentiert Dunja Bialas

den Roman und trifft damit den Punkt; denn hier, knapp zwanzig
Seiten vor dem Ende, greift der Ich-Erzähler noch einmal ein, um
zu sagen: »*Ich ahnte von Anfang an, dass Tom Robert war, und dass es
Robert nie gegeben hatte*« (*E*, 106). Damit ist auch der Mord eine Fiktion – so fiktiv wie die Satire vom 'Haus im Süden' (*E*, 82–94), in
dem das fiktive Mordopfer R. in seinen Aufzeichnungen alle Ver-
satzstücke US-amerikanischer Gruselstories nutzt, um drei Personen, John, Jane und Klara wie auf einem Schachbrett hin- und
herzuschieben, bis ihm die Phantasie einer mörderischen Sex-
geschichte zu gelingen scheint.

Nichts 'fügt' sich in logischer Manier ans andere, sondern es
bleibt tatsächlich den Lesenden überlassen, die einzelnen Texte in
einen Zusammenhang zu bringen. Der nun wiederum liegt in der
Ironie, mit der Sexualität und Kriminalität miteinander verbunden
und, zum Teil, *ad absurdum* geführt werden. Denn nichts hat sich
wirklich ereignet, sondern nur im Kopf des Erzählers, der während
des Schreibens nach wie vor auf der Suche nach der wirklichen
Geschichte ist – und immer wieder neu ansetzt. Das wiederum ist
nun in der Tat ein orientalisches Element – in dem Sinne, dass
thematisiert wird, man könne eine Geschichte auf diese oder jene
Art schreiben oder erzählen – oder auch ganz anders. Im Verlauf
der Lektüre und bei genauem Lesen wird eins deutlich: Der rote
Faden ist die Einsamkeit, aber auch die Verzweiflung des in seiner
Einsamkeit Schreibenden, dass die Welt sich ihm entzieht. Selbst
die Topographie ist selten eindeutig.

Die Suche nach der eigentlichen Geschichte, eine Suche, die
jedes geradlinige Erzählen in Frage stellt und dazu führt, dass
Geschichten entworfen und verworfen, aber selten wirklich ausge-
führt werden, prägt auch Zafer Şenocaks Roman um jüdisch-
türkisch-deutsche Gemeinsamkeiten, *Gefährliche Verwandtschaft* von
1998. Beide Bücher haben den Charakter von Vorstudien zu einem
zu schreibenden Roman, den Charakter einer Materialsammlung
aus Versatzstücken. Personen werden vorgestellt, ihre Wesenszüge
angedeutet, Sentenzen werden eingeschoben, Aphorismen, Texte,
die wie Essays wirken, Szenen reihen sich aneinander, verbunden
durch den Grundgedanken der Notwendigkeit, sich zu erinnern,
da geschichtslose Gegenwart einem Schweben im luftleeren Raum
gleich käme.

Ironische Melancholie

Ein Mord wird rekonstruiert, ein fiktiver Mord an einem Menschen, der seine Authentizität, seine ursprüngliche Person verloren und seinen Tod selbst gesucht hat. Rekonstruiert wird der Mord von einem Staatsanwalt, der diesen Mord erfunden hat, um sich an einem literarischen Sujet zu versuchen; der sich selbst als 'Tayfun' ausgelöscht und in einen 'Tom' verwandelt hat, um sich mit dem Staat, in dem er lebt, bis zum Äußersten zu identifizieren; der auch noch Beamter dieses Staats, Ankläger von Staats wegen geworden ist (*E*, 8).

Darin liegt die Ironie. 'Tom' ist die personifizierte Überanpassung. Ironisch ist aber auch diese permanente Fiktion in der Fiktion, eine Welt am Draht, deren Fäden nur der Verfasser in der Hand hält, jener Ich-Erzähler, der die Wärme der Gemeinschaft in einer großen, hellen Wohnung mit zwei Frauen, die sich weigern, ihm als 'Muse' zu dienen, verlassen muss, weil die beiden Frauen ihn nicht mehr aushalten. In die Kälte der Einsamkeit des Schreibenden zurückgeworfen, bleibt ihm nur die Auseinandersetzung mit seinen fiktiven Gestalten. Tom alias Mordopfer R. alias Robert gewinnen dabei die Oberhand und verwickeln ihn immer tiefer in einen Fall, dem er nur dadurch auf die Spur kommen kann, dass er Papiere, Dokumente und seine eigenen Gedanken sortiert, wie 'Der Antiquar', der Ordnung in die Zeiten, in die Geschichte der Menschheit bringen will.

Dass dies ein hoffnungsloses Unterfangen ist, weiß der Ich-Erzähler und tritt die Flucht, besser gesagt, den genau kalkulierten Weg in die Distanz an, an einen Punkt außerhalb der Geschichte und der Geschichten, indem er das probate Mittel der Ironie wählt. Nichts ist eigentlich wirklich, nur das, was er mit einem deutlich spürbaren inneren Abstand erzählt. Dieser Abstand entsteht durch Präzision, durch die Exaktheit der Worte und der Syntax, durch gestaltete Sprache. Jede Koketterie, jedes überflüssige Wortgeklingel ist dem Verfasser fremd. Er erfindet eine Welt am Draht, bewegt diese Drähte nach Lust und Laune -- und einer Logik, der seine Leser und Leserinnen nur durch akribische Lektüre auf die Spur kommen: »Wer Geschichten schreiben will, muss Geheimnisse haben, mit denen er die Leser locken kann. Man kann nur in einer Sprache Geheimnisse haben« (*E*, 121).

Sein Geheimnis ist die innere, ist die ironische Distanz. Gelockt werden die Leser aber auch dadurch, dass der Verfasser ihre Lüsternheit hervorkitzelt. Genauso, wie das 'Mordopfer', oder wie

Robert, von erotischen, wenn nicht pornographischen Szenen, sei
es in japanischen Sexfilmen, sei es in Peep-Shows, magisch ange-
zogen wird, um Positionen, die im eigenen Repertoire noch fehlen,
zuerst einmal theoretisch kennen zu lernen, sind Leserinnen wie
Leser auch im Jahr 2001 noch von neuen, ihnen unbekannten Kör-
perstellungen beim Bumsen zu begeistern, selbst wenn etwa im
Kamasutra oder in Boccaccios *Decamerone*, zum Teil auch im Alten
Testament schon fast alles beschrieben ist, was man oder frau wissen muss. Und dennoch lockt es, immer noch. Aber selbst wenn
die spannendsten Sex-Szenen detailliert ausgemalt werden, bleibt
ein kühler Hauch. Die innere Hitze, die Totalität der authentisch
Liebenden, gleichgültig, ob in der Kombination Mann-Frau, Mann-
Mann oder Frau-Frau, fehlt. Auch hier dominiert die Kälte des
distanziert Beobachtenden. Der Verfasser kommentiert Liebe, wie
er sie sieht, mit den Worten:

> Ich liebe die deutsche Sprache für Worte wie»Selbstaufgabe«,»Selbst-
> vergessenheit«,»Selbstlosigkeit«. Wird in diesen Worten nicht der
> wahre Charakter von Liebe deutlich? (*E*, 121)

Dieser Kommentar lässt sich als Schlüsselsatz werten; das liebende
Subjekt, dem ein geliebtes Objekt – fast durchgängig – fehlt, sucht
ein anderes, ihn liebendes Subjekt, dem es sich bedingungslos un-
terwirft, auch um den Preis der totalen 'Selbstaufgabe', des Todes.
Übrigens ohne Auferstehung; von Transzendenz im christlichen
oder islamischen Sinn ist nirgendwo die Rede. Die Grundhaltung
ist existenzialistisch: ein Leben nach dem Tod wird aus-
geschlossen. Tod ist Ausgelöscht-Werden.
     Es ist, ob erotisch oder im Sinne der Todessuche, eine Welt am
Draht. Manches Mal aber gleiten dem Verfasser die Drähte aus der
Hand, verwirren sich, und der oder die Lesende ist aufgefordert,
Ordnung in die Zeiten, in die Texte und die Personenspaltungen
zu bringen. Aber selbst wenn die Drähte, die Handlungsfäden sich
nicht immer nach dem Geheiß ihres Marionettenspielers richten, so
bleibt ihm doch immerhin eins: die Souveränität dessen, der
entwirft und verwirft, Personen und Geschichten ein Stück weit
erfindet und dann ins unausweichliche Leere laufen lässt. Dies
wiederum bedingt eine ironische Melancholie, eine Trauer um den
Verlust, um Personen, die dadurch verloren gehen, dass sie sich
scheinbar selbst aufgeben, in der (fiktiven) Wirklichkeit aber vom
Verfasser aufgegeben werden, eine Trauer um die Geschichten, die

ihm aus der Hand gleiten, weil sie sich nicht auf süffig-
konventionelle Art und Weise weiterentwickeln lassen.

Interkulturalität als Zeichen der Zeit

Der interkulturelle Riss, der die Spaltung der Figuren bestimmt,
geht durch das gesamte 'Findelbuch' und macht seinen Reiz aus.
Wenn Karin Yeşilada davon spricht, dass »Archivieren und Aus-
graben von Geschichte [...] zentrale Leitmotive nicht nur in Şenocaks Lyrik seit Beginn der neunziger Jahre, sondern auch in seinen
Essays« sind, wenn sie von einer »gebrochen reflektierten Inter-
kulturalität« spricht, »deren Randpunkte und Bruchstellen der
Autor zu benennen versucht«,[4] so lässt sich ergänzen, dass dies
nicht nur für die Gedichte und die theoretischen Texte des Autors
gilt, sondern vor allem auch für die Romane.

Um die literarischen Einflüsse auf das Werk Zafer Şenocaks
oder auch nur auf seinen letzten Roman zu untersuchen, fehlt hier
der Platz, zumindest, um sie auszuloten. Hier kann nur einiges von
der Vielschichtigkeit angedeutet werden. Das Spektrum der Kulturen, in denen der Autor – schreibend – zu Hause ist, wäre mit
der Dichotomie Türkisch-Deutsch zu kurz gegriffen. Aber außer-
ordentlich 'deutsch' ist allemal die ironische Grundhaltung, die
beispielsweise Friedrich Schlegel und Ludwig Tieck in ihren
Jugendjahren bis zum Exzess getrieben haben; genau davon finden
sich deutliche Spuren, wenn man die erzählerische Strategie der
Fiktion der Fiktion in der Fiktion betrachtet. Signifikant ist auch
der Einfluss der sogenannten 'Kahlschlagliteratur' nach der
'Stunde Null', nach 1945. Dies zeigt sich in der lakonischen Sprache, in dem bewussten Verzicht auf jedes Brimborium, auf alle
Manierismen, und eine Sprachdisziplin, die jedes Wort abklopft,
um nicht in das Vokabular aus dem Wörterbuch der Unmenschen
aus der Zeit des Nationalsozialismus zu verfallen.

Türkisch ist – auf jeden Fall – die Lust am Fabulieren, auch die
Lust an Spiegelbildern, Spiegelbildern des Ich im Anderen, und
die Lust am Beobachten aus der Distanz. Hier ließen sich viele
literarische Vorbilder nennen, wären da nicht auch zwei Hinweise
im 'Findelbuch' auf Nâzım Hikmet, einen Dichter, dem Şenocak
sich schon allein dadurch verwandt fühlen dürfte, dass er kosmo-
politisch gedacht und geschrieben hat.

Nicht zu unterschätzen ist aber auch der Einfluss zeitgenössischer amerikanischer Autoren. Lässt man sich genauer auf die Persiflage 'Das Haus im Süden' ein, wird man an Don DeLillo oder

Paul Auster erinnert. Hier werden paranoide Mord- und Sexual-
phantasien so zynisch ausgebreitet, dass man sich des Eindrucks
nicht erwehren kann, dass der Berliner Schriftsteller aus türkischer
Familie alle Register seines europäisch-orientalischen Kulturver-
ständnisses zieht, um sich über eine Gesellschaft lustig zu machen,
die außer Sex und Nekrophilie nichts anderes mehr im Kopf zu
haben scheint.

Souverän geht der Autor mit seinem persönlichen 'interkul-
turellen Riss' um, indem er ihn nicht als Riss begreift, sondern als
Chance, als Möglichkeit, die sozialen und persönlichen Brüche
einer Gesellschaft im Wandel zu beschreiben, indem er von der
Wahrnehmung des Aktuellen, der Gegenwart, immer wieder in
Vergangenes eindringt und darstellt, wie die Personen zu ihrer
meist nicht ganz freiwillig angenommenen oder aufoktroyierten
Identität kamen. Lesern und Leserinnen wird bewusst, was diesen
Gestalten fehlt, denen die soziale wie kulturelle Substanz verloren
gegangen ist. Aber bei der Lektüre schleicht sich ein anderes Gefühl des Verlusts ein: Warum wird nicht ein einziges Mal eine
Geschichte zu Ende erzählt, warum nur reiht sich Entwurf an
Entwurf? Gewiss, oben wurde ausführlich dargelegt, dass es sich
dabei um eine Strategie des Erzählens handelt, aber man wünschte
sich, dass aus dem Puzzlespiel eines Tages ein Panorama würde, in
dem die einzelnen Handlungsdrähte dieser fiktiven Welt stärker
miteinander verbunden würden.

Anmerkungen

[1] Karin Yeşilada, 'Zafer Şenocak', in *Kritisches Lexikon zur deutschsprachigen Gegenwartsliteratur* (Göttingen, edition text+kritik, 1987–), 58.
Nachlieferung (1998), 4.

[2] Vgl. 'Der Dichter und die Deserteure', *Hitler*, 21–8.

[3] Dunja Bialas, 'Zafer Şenocak, *Der Erottomane*', in *Münchner Stadtmagazin*, Januar 2000.

[4] Yeşilada, 'Zafer Şenocak', 4.

8

Zafer Şenocak's Essays and Early Prose Fiction: From Collective Multiculturalism to Fragmented Cultural Identities

JAMES JORDAN

Zafer Şenocak stands as one of the most articulate and perceptive observers of Germany's struggle to come to terms with its increasing ethnic plurality. In *Atlas des tropischen Deutschland* (1992) and *War Hitler Araber? IrreFührungen an den Rand Europas* (1994), he comments on the state of relations between the German and Turkish communities and explores the principles which might underpin a society capable of accommodating both cultural traditions constructively. While these principles are predicated on stable and definable group identities, Şenocak already shows an awareness that collective political solutions to the problems of multiculturalism are inadequate in themselves to describe, let alone resolve, the dilemma of those whose cultural allegiance is split between two or more traditions.

Shortly after the publication of these essays, Şenocak began writing prose fiction. The fragmentary and enigmatic *Der Mann im Unterhemd* (1995) was followed by *Die Prärie* (1997) and *Gefährliche Verwandtschaft* (1998), novels which can justifiably be seen as a pair. The novels depict fragmentations of key elements of individual identity, and in particular the struggle of characters to resolve the contradictions and incompatibilities of their multiple cultural backgrounds. These prose fiction works are, in essence, an exploration of the limitations of the politics of multiculturalism in addressing individual rather than collective needs.

This essay will look first at Şenocak's views of German–Turkish relations in the aftermath of unification and the ensuing rise of xenophobic violence in the early 1990s. Against this background it reviews his attempts to outline a multicultural solution to the problems arising from these relations, which could overcome the alternating exoticization and demonization of the Turks in Germany. The prose fiction works will then be shown to develop Şenocak's understanding of the more individual problems of second- and subsequent-generation migrants, who seek to reconcile in their personal sphere traditions whose relationship in the public sphere is still uneasy and unresolved.

Şenocak's critique of German and Turkish attitudes towards integration and multiculturalism needs to be seen against the background of the unification of Germany. The enormity of the events of 1989–90, along with the prolonged period of national introspection which followed them, distracted attention from consideration of the shape of an ethnically plural society. As he put it in 1993: 'Nun droht in Deutschland vor lauter Einheit die Vielfalt verlorenzugehen.'[1] The relegation of multiculturalism in the order of national priorities, combined with the rejection of immigrants as fully enfranchised citizens, had led to increased social and ideological polarization, he argued. Immigrants had been reclassified globally as non-Germans, and had for their part lost confidence in the country's institutions. Some were turning to violent and intolerant ideologies. Confronted by constant reminders of their impermanent status, they had failed to engage in the process of integration which would normally follow immigration. Germans, in Şenocak's view, had also abandoned attempts to find common ground. The discourse of unification centred on concepts such as 'Nation' and 'Volk', inadequate for a situation in which historical and social continuities were fragmenting (*Atlas*, 40). Moreover, it was in part the ethnically exclusive nature of German nationhood that led to fascism. The preoccupation with nation in the post-unification era risked a return to dangerous tendencies towards exclusion (*Atlas*, 56–61).

The political trends of the early 1990s compounded what Şenocak saw as a deep ambivalence amongst Germans towards Turks. On the one hand was the condescension of an industrially advanced nation towards the 'Hilfsarbeiter Türke', exploited by ruthless German entrepreneurs and unable to articulate his needs and rights.[2] In this respect, Günter Wallraff's exposé *Ganz unten* (1985), while intended to highlight the plight of low-paid and black-economy workers, merely reinforced notions of the Turks as incapable of advocating their own cause, an image which German media subsequently failed to correct or put into perspective.[3] Parallel, and apparently contradictory, to this view of the Turkish population was an exoticization of selected aspects and perceptions of Turkish culture. This enabled German society to reject and oppress its Turkish minority while convincing itself that it was fundamentally positively inclined towards Turkish culture and the Turkish presence in Germany. This contradictory approach was only possible in an unequal relationship: 'Verteufelung und Glorifizierung des Fremden liegen nah beieinander, beides sind Abwehrmechanismen, die nicht auf einem partnerschaftlichen Verhältnis, sondern auf einem Herrschaftsverhältnis fußen' (*Atlas*, 11).

Concurring with Edward Said's critique of orientalism, Şenocak saw the maintenance and reinforcement of selected images of Turkey principally as an exercise of power which ignored all images and ideas which did not contribute to the retention of that power.[4] Şenocak was particularly critical of *Das Leben ist eine Karawanserei* (1992) and its author, Emine Sevgi Özdamar.[5] Her work, he argued, pandered to the fairy-tale orientalism of the German reading public, who took Turkish writers seriously only when they conformed to their preconceptions. In this way, she retarded any authentic cultural encounter between Germans and migrant and post-migrant Turks. As he expressed it in a poetic essay on her novel: 'verstehen ist anders / aber rauschen ist schöner'. Turks, he suggested, must look for other sources of validation than conformity to German clichés:

ein anderes Leben haben wir unter euch
und unter euch ist unser Leben illegal
ein Leben ohne Zauber ohne Märchen ohne Tricks ist illegal
nur eure Phantasie verleiht unserem Leben Legalität (*Hitler*, 55)

One of the clear implications of his argument is that, far from advancing a differentiated and realistic understanding of migrant and post-migrant culture, Özdamar's success created a model by which authors could achieve acknowledgement without challenging the preconceptions of their German readership.

This development was especially unhelpful to the second generation of migrants, who faced great difficulty in establishing a space in which they could develop work which addressed their needs and problems. There was little for them in the German media which, in exoticizing and demonizing Turks by turns, reflected the wider attitudes of German society. Their only other source of information and opinion came from Turkey's media, whose concerns were remote from those of the second generation of migration: 'Die Medien und die öffentliche Meinung der Türken in Deutschland sind verlängerte Arme türkischer Medien, türkischer öffentlicher Meinung, türkischen Bewußtseins und sind bisher ohne jede Eigenständigkeit, eigene Vision' (*Atlas*, 9). The second generation's efforts to produce more relevant work, Şenocak reluctantly concluded, had been sparse and had little success.

Two specific strategies appeared crucial to Şenocak at this stage. The first generation could at least relate to the issues covered by the Turkish media, but the second generation were 'die eigentlich Fremden, weil ihnen der Blick in den Rückspiegel versperrt ist' (*Atlas*, 11). They must therefore challenge the 'Alleinvertretungsanspruch der Türkei' by divesting themselves of 'das Obrigkeitsdenken der Eltern' and relinquishing 'eine einseitige Türkei-orientierung' (*Atlas*, 13). The second strategy links in directly with this. Turks, particularly the younger generation, had for the most part failed to engage critically and positively with the wider problems of German society and history. They must assert their right to comment on the general issues confronting their adopted society and must be visible in so doing. Obeying his own enjoinder, Şenocak's essays in the early 1990s address issues such as 'Vergangenheitsbewältigung' and unification.

The racist murders in Mölln and Solingen and the attacks on hostels for asylum seekers, for example in Hoyerswerda, prompted Şenocak to move beyond criticism and analysis of relations between Germans and 'Ausländer' and to engage with the more conceptual debate surrounding multiculturalism. He rejected the demonstrations of solidarity with foreigners shown by Germans in the aftermath of these attacks: 'Mit Sprüchen wie »Mein Freund ist Ausländer« wird diese kulturelle Debatte kaum zu führen sein. Darin wird lediglich nur jene Wirklichkeit sprachlich (semantisch?) reproduziert, in der »der Ausländer« funktionalisiert wird.'[6] The unthinking use of such terms as 'Integration' and 'multikulturelle Gesellschaft', he further argued, was misguided and potentially counter-productive. The aspiration that foreigners should integrate into German society meant no more than assimilation, while multiculturalism had to mean more than 'das berührungslose Nebeneinander von Kulturen und Lebensanschauungen' (*Atlas*, 10).

The problems did not, however, exist solely on the side of the majority community. The pressure of the majority on the minority to assimilate was balanced by an equal pressure from minorities to preserve their 'identity', founded on the illusory notion that such things are discrete and unfragmented (*Atlas*, 43–4). In their enthusiasm to deal with clear group identities like individual figures on a chess board, majority and minority communities begin to share a discourse of 'das Eigene und das Fremde' in order to distance themselves from one another and to demarcate the boundaries of their (perceived) identities. Both had become divorced from the reality of modern societies of immigration: 'Die Wirklichkeit ist aber synkretisch. Es ist die Wirklichkeit der Mulatten, der Bastarde' (*Atlas*, 42). A conception of the multicultural society which excluded cultural fusion was condemned to irrelevance.

A central problem for Şenocak in the discussion of multiculturalism was the concept of culture itself. He follows Raymond Williams: 'Sie war der Ausdruck für eine bestimmte Art und Weise zu leben' (*Hitler*, 63). It is more than the creative achievements of a society: it is actually the ground on which these are built. But a society's conception of 'Kultur' springs inevitably from its own cultural context and perspective. Other forms of 'Kultur' recognized as such by one's own culture are those forms which accord with the expectations of one's own culture: 'Schon hinter der Definition anderer Kulturen als Kultur steht eine bestimmte Vorstellung von Kultur, die auch für die anderen gültig sein soll' (*Hitler*, 62). There is an inherent inability to recognize as valid cultures radically different from one's own. If the concept of 'Kultur' is no longer valid, then neither can be concepts requiring combinations of discrete 'Kulturen', such as symbiosis.

Şenocak argued that two main options are available if one accepts this initial premise. One is to reject the relativization it implies and to adopt one's own culture as the qualitative yardstick for all others. Another, though, is to accept that the language we use to describe our own culture is inadequate to define any other, because it contains underlying presumptions particular to our own cultural context. Thus: 'Wir und die Anderen sind alle gleichermaßen sprachlos, wenn wir einander betrachten' (*Hitler*, 62). If we accept the inadequacy of language for this task, then we liberate ourselves from the perceived need to define the Other before we can approach a definition of ourselves. A new language, created jointly with the Other, is necessary. But this cannot be achieved by conventional means: scientific objectivity is compromised by its cultural particularity; subjectivity is equally questionable; and dialectics are inappropriate in a task which aims at the removal of 'Gegensätze' (*Hitler*, 62).

A first step in this process might be to overcome the inherent fear of the cultural superiority of the Other and accept a tabula rasa in which we are 'stumme Zeitgenossen' who need to communicate not with language but with 'einer Art von Zeichensprache' (*Hitler*, 63). Those wanting to reach a new understanding must acknowledge their 'Sprachlosigkeit', a difficult step given that such a confession implies a loss of power – of the power to determine and thus to dominate the Other. Admitting our 'Sprachlosigkeit' raises fears that the Other will force its language on us, and so dominate us. Such fears rest on a dialectical world view based on power relations in which dominance is validated by subordination.

Şenocak sees a meaningful process of engaging with the Other as comprising three stages. Perceiving the Other ('Erkennen') relativizes one's own standpoint and makes assumptions of cultural particularity impossible. By getting to know the other culture ('Kennenlernen'), fears of cultural domination are overcome. And the recognition of the validity of the Other ('Anerkennen') removes the possibility of presumptions of cultural superiority. Thus the starting point of and key to the process is taking leave of the concept of 'Kultur' and accepting the relativizations which this necessarily brings with it:

> Wer sich vom Begriff der Kultur verabschiedet hat, hat seine Festung abgerissen, wird seinen Standpunkt nicht verabsolutieren können, denn er ist ebenso nackt und unberührt wie der Andere. Nicht mehr an seinen Schuhspitzen orientiert er sich, sondern am Horizont, dort wo dieser sich mit dem Horizont des Anderen verschmelzen kann. (*Hitler*, 64)

This is the 'fusion of horizons' advocated by Charles Taylor in his seminal essay 'Multiculturalism and the politics of recognition', where he argues forcefully that multicultural models cannot be orientated around the perceptions of a dominant culture. A key starting-point for Taylor is a presumption of value in other cultures, and this requires the abandonment of notions of intrinsic cultural superiority.[7]

Şenocak was far from alone amongst German intellectuals in the early 1990s who turned to North American and Anglo-Saxon sociologists and philosophers such as Taylor, Stephen Castles and John Rex. Until the late 1980s the 'multicultural' debate in Germany was relatively simplistic, centring on how guest workers and their children (along with some political exiles) might be best integrated into German society. The waves of de facto immigration in the late 1980s and early 1990s, consisting mainly of large numbers of asylum seekers and returning 'Aussiedler', fragmented the established pattern of immigration. The official insistence that united Germany was not a country of immigration had by now clearly become untenable. Seeking to develop a debate on multiculturalism, intellectuals such as Jürgen Habermas, Ulrich Herbert and Klaus J. Bade, and of course Şenocak with them, turned to existing models which might be adapted to Germany's changed circumstances. The problem was that these models were based on radically different initial conditions, such as the integration of post-colonial migration in Britain, or the resolution of the Quebec question in Canada. It became apparent that no existing model fitted the conditions in Germany, namely, a highly industrialized welfare society with a deeply problematic ethnic and national identity of its own, attracting large numbers of (soon to be permanent) immigrants from very different societies.

This was not the only problem posed by the adoption of these multicultural models. By now, many guest workers and asylum seekers had either started families in Germany or had fetched their spouses and children from their home country. These children (amongst them Şenocak himself) grew up having to acknowledge both German society's formative influences upon them and the sense of otherness arising from their family's cultural heritage. Multiculturalisms based on clearly defined collectives ascribed them automatically to the community of their parents' generation and ignored their difficulties in establishing their own personal identity. It is the needs and confusions of the second and subsequent generations which Şenocak sought to address in his prose fiction from the mid-1990s onwards, to which we now turn.

Despite a certain quality of elusiveness, the opening sequence of *Der Mann im Unterhemd* initially promises familiar territory to the reader. The narrator, we learn, is a Turkish private eye based in a bureau in Berlin who specializes in missing persons, particularly

Turkish girls. The immediate association is not with Raymond
Chandler but rather with Jakob Arjouni and his Turkish private
detective Kemal Kayankaya.[8] The reader is led to anticipate an
exploration of issues facing the detective figure, by now conventional in 'Migrantenliteratur'. How does the detective relate to
living and working in Germany? What kind of associations and
dislocations are caused by the requirement of commuting between
his adopted country and his country of origin? What kinds of cultural adjustment are necessary in his situation, and what personal
cost do these exact? These are, as it were, the standard issues addressed by the 'Migrantenliteratur' of the late 1980s and early
1990s, relating principally to a conception of the migrant as caught
between two distinct cultures. Şenocak himself expressed this dilemma pungently in a poem published in 1983 and subsequently
much quoted: 'ich trage zwei Welten in mir // [. . .] die Grenze
verläuft / mitten durch meine Zunge'.[9]

What shatters both the assumptions of the reader and the familiar bipolar conception of the position of the migrant is the complex and multivalent figure of the woman who is the object of the
narrator's quest. At the end of the opening chapter, after the nar-
rator/detective's search is called off by his office, she appears as a
stewardess on a return flight from Istanbul to Frankfurt. It can be
inferred in subsequent chapters that the narrator has embarked on
a personal search initiated by the enquiries after this woman –
called Lisa in one sequence of stories – and the transition he experiences between Germany and Turkey. The attempt to establish
Lisa's location and motivation triggers a series of reflections on an
interconnected range of problems which have been troubling him.
The shifting of time frames between the present-day Lisa and her
grandmother (also Lisa) prompts the narrator to reflect on his own
relationship with his father and grandfather. Lisa's sexuality, at
times passive and accommodating, at others aggressive and selfish,
causes the narrator to consider traditional conceptions of the male
and female and to reflect on the locus of power in sexual relationships. The narrator also explores the question of the writer as a
sexual participant, experiencing the primal drives of sexuality but
at the same time emotionally distanced from the act itself by his
need to analyse and depict experience. In all, this first major prose
fiction work represents a radical questioning of Şenocak's positions up to that point, using the power of fiction (Kafka is ever

present) and in particular of metaphor to explore a wide range of the facets of the experience of the migrant, the male and the writer. Şenocak sums up this sea change in his attitudes in the final, auto-biographical chapter of the work, by quoting Salman Rushdie: 'Was ist das Gegenteil von Glaube? Nicht Unglaube. Zu endgültig, gewiß, hermetisch. Selbst eine Art Glaube. Zweifel' (*MiU*, 141).

If *Der Mann im Unterhemd* appears to reject attempts to rationalize the world and its phenomena and to weave this understanding into a hermeneutically complete narrative, then Şenocak's first novel *Die Prärie* represents the search for a new beginning in the reconstruction of an identity. The central figure, Sascha, relates in detail his sexual adventures in Germany in a restless search for a stable relationship with a woman. The focus on his sexuality eclipses other intriguing details about him: for example, that he is of Turkish origin, living in Berlin, a writer jobbing between advertising agencies and journalism, wishing to become a serious novelist. The fact that these other aspects of him are given so little prominence and are explicitly not problematized suggests that his preoccupation with his sexual life represents a transference of emphasis away from other issues in his life which he is unable satisfactorily to resolve.

This tendency is confirmed when he takes up a post as writer-in-residence at a North American college at the very end of the 1980s. He dismisses any possibility that German unification will open up prospects for meaningful change, either in the personal or public spheres: 'Wenn man sich verändern will, muß man erst einmal die Orientierung verlieren' (*P*, 69). What better place to do this than in the featureless North American prairie landscape, the externalization of Sascha's aspiration to divest himself of his cultural and historical antecedents? At first Sascha seems convinced that moving to America has helped to resolve the inconsistencies in his own cultural identity because he is no longer confronted with the need to commute between two communities:

In Amerika gelang mir die Flucht aus Deutschland. [. . .] In der Türkei, ich hatte es auch dort einmal versucht, war mir die Flucht mißlungen, da die Türkei, wie Italien, ein unbedeutender Ort in Deutschland ist. Täglich werden die Grenzen zwischen der Türkei und Deutschland von Tausenden von Menschen aufgehoben. Bei diesen Aktivitäten zwischen zwei Ländern verlagern sich die Grenzen nach innen. In jedem menschlichen Körper gibt es einen Grenzverlauf, der mit den

Staatsgrenzen korrespondiert. Diese Grenzen werden dort für immer aufgehoben. Man wird sie weder durch Staatsverträge noch durch Gedächtnisschwund los. Wenn Sie Deutschland meiden wollen, müssen Sie die Türkei loswerden und umgekehrt. (*P*, 73)

But Sascha is only avoiding confronting his problems, as he is reminded when a former editor telephones him to commission an article on American views of the attacks in Mölln and Solingen. Attempting to avoid the issues, Sascha tells the editor that there are no Turks in his part of America, receiving the reply: 'Türken gibts überall. Die heißen da halt nur anders' (*P*, 87).

In a final attempt to escape his problems, Sascha takes up hunting in order to melt into the American way of life. In order to do this, he must acquire a driving licence. Describing where he comes from to the American driving examiner, Sascha refers to Turkey as: 'Weit weg im Osten. Alles, was weit weg ist, ist doch im Osten' (*P*, 88). The American brings home to him how different American cartography is, pointing out that Japan is far away both geographically and culturally but also lies, from his perspective, in the West. The remark relativizes and throws back into confusion Sascha's assumptions about the correlation between geographical relationships and cultural identities. In the New World, Eurocentric critiques of orientalism do not apply in the same way.

The novel concludes in Sascha's failure to resolve or escape his cultural contradictions. This outcome was already indicated when he related a dream he had had in Berlin, in which he is confronted by a stranger who tells him he is going to change both his identity and his gender. Sascha reflects: 'Ja, beim Geschlecht ist es einfach: Da gibt es nur zwei Möglichkeiten. Aber bei der Identität? Da ist man fast so ratlos wie vor den Auslagen in einem Supermarkt. Endlose Kreuzungen, großes Durcheinander' (*P*, 63). Sascha may have failed, but he has become aware that the solution cannot lie in trying to escape either his own Turkish cultural traditions or the conflicts which arise when these are transposed into German society. The novel is not so much a warning against 'die Gefahren eines globalen Multi-Kulti-Mix', as Hans-Jürgen Heise has put it, as against hopes that the consequences of one's own cultural background can simply be avoided.[10]

Şenocak's second novel *Gefährliche Verwandtschaft* is clearly a sequel to *Die Prärie*. Sascha returns to Berlin with the German-born linguist Marie, now his wife, hoping she will be of assistance to him in his 'Heimatsuche' (*GV*, 20) – his attempt to clarify his relationship towards his cultural backgrounds. The catalyst in this process are the diaries of his paternal grandfather, which are bequeathed to him. Sascha Muhteschem's acceptance of the silver casket containing the diaries is a symbolic acknowledgement of the legitimacy of part of the cultural heritage he had sought to escape from in the United States. Berlin is to be the scene of his bid to establish a clear identity for himself:

> Ich hatte keine Identität. Damit hatten Menschen in meiner Umgebung zunehmend Probleme. Es war, als hätte der Fall der Mauer, der Zusammenbruch der alten Ordnung, nicht nur eine befreiende Funktion gehabt. Ohne Mauer fühlte man sich nicht mehr geborgen. Identität ist zum Ersatzbegriff für Geborgenheit geworden. Man fixiert sich, den anderen, seine Herkunft, um Nähen und Distanzen zu bestimmen. Überall konnte man auf unsichtbare Mauern stoßen, die nach dem Fall der Mauer errichtet worden waren. Die Welt war komplizierter geworden, die Wege labyrinthartiger. Früher hätte man sich sorglos dem Spieltrieb hingegeben, sich auf Irrwegen wohlgefühlt, die Mauer schützte einen vor dem Abgrund. [. . .] Mein Weg würde mich also unweigerlich in die Vergangenheit führen. Ihre Vergegenwärtigung schien mir unvermeidbar. (*GV*, 47)

Sascha's hope at this stage is that by opening himself to his family's past – the opposite of what he tried in *Die Prärie* – the connections will establish themselves naturally, and that there is an already extant identity waiting to be rediscovered.

As the novel unfolds, this assumption proves to be premature. For a very long time Sascha fails to make any serious effort to decipher the diaries, written partly in Arabic and partly in Cyrillic script. Will the diaries prove to be merely banal reminiscences? Or will they reveal secrets so personal to his grandfather that they are irrelevant to Sascha in his quest? He muses, beginning to consider himself the novelist of his grandfather's biography:

> Ein Tagebuch ist kein Buch. Es ist vielmehr ein Organ seines Verfassers. Es legt offen, was ein Erzähler vor seinen Figuren verheimlicht. Die entscheidende Frage beim Erzählen ist, ob Schreiber, Figuren und Leser im Bann des Erzählens sich selbst finden können. (*GV*, 41)

He is distracted by accepting a journalistic commission to produce monologues by young Turks in Germany in order to give them a voice. The monologues feature three young Turks and then 'Zafer, Schriftsteller' (*GV*, 102).[11] Zafer's 'monologue' consists of excerpts from articles and essays which Şenocak himself had previously published, teasing the reader into identifying Zafer and, by extension, Sascha (the similarity of the names is not unintentional) with Şenocak himself. The exposure to the views of other Turks and the sometimes distorting attitudes of German journalists and readers renew Sascha's urge to understand the diaries. He commissions a translation, but this will be delivered in a long series of weekly instalments. The process of encounter with his cultural heritage is to be a gradual one, no Damascene revelation. Sascha moves out of his shared flat with Marie and returns to his creative writing, implying that establishing an identity is more than a simple act of discovery: it requires a creative contribution from the individual in assembling elements of his own heritage into a personal rather than a collective identity. As Barbara Frischmuth notes, the novel is less the story of the grandfather than of the process by which Sascha reflects on himself.[12]

The need for individuals, and in particular writers, to participate actively in constructing their own understanding of their identity is expanded upon in the essay 'Welcher Mythos schreibt mich?' (*Zunge*, 97–103).[13] Here Şenocak reacts against those who seek to understand a writer's work by relating it directly to his or her biography. Instead, he argues, they should explore the writer's 'mythische Grundlage' which has given rise to an individual 'Schreibmythos'. By this he means the range of experiences and influences which underpin the writer's conceptual world. In his case this is a deep ambivalence arising from a family divided by tradition and modernity, rationality and mysticism, tolerance and conformity. From the remains of these conflicts Şenocak constructed his personal approach, which sees interchangeability rather than polarity, fluidity rather than rigidity. Fundamentally sceptical, he develops an eclectic technique, and he argues that the writer's task is to assemble the elements of diverse styles, historical periods, and so on, coherently:

> Unsere Welt hat sich in eine Baustelle verwandelt. Doch läßt es sich dort nicht nach einem bestimmten Plan bauen. Keine schlechte Zeit für Autoren. Sie werden herausgefordert, Pläne zu entwerfen, die weniger nach Gültigkeit als nach ihrer Phantasieleistung zu beurteilen sind. (*Zunge*, 102–3)

This is the position in which Sascha finds himself at the end of *Gefährliche Verwandtschaft*. His grandfather's diaries are not the key to his identity problems, but just one more element which he has the responsibility to combine into his own 'Schreibmythos'. The extract from his new novel shows that he has begun this process. The close of his novel marks a new beginning for Sascha.

In terms of the development of Şenocak's thinking on multi-culturalism and cultural identity, much of the inspiration for his protagonist's German-Jewish-Turkish background comes from ideas formulated in essays in *Atlas des tropischen Deutschland* and *War Hitler Araber?*, and summarized at the start of chapter 25 of *Gefährliche Verwandtschaft* (*GV*, 89–90). The opening out of German–Jewish dialogue into a three-cornered discussion involving the Turks in Germany would prevent the Turks from being drawn into 'die Fußstapfen der deutschen Juden von einst' (*GV*, 90). Sascha goes on to comment: 'Solche Phantasien habe ich nur, wenn ich gut gelaunt bin. Die Wirklichkeit gibt mir keinen Anlaß zu solch konkreten, optimistischen Überlegungen' (*GV*, 90). Here Şenocak draws a clear distinction between a rational, optimistic and objective analysis of Germans, Jews and Turks as distinct communities, and the reality for individuals coping with fragmented cultural identities, especially when these are freighted with partly traumatic shared histories. The inner divisions are the most difficult to deal with: 'Ich lebe in der Leere, die keine Haltepunkte für meine immer dünner werdenden Fäden bietet, die mich mit den drei Teilen meiner selbst verbinden sollen' (*GV*, 90). The three cultural heritages in which Şenocak places Sascha serve a number of purposes: they differentiate Sascha from other central figures in works of 'Migrantenliteratur' who suffer from the 'zwei Welten' dichotomy; they make Sascha's case more complex, and thus more interesting; and they make explicit the shift in Şenocak's focus from collective multiculturalism to an interest in the problems of individual cultural identity.

This chapter has concentrated on the shift in focus of Şenocak's interest from collective to individual identities during the course of the 1990s. This is only one part of a range of developments in Şenocak's thought and writing in this period. The essay is, of course, the classic vehicle for reasoned and objective arguments on social, political and cultural themes. Şenocak needed to adopt fiction too in order to be able to explore the enigmatic and ineffable aspects of cultural identity, in particular its relation to the subconscious. Prose fiction allows for uncertainties, discontinuities and dislocations, which are out of place in essayistic prose.

These developments also coincide with Şenocak's clear and explicit abandonment of Modernist rationalism. In 1988, in his acceptance speech for the Adelbert-von-Chamisso-Förderpreis, he expressed the following aspiration for his poetry. It was, he said,

> Ein Versuch, mich und mein Dasein in seiner vielschichtigen, in sich widersprüchlichen Gesamtheit zu empfinden und sprachlich zu erfassen. Für Augenblicke den ganzen Menschen wieder herstellen, der sich weder in der Phantasie und im Empfinden, noch in der Rationalität empirischer Wahrnehmung und abstrakter Denkmuster erschöpft. (*Atlas*, 99)

By 1999, Şenocak had distanced himself from the aspiration that the whole person, with all attendant intricacies and contradictions, could be represented through writing. There remained 'Mysterien' which could not be explained through rationality: 'Ein Unbehagen an Sehweisen der Aufklärung breitete sich in den Geisteswissenschaften aus. Für all die Phänomene wurde ein Epochenbegriff geschaffen: die Postmoderne' (*Zunge*, 102).

Şenocak's prose fiction also reflects a change of emphasis from sociological to cultural approaches to multicultural issues. Efforts continue to go into the creation of political solutions to the problems of ethnically plural societies, and Şenocak continues to publish journalistic essays: for him, clearly, the political arena cannot be abandoned. But his more intense interest has moved to questions of cultural identity and hybridity, and Şenocak's prose fiction demonstrates that here too the creative writer has a significant role to play.

Notes

[1] 'Deutsche werden – Türken bleiben', in Claus Leggewie and Zafer Şenocak (eds), *Deutsche Türken / Türk Almanlar: Das Ende der Geduld / Sabrın sonu* (Reinbek, Rowohlt, 1993), 9–16 (11).

2 'Samuel-Emil-Nordpol-Otto-Cäsar-Anton-Kaufmann', in Bahman Nirumand (ed.), *Deutsche Zustände: Dialog über ein gefährdetes Land* (Reinbek, Rowohlt, 1993), 11–18 (12).

3 Günther Wallraff, *Ganz unten* (Cologne, Kiepenheuer & Witsch, 1985).

4 'Samuel-Emil-', 12.

5 Emine Sevgi Özdamar, *Das Leben ist eine Karawanserei / hat zwei Türen / aus einer kam ich rein / aus der anderen ging ich raus* (Cologne, Kiepenheuer & Witsch, 1992).

6 'Samuel-Emil-', 17–18.

7 Charles Taylor, 'The politics of recognition', in Amy Gutmann (ed.), *Multiculturalism: Examining the Politics of Recognition* (Princeton, Princeton University Press, 1994). Originally published in 1992 under the title 'Multiculturalism and the politics of recognition'.

8 Arlene Teraoka, 'Detecting ethnicity: Jakob Arjouni and the case of the missing German detective novel', *German Quarterly*, 72 (1999), 265–89.

9 'Gedicht XIV' in *Verkauf der Morgenstimmungen am Markt* (Munich, Edition Literazette, 1983) [Haidhauser Werkstat(t)texte 4].

10 Hans-Jürgen Heise, 'Mit kalkuliertem Unschuldsblick: Prosa und Verse von Zafer Şenocak', *Süddeutsche Zeitung*, 23 October, 1997, 14.

11 These monologues parody the genre of Dursun Akçam's *Deutsches Heim – Glück allein* (Bornheim, Lamuv, 1982), Metin Gür's *Meine fremde Heimat* (Cologne, Weltkreis, 1987) and numerous other anthologies of migrant voices, anticipating Feridun Zaimoğlu's *Kanak Sprak: 24 Mißtöne vom Rande der Gesellschaft* (Hamburg, Rotbuch, 1995).

12 Barbara Frischmuth, 'Der Blick des Rundgängers: Ein Roman von Zafer Şenocak', *Neue Zürcher Zeitung*, 7 April, 1999, 35.

13 First published as: 'Der Schriftsteller ist ein Archäologe: Ein Essay über Schreiben in Deutschland und überhaupt', *Die Welt*, 5 June 1999, 11.

9

Istanbul: Imagination Itself

PIERRE PACHET

'The vertical sea':[1] we can all instantly recognize this as the way the sea may appear at the end of a narrow street leading down to a harbour. A surprising vision, yet perfectly natural, tied to an angle of view.

Şenocak loves surprising angles. That is surely the first thing we need to recognize and understand, rather than categorizing him as an 'expressionist' or a 'neo-surrealist'. Neither label really suits him at all.

To see the sea from this disconcerting angle, a city is required, with its walls, its surprises, its empty spaces framing 'views': 'in the gaps between buildings on the horizon / black-haired ships pass' ('Das senkrechte Meer III', *SM*, 17). So here we have poems tied to a city, the perspectives it opens, its vistas, rather than sea-side panoramas. The city is Istanbul: numerous details the poet recalls confirm it.

The views are partial, sometimes dislocated or aggressive, and the gaze to which they present themselves is not meditative. It is neither satisfied, nor seeking satisfaction. (Şenocak is young – he was only thirty when this collection appeared.)

What the poet's gaze encounters, often, he was not looking for: something interposes itself, disappointing his expectations, or on the other hand, repaying a glance unexpectedly fully: 'one quiet minute in the harbour unleashes the longing to escape / the gaze shifting away from one of these hills in a vague direction / ends in hectic bus stations …' ('Archivisten in Istanbul II', *SM*, 9); 'my tête-à-tête with the window / revealed a view of sails' ('Zweiund-siebzig Sprachen IV', *SM*, 32).

He was not seeking what imposed itself. What then was he seeking? What use is an 'archivist' in a city like Istanbul, or in similar cities, since today no city exists that is not torn between its ancient origin and its modern destiny (even New York), between abandoned poverty and the urbanist ambition of modernism. The archivist's first task is to collect what is being effaced or lost, to perceive what but for him would be covered over or neglected: 'shreds of film posters recall / the wall that stood here' ('Das senk-rechte Meer III', *SM*, 17). For Şenocak, clearly, maps and plans are not enough. This poet's work is not office work. He surveys:

> I consult a worn street-map
> rearrange the streets
> forage for scraps of the sun
> only at night they recall a past life
> ('Das senkrechte Meer VI', *SM*, 19)

He tries to see what hides behind the façades of a street, or, rather, to show the tranquil coexistence of various planes or spheres of life which slide over one another, favouring the city's great discretion, where everything is hidden because everything is shown.

> behind the shop where fruit-stalls grow
> no one suspects a cemetery
> a rendez-vous for conspirators
> at best a mulberry tree
> matching the grey stone
> ('Archivisten in Istanbul VI', *SM*, 13)

But his work is more than this quest for remains or relics. The strangeness of Şenocak's lines presses encounters on the reader which are incongruous, unacceptable, incomprehensible. Perhaps he is, after all, a beautiful surrealist, as defined by Lautréamont: 'the meeting of an umbrella and a sewing machine on a dissection table'.

Does the poet mean to aim blows at us, to wound our eyes and our intelligence? Does he want to shock us? I have said that he is young: he may have wanted to shock 'bourgeois' readers, but is he not also trying to seduce them, to convince them, and, by seizing their attention, to educate his own eyes, his own attention, his sensibility? This is what I believe. It is as if he wants to inflict on the reader the same violence which the city made him inflict upon himself (is this not, in part, what 'expressionism' is?).

For example, in a spontaneous poetic movement, a city with a harbour becomes the harbour, the sea becomes the city, objects change places (as in a seaside landscape), and the beauty revealed by this unstable and troubling exchange is strangely familiar, because it matches the instability of a soul: 'we live in a city made of sunken ships / many signs make up the image of a ship / dead ships have human features' ('Das senkrechte Meer IX', *SM*, 22).

The big city unsettles images and brings them together in 'convulsive' encounters (to use André Breton's word). The city thereby produces quasi-mythical or chimerical beings which do not exist in the ordered nature of yesterday's world (the one where supposedly there was a clearer separation between town and country, present and past, city and court, land and sea, industry and luxury). More importantly, what these beings actually are is the imagination revealed to itself.

This can best be seen in the image of the 'goat-stag' ('Tragelaph', in 'Zweiundsiebzig Sprachen VIII', *SM*, 36), borrowed by Şenocak from Greek thought. This 'goat-stag' comes from the ancient Greeks' debates on aesthetics, and the distrust they manifest towards the oriental imagination, supposedly excessive and too much given to hybridization through incongruous encounters. Thus in Aristophanes' comedy *The Frogs*, the tragedian Euripides reproaches Aeschylus, his elder, with having presented in drama the goat-stags 'as they have them on carpets from Persia'. In Plato's *Republic*, which Şenocak must have read as a philosophy student, Socrates wants to describe something difficult to describe (namely, the position of philosophers in a city), and requests permission to use a composite image such as the 'goat-stags' depicted by painters. (Were these Persian painters? Or just Persian-oriented?) These products of the imagination, obtained by combining or agglutinating real elements, bear witness to the powers of the mind, as indeed does the city. The Persian or Turkish city, Istanbul, more than any other, according to Şenocak, has been fashioned by these fearsome and admirable powers. It has bred in him, as Paris bred in Baudelaire, a melancholy attentiveness: 'the deaths of cities as painful as deaths of friends / the cities will be born again in a wink / no one will recognize them' ('Portraits in Handschriften und Versatzstücken IX', *SM*, 50).

Human omnipotence, then, the talent for recombining and bringing into being chimeras, goat-stags and cities, carries with it a terrible risk: that of falling out of reality, losing it. Then images freeze, they become nothing but images for 'image-hunters' ('Zweiundsiebzig Sprachen VIII', *SM*, 36); everything seems artificial, as if produced 'on demand', without difficulty, and so without reason. Literary creativity too can be contaminated by this cynical ease: 'fine writing gaseous and cynical / summer films censored by an office junior / shoe boxes full of snow on demand' ('Das senkrechte Meer I', *SM*, 15).

Elsewhere, we see the poem turning back, seeking and guarding the trace of:

> the forgotten alphabet of the white language
> roof-gables birds of passage blurred shores
> what still moves on the pictures
> memory
> the lost white
> the whitest language
> ('Zweiundsiebzig Sprachen VIII', *SM*, 36)

Poetry is often devoted to bearing witness to what is most real, most moving, what is there just as it is. Often it seems that only poetry is able to give us a precise sense of this. But there are also cases (moments of weakness, confusing situations, environments which are over-artificial, over-equivocal) where reality conceals itself and cannot be immediately recognized or grasped. Then it can be part of poetry's duty, provided it has the strength and does not cheat, to bear witness to this concealment of reality:

> a van delivered reality to my door
> [. . .]
> the vehicle which delivered reality departs again empty
> in the background a tape-deck keeps the buzz of cicadas going
> ('Losung', *SM*, 75-77)

These moments are very strong in Şenocak's poetry. It seems that a curtain of images too beautiful or too incongruous is suddenly torn, and a sensibility speaks which is stripped to the bone, attentive to destruction and dispossession:

> it is hard to tour cities that no longer exist

still harder to find a way out of them
the wall will last long
long after the city is weathered away
('Berlin vor dem schwarzen Frühling I', *SM*, 78)

These lines, as illuminated by the title of the poem, must have
resonance for a German or a European reader: as if Istanbul were
coming to illuminate Berlin, indeed to reveal a strange kinship
among all contemporary cities. A city signifies cities, just as the
city represents and reveals to the poet his mind and, beyond that,
his reader's mind: 'it's me / me the city / or is it you / am I no one
in me' ('Berlin vor dem schwarzen Frühling XIII', *SM*, 92).

If reality is threatened and covered over by modern prolifera-
tion, this is not least a threat to language itself, to languages, to the
riches of the 'seventy-two languages' evoked in the reading of a
text by Kleist ('Zweiundsiebzig Sprachen XII', *SM*, 41). The city's
attack on reality does not leave language intact; how much more
again in the case of an émigré! At this level, the dispossession can
seem total:

I lend my mouth
get it back
with another's tongue
get by nameless
('Synonyme I', *SM*, 53)

Encircled by images, by 'photo-chains' ('Das senkrechte Meer XII',
SM, 25), devalorized by the mass diffusion of commonplaces,
scrambled by media squawking, words are as threatened as natural
elements. The beauty of Şenocak's poems deliberately reconstitutes
the power of words, gives them another chance. But not some-
where beyond the city streets, their brouhaha and confusion. He
wants that noise, destruction, disharmony, not in order to accentuate it cynically, but to catch hold of whatever it is that holds out in
amongst it all, or even thrives on it all, by way of solid, true, humorous, good things. He makes contemporary chaos seem habit-
able again, as indeed it really is, and lost reality is found again,
gaily, as in this message left by a joking traveller:

our dreams are behind bars sweetheart
I'm travelling till further notice
in the freezer there's a bottle of my sperm

help yourself
('Losung', *SM*, 75-77)

The force of Şenocak's poems crosses the darkness towards us like this, talking, wanting to talk. Each poem stretches towards a listener, a correspondent: it may be a postcard, a letter, a message in a bottle, a note, or simply a word: 'pronounce a long word / about the tiredness that keeps you awake' ('Das senkrechte Meer VI', *SM*, 19).

If Şenocak's words keep readers awake, this is no doubt because of the painful trials they have suffered, and are still suffering: the threats to 'words in distress' ('Das senkrechte Meer XIII', *SM*, 26), threats of calcification, of loss, of silencing:

you ask why do our poems resemble letters
because we lose our words as well as our friends
[...]
you ask why our words resemble images
so even the dumb may understand one another
('Archivisten in Istanbul I', *SM*, 7)

The experience of such distress of language is clearly not faked. It is not only visible to the eye, one can almost touch it, like 'calcified language on the dumb tongue' ('Zweiundsiebzig Sprachen XIV', *SM*, 42). Şenocak surprises his reader, but not to intimidate: only to move and touch.

Notes

1 'Istanbul, l'imagination même' appeared as the preface to Timour Muhidine's translation of *SM*, *La Mer verticale* (Paris, L'Esprit des Péninsules, 1999), 7–14. All translations here by Tom Cheesman.

10

Poetry on its Way: aktuelle Zwischenstationen im lyrischen Werk Zafer Şenocaks

KARIN E. YEŞILADA

Zu Beginn meines Beitrags möchte ich (m)ein Mantra verkünden, das mich bei der Beschäftigung mit Şenocaks Werken stets begleitet: *Zafer Şenocak ist Lyriker.* Das mag ein wenig aus dem Blickfeld geraten, wenn die meisten Beiträge dieses Bandes sich mit dem umfangreichen Prosawerk eines Autors beschäftigen, der auch in Deutschland im letzten Jahrzehnt eher als 'public intellectual' wahrgenommen wird denn als Lyriker.[1] Ich möchte dementgegen nun eine Lanze für die Poesie brechen – und sie auch gar nicht brechen, sondern sie mit voller Kraft auf die *Wortschatzinsel* werfen, um zu sehen, welchen Schatz sie dort antrifft.

Seit den letzten großen Lyrikpublikationen Mitte der 1990er Jahre (*Das senkrechte Meer*, 1991 und *Fernwehanstalten*, 1994) erschienen Gedichte von Zafer Şenocak in Deutschland nur noch vereinzelt in Zeitschriften und Anthologien.[2] Somit scheint es um den Lyriker Şenocak hierzulande tatsächlich still geworden zu sein, was Ulrich Beil in seinem Beitrag zu der berechtigten Vermutung veranlaßt, der Lyriker sei dem Prosaautor gewichen. Doch ist der Lyriker gar nicht so weit entfernt – hat nicht sogar Sascha eine ganze Gedichtsammlung ins zweite Buch der Prosa-Tetralogie,[3] in *Die Prärie* (105–12) geschmuggelt? Einige aktuelle Lyrikproduktionen wurden noch gar nicht richtig 'entdeckt', etwa der dreiteilige 'Futuristen-Epilog', den Şenocak gemeinsam mit dem Münchner Künstler Berkan Karpat geschrieben hat.[4] Sicherlich, in der wissenschaftlichen Literatur sucht man Beiträge zu Şenocaks Lyrik fast vergeblich: Wenn sie denn rezipiert wird, so oft unter wundersamer Umgehung seiner aktuellen Lyrik; stattdessen verharrt man gern im Frühwerk. Doch auch wenn die Rezeption in der Sackgasse zu sein scheint, so befindet sich Şenocaks Lyrik, pardon, seine *poetry well on its way*. Wir wollen diesen Weg ein wenig mitgehen.

Betrachtet man die Entwicklung, die Şenocaks Poesie auf ihrem Weg von den 1990ern bis heute genommen hat, so fällt zunächst auf, daß die unter dem Eindruck der deutschen Vereinigung entstandene 'Metropolenlyrik'[5] allmählich wieder aus dem Blickfeld verschwindet: Einige der neuen Gedichte handeln zwar noch in der großen Stadt, doch dies sind nicht mehr die verschwisterten Metropolen Berlin und Istanbul. Stattdessen eröffnet sich gegen Ende der 1990er eine andere Topographie, welche auch in der Prosa zum Ort des Erzählens wird: Die endlose Weite der nordamerikanischen Prärie. Sie ist Ort der Meditation und Selbstspiegelung eines lyrischen Subjekts, das sich zunehmend auf sich selbst konzentriert, so lange, bis das Ich wieder ganz in den Mittelpunkt der poetischen Dichtung rückt. War zuvor noch das mit der Metropole Istanbul verbundene Meer eine zentrale Metapher, so scheint sich das Ich nun eher als einsamer Ruderer auf einem endlosen Ozean zu befinden, auf dem Weg zu neuen Ufern und Schatzinseln, mit neuen Themen und Motiven an Bord.

Bevor wir uns den einzelnen Gedichten, die der Autor für diesen Band zusammengestellt hat, zuwenden, sollten wir uns aber ins Gedächtnis rufen, daß in Şenocaks Werk die Lyrik immer präsent ist – siehe das eingangs erwähnte Mantra! – und damit auch bis in die Prosa hineinreicht. So werden wir zahlreichen Bezügen zwischen Motiven der Lyrik und den Büchern der Tetralogie begegnen. Ebenso wird es niemanden verwundern, wenn auch in den Essays literarische Gedanken auftauchen. Dies gilt insbesondere für Şenocaks jüngste Essaysammlung *Zungenentfernung* (2001). Es sind fast durchweg literarische Themen, die im Kapitel 'Jenseits der Landessprache' (*Zunge*, 81–103) entfaltet werden, und bereits im Titel des gleichlautenden Textes[6] manifestiert sich Şenocaks poetischer Standpunkt: typischerweise für ihn ist dieser Standort bereits eine Metapher. Die Sprache als »verlassenes Haus«, in dem man »sich einrichten« kann, das scheint eine Vision zu sein für den Dichter unterwegs, dessen neuere Lyrik ortlos ist, oder an imaginäre Orte wandert wie die Wortschatzinsel. Zentral ist auch der Essay 'Welcher Mythos schreibt mich?' (*Zunge*, 97–103). Hier geht Şenocak auf die Ursprünge seines Schreibens ein und gibt uns einen entscheidenden Hinweis: »Meine Essays sind

Krücken, auf die sich viele stützen, wenn sie auf den Pfaden meines Arbeitsfeldes balancieren wollen. Doch was in den Essays ausgedrückt wird, ist lediglich die nach außen gewandte Seite meiner Literatur. Wege nach innen gehen von der Lyrik und der Prosa aus« (*Zunge*, 99). Seinen eigenen Schreibmythos beschreibt Şenocak dann als »die Ambivalenz zwischen rationaler und mystischer, moderner formuliert, mysteriöser Welterfahrung, zwischen Physik und Metaphysik«, die er später auch als »Trümmerfeld« bezeichnet (*Zunge*, 99, 100). Ähnlich wie auch im Text 'Jenseits der Landessprache' erscheint dieses Trümmerfeld jedoch wie »ein Spielfeld mit unendlichen Möglichkeiten«. Eine dieser Möglichkeiten wäre vielleicht das märchenhafte Genre, das uns zu der »Wortschatzinsel« führt, in jenen Bereich mysteriöser Welterfahrung, der dem Entdecker einen Schatz verspricht.

Die Spur zum Schatz jedoch legt der Autor selbst: »Wege nach innen gehen von der Lyrik und der Prosa aus.« Meine nachfolgende Interpretation versucht also auch, etwas von jenem »Schreibmythos« aufzuspüren, der sich wie ein Strang durch fast alle Bücher von Zafer Şenocak zieht.

'Wortschatzinsel'
Die vierzehn hier im Band zum ersten Mal veröffentlichten Gedichte aus dem Zyklus 'Wortschatzinsel' sind ursprünglich Bestandteil einer neuen Lyriksammlung unter dem Arbeitstitel 'Schlafreflexe', die bislang noch unveröffentlicht ist.[7] Es sind kürzere Gedichte, keine Poeme mehr wie Anfang-Mitte der neunziger Jahre, und auch die Metropolenthematik ist nicht mehr vorrangig. In den Gedichten der 'Wortschatzinsel' geht es um Liebe und Freundschaft, um das lyrische Ich in seinen Beziehungen zum Du, zu anderen, und um seine eigene Einsamkeit; es geht um Reisen und Unterwegssein, um den Generationskonflikt und immer wieder um das Schreiben selbst. Und auch um Märchenhaftes geht es auf der 'Wortschatzinsel'.

Die Liebesgedichte nehmen zunächst den größten Teil des Zyklus ein. »Wir gehen durchs Glas«, heißt es im ersten Gedicht (*Ş*, 1), und schon hebt der Divan an mit einer jener Metaphern, die Ulrich Beil in seinem Beitrag als Essenz der Şenocak'schen Poesie ausmacht. Liebe befähigt hier im Gedicht zur Grenzerfahrung, Grenzüberwindung, und schafft eine mystische Aura der Vereinigung im Licht: Hier wie auch in anderer Lyrik Şenocaks steht die Sonne als Symbol für das mystische Empfinden.[8] Das 'wir' des ersten Gedichts löst sich auf in das lyrische 'ich' und 'du', etwa im philosophischen »denk mich zu dir« (*Ş*, 6), einem kurzen und klaren Liebesgedicht, fast ein Aphorismus, der zur Chiffre für die Begegnung von Kulturen wird, und damit an einen verwandten Essay, 'Berühren oder Begegnen?' (*Zunge*, 62–3) erinnert. Das erotische Berühren wird im Gedicht 'nicht zuende sprachst du' (*Ş*, 6) zur Metapher, wenn sich zwei Liebende »im Halbwort« vereinen wie Ying und Yang: Der Eros fällt der Sprache ins Wort. Das Bild vom rohen Fleisch erinnert dabei an Szenen im Erzählband *Der Mann im Unterhemd*.[9] In einem anderen Gedicht ('Feigen aßen sie', *Ş*, 4) geht es ebenfalls um die erotische Liebe; der Verkehr wird zum Verzehr und zur Metamorphose. Die Liebend-Vereinigten nehmen eine neue Gestalt an, werden zu »Blättern an einem fremden Stamm«. So sind sie an einem dritten Ort versteckt. Diese Liebe im Verborgenen ist fragil, kann enttarnt werden durch einen anonymen »jemand«, der brüllt, Aggressionen in die Idylle einbringt und sie somit zerstört. Daß die liebende Vereinigung zu etwas Neuem, Drittem transzendiert, ist auch im späteren Gedicht 'Die Pilotin' (*Ş*, 11–12) wieder der Fall. Es scheint zu Şenocaks Konzept einer Existenz »jenseits« von allen Grenzen zu gehören und dem zu entsprechen, was Leslie A. Adelson mit dem Begriff »Orte des Umdenkens« beschreibt.[10] Jedenfalls arbeitet Şenocak hier, wie bereits in den frühen Gedichtbänden auch, mit Naturbildern (wie der Mimikry der Liebenden) und kombiniert sie nun mit archaisch-religiösen Anspielungen (die Feigen als verbotene Früchte).

Ironisch ist dagegen die Bewegung hin und zurück, aufeinander zu und voneinander weg im zweiten Gedicht des Zyklus, 'Sie kam auf einem Rad' (*Ş*, 1). Hier ist die Beziehung ein Perpetuum mobile. Ruhig und kontemplativ ist die Betrachtung über den Weg der Liebenden von Trennung und Wiederbegegnung in 'Oft sitzt man Rücken an Rücken' (*Ş*, 3). Dieses Gedicht könnte auch eine philosophische Beschreibung von Freundschaft sein: Ist dies hier ein Liebender oder ein Derwisch, der da spricht?

Das Motiv des einsamen Wanderers auf dem Lebensweg klingt öfters an bei Şenocak, der als Übersetzer der Gedichte des türkischen Mystikers Yunus Emre mit der mittelalterlichen Mystik vertraut ist. Der einsame Derwisch ist unterwegs, immer ein wenig leidend, ob an der Welt, oder am eigenen »Lebenswiderspruch«

(so ein weiteres Gedicht aus dem Zyklus, *Ş*, 3). Er ist selbstgenüg-
sam (»ich brauche keinen Boden zum Liegen«) und sagt über seine
Beziehung zu anderen lakonisch: »sollte ich auf keinen treffen habe
ich Platz genug«. Hier spricht kein egoistischer Kämpfer aus der
New Economy zu uns, sondern ein abgeklärter Wanderderwisch.
Und der widmet auch den Menschen am Wegrand seine Poesie,
etwa dem »Grenzsteinbesitzer auf seinem uralten Grenzstein« (*Ş*,
4). Sehnsuchtsvoll wird hier der Ton, und märchenhaft, und durch
und durch poetisch!

Der Weisheit des Derwischs steht in manchen Gedichten aber
auch die Verzweiflung einer einsamen Seele gegenüber: Da ist das
Reisen nicht mehr Wanderschaft sondern Flucht. Schon im Gedicht
'Mein Lebenswiderspruch' wird selbiger zum Grund des Reisens,
aber: »ich wollte nicht fort«, heißt es da. Warum dann der Aufbruch? Einen Schlüssel dazu liefert das Gedicht 'Das reisende Kind
in mir' (*Ş*, 2). Für ein entkommenes Kind zieht das Ich nun »ein
gefesseltes Kind« in sich groß, eine traurige Schizophrenie. Ist das
eine Klage über den Verlust von Kindheit? Zentrale Begriffe sind
hier »fesseln« und »wachsen«. Aus den Fesseln wachsen oder sich
'entfesseln', das könnte das Erwachsensein darstellen oder die
Libido, vielleicht aber auch die befreite Identität. Immer wieder,
und gerade in der literarischen Prosa, spielt Şenocak mit dem Motiv der festgeschriebenen Identität (als Türke, als Orientexperte, als
Liebhaber), der sich der Ich-Erzähler immer wieder auf's Neue
entzieht. Auch Sascha Muhteschem ist so ein »reisendes Kind«. Im
Roman *Gefährliche Verwandtschaft* gibt es ebenfalls eine interessante
Entsprechung. Dort in den Porträts verschiedener Deutschland-
türken sagt die junge Modedesignerin Kamile über sich: »Ich war
zweimal Kind, einmal auf türkisch, einmal auf deutsch« (*GV*, 98).
Sie beschreibt dabei die identitätsspezifische Schizophrenie dessen,
was gern mit dem plakativen Begriff 'Leben zwischen zwei Kulturen' bezeichnet wird. Hier wird es in einer Metapher aufgelöst.
Das türkische Kind existiert nur (noch) für die türkischen Eltern,
die sich vor dem deutschen Kind fürchten. So wird das türkische
Kind nur sieben Jahren alt und danach »unsterblich«. Auch dieser
Text ist von einer starken Poesie getragen und zeigt, daß Şenocak
statt platter Zuordnungen lieber eine poetische Chiffre wählt. So
als entzöge er sich. Wie das dreiarmige Kind, das sich im Gedicht
'Wen wundert's' (*Ş*, 8) selbst gebiert und sich auch selbst aus der
Welt schafft.

Für dieses Entziehen gibt es wiederum in der neuesten Lyrik
einen Schlüssel, der übrigens auch in dem Ende der neunziger
Jahre zusammen mit Berkan Karpat geschriebenen, dreiteiligen
'Futuristen-Epilog' zu finden ist: Es ist das Thema vom Konflikt
der Generationen, genauer, der Väter und Söhne. Im dritten Poem
des 'Futuristen-Epiloges' geht es um die Auseinandersetzung mit
Mustafa Kemal 'Atatürk', dem 'Vater aller Türken'.[11] Im Zyklus
'Wortschatzinsel' gehen zwei Gedichte über den leiblichen Vater,
ein kurzer Dreizeiler (Ş, 2) und ein längeres Gedicht von sechzehn
Zeilen.[12] Zunächst drei Zeilen:»Man bewegt sich nicht / in Gegenwart des Vaters / doch wie wächst man dann« – das ist schon die
alles sagende Benennung des Konflikts, aus dem das Kind nur zu
entkommen scheint, in dem es auf Reisen geht. Dieses Dilemma,
man könnte es auch 'Lebenswiderspruch' nennen, ist im längeren
Gedicht 'Vater' (Ş, 5) näher beschrieben. Motive aus dem Atatürk-
Poem klingen an, etwa die berühmten strengen Augen, oder die
Abwesenheit mütterlicher Wärme. Bemerkenswert ist die Verknüpfung von Generationsfolge und »Schrift«: Nachdem das lyrische Subjekt gegangen ist, wird die »Schrift auf (seiner) Haut«
unlesbar; für die endgültige Loslösung vom Vater muß dieser das
Ich aus seiner Schrift löschen:»häute mich / daß kein Wort uns
erinnern kann«. Der Bruch geht hier durch die Schrift, durch die
Sprache, befindet sich also nicht im materiellen, sondern im zu-
tiefst mythologischen Bereich. Von der Bedeutung der Sprache für
den eigenen Schreibmythos spricht Şenocak auch in dem bereits
erwähnten Essay 'Welcher Mythos schreibt mich?' Dort erwähnt er
die Wirkung der zwei unterschiedlichen »Sprachen« von Mutter
und Vater, von einer »warmen« und einer »kalten« Sprache, und
der Suche nach dem Eros in beiden (*Zunge*, 101). Bekannte Po-
laritäten verschwimmen dabei, und auch dies scheint ein häufig
anzutreffendes Motiv zu sein bei Şenocak. In den lyrischen Skizzen
'Jenseits der Landessprache' heißt es in der XIV. Sentenz:»Ich habe
meinen Vater in eine Mutter verwandelt und ihren Körper in Sprache« (*Zunge*, 89). Wenn es am Schluß unseres Gedichts heißt:
»Nimm die Hände aus meiner Sprache / damit ich mein eigenes
Haus bauen kann«, dann ist dies nicht nur der mythologische
Vatermord.[13] Sondern Şenocak gebraucht eine seiner zentralen
Metaphern: Die Sprache als »Haus«.[14] Steht es leer und offen, so
kann sich der Dichter darin einrichten:»ein seltener, glücklicher
Moment«, wie es dazu in der XVIII. Sentenz von 'Jenseits der Lan-

dessprache' heißt (*Zunge*, 90). Der Vaterkonflikt ist also der Ausbruch des lyrischen Subjekts aus dem Korsett der Generationshierarchie, d.h. sein Aufbruch zur Entdeckung der 'Wortschatzinsel'.

Und diese steht ihm zur Suche offen, wie jenes Haus, das die Sprache ist. Das Titelgedicht, 'Tagsüber die Suche nach Wörtern' (Ş, 7), befindet sich selbst wie eine metaphorische Insel im Zyklus: Umspült von benachbarten Themen birgt sie den zentralen S(ch)atz: »ich lese und grabe / bis ich das erste Wort greife«. Es klingt nach religiöser Offenbarung, wenn da »eine Stimme« zum lyrischen Ich spricht; das könnte aber auch seine eigene innere Stimme sein. Das Graben als Erinnerungsarbeit berührt ebenfalls eine zentrale Metapher in Şenocaks Werk: So sind die Dichter der Metropolenlyrik »Archivare«, die das Stadtgedächtnis zutage heben,[15] und Sascha Muhteschem vergräbt sich im Roman *Gefährliche Verwandtschaft* sprichwörtlich in die Tagebücher seines Großvaters, bevor er zu schreiben beginnt. Graben heißt 'erinnern', das paßt zum »"lies, was du nicht siehst!"« des Gedichts. Erinnerung als archäologischer Prozeß im Unterbewußtsein[16] braucht keine visuellen Eindrücke, es genügt, wenn das Ich sein Auge nach innen richtet. »Man kann nur durch Erinnerung erkennen«, heißt es im Roman (*GV*, 93). In einer 'Poetologische(n) Skizze' im neuen Essayband bezeichnet Şenocak das »Erinnern« als eines von drei Beinen, auf denen seine Texte stehen. Die anderen beiden Beine sind »Erfinden« und »Spielen« (*Zunge*, 93). Schreiben geschieht zwischen Sturz und Balance. Wieder eine Metapher.

Der Zyklus 'Wortschatzinsel' erscheint wie eine Traumlandschaft inmitten der 'Schlafreflexe' (so der gewählte Arbeitstitel für die vollständige Gedichtsammlung). Es sind Träume von Liebe, Erotik und Freundschaft, von Begegnen und Berühren. Das lyrische Subjekt (schlaf)wandelt aber auch allein des Wegs, gelassen wie ein Wanderderwisch, einer, der erwachsen geworden und zu neuen Ufern aufgebrochen ist. Der Traum führt zur sagenumwobenen Wortschatzinsel, wo der Lyriker ganz Archäologe ist und nach dem Schatz gräbt. – Es ist klar, was sich außer Wörtern noch in der märchenhaften Schatztruhe befindet: Metaphern!

Auch jenseits der 'Wortschatzinsel' gibt es poetische Landschaften – so sind dem Zyklus hier noch weitere fünf Gedichte hinzugefügt (Ş, 9–15). Es sind fünf Gedichte unterschiedlicher Länge, die im Gegensatz zu denen des vorangegangenen Zyklus alle mit Überschriften versehen sind. Wir wollen auch hier Themen und Motive aufspüren: Gibt es Ähnlichkeiten? Was ist neu? Und auf welchen Wegen befindet sich Şenocaks Lyrik hier?

'Die schlafende Generation'

Mit seinen vierzig zum Teil längeren Versen ähnelt dieses Gedicht (Ş, 9–10) den Poemen der beiden letzten Lyrikbände der frühen neunziger Jahre. Das komplexe Thema und die dichte poetische Sprache erinnern auch stark an den Ton der 'Metropolenlyrik'.

Ein lyrisches Subjekt meldet sich von seiner Reise aus zu Wort und kommentiert Eindrücke und Begegnungen, bevor es am Zielort wieder in den Schlaf fällt. Um was geht es hier? Um die schlafende oder die reisende Generation? Und was bedeuten die Orte?

Zunächst zum Grundzustand des lyrischen Ichs: Es schläft, »da Poesie keiner Worte bedarf« (Zeile 1).[17] Demnach ist Poesie das Schlafwandeln, das Reisen im Raum zwischen Wachsein und Tiefschlaf, im Traum. Die Topographien dieser Reise sind symbolträchtig; sie bilden den Rahmen des Gedichts. Zentrale Topographie wäre da zunächst die Nicht-Verortung, die Reise selbst, also ein transitorischer Ort zwischen Abfahrt und Ankunft, eine Art topographische 'twilight zone'.[18] Das lyrische Subjekt befindet sich irgendwo zwischen Transsylvanien und dem Himalaya, in südöstlicher Fahrtrichtung: Eine Anspielung auf die Seidenstraße, oder auf die Route der Mongolen? Mit den Koordinaten Konstantinopel, Schwarzmeer und Berlin wird eine markante Linie, ein Ostmeridian festgesteckt. Und es werden Verbindungen hergestellt: Zur Geschichte zweier Städte, und zur eigenen Lyrik, in der sich Şenocak diesen Städten genähert hat. Was in der Metropolenlyrik zentrales Motiv ist, nämlich die Beschäftigung mit der Geschichte und der historischen Schuld zweier ehemaliger Reichsmetropolen, wird hier im Gedicht jedoch völlig ausgelassen und erscheint höchstens in Andeutungen. Konstantinopel: Hauptstadt des Osmanischen Reiches, Erbin Ostroms, Umschlagplatz für all jene Luxusgüter, die auf der Seidenstraße aus Asien nach Europa gebracht wurden und den Handelsmächten der Levante zu Ruhm und Reichtum verhalfen. Ist der im Gedicht erwähnte »Mann mit einem schmalen levantinischen Gesicht« (Z. 6) vielleicht ein Nachkomme jener Händler?

Konstantinopel, das ist ein Begegnungspunkt zwischen Ost und West, zwischen 'orientalischer' und okzidentalischer Kultur. Den alten Namen der Stadt benutzend, spielt Şenocak mit den Bildern im Kopf: 'Istanbul' ist die ausgeblendete türkische Realität; »Konstantinopel« dagegen ist der europäische Traum vom Orient – den die schlafende Generation träumt? Berlin als topographisches Pendant wiederum wird kaum ausgeschmückt; das lyrische Ich begnügt sich mit der lakonischen Warnung »vor Fahrraddieben«. Im Vergleich zur Metropolenlyrik wirkt diese Ellipse ironisch. Was aber ist mit »Transsylvanien« gemeint? Als Heimat des berühmten literarischen Grafen Dracula assoziiert sie zunächst die literarische Tradition der gothic novel, zugleich ist sie eine Topographie des dunklen, unheimlichen Europas. Ein zweiter Begriff verstärkt diese Vermutung: Der Balkan steht für den jüngsten, grausamen Krieg, den Şenocak in knappe, lyrische Bilder preßt: »auf dem Balkan schneite es / der Schnee roch nach Qualm / [. . .] / die Bäume am Wegrand rauchten ihre letzten Blätter« (Z. 23–4, 34). Krieg, Tod und Zerstörung als reale Katastrophe der jüngsten Vergangenheit stehen hier neben der albtraumhaften literarischen Topographie, der Landschaft eines unheimlichen Blutsaugers. Eine gewollte Parallele?

Orte und Personen des Gedichts bleiben verschlüsselt, und offenbaren sich doch durch ihre Anspielungen. Die Zeit des Gedichts ist zweigeteilt, in eine erzählte Traumzeit und eine reale Zeit, im Kontext der 1990er Jahre: die Zeit des Aufbruchs, der Völkervereinigungen (deutsche Wiedervereinigung), aber auch eine Art Endzeit, mit Kriegen und Völkermord. Migrationen sind hier gespiegelt, auf einer unsichtbaren Achse von Europa in den Südosten, bis nach Asien. Der Mann »mit dem levantinischen Gesicht« könnte auch einer jener Millionen Gastarbeiter sein, die sich in den sechziger Jahren auf den Weg nach Deutschland machten. Die »zwei Schwarzmeerfrauen« (Z. 17–19) wiederum erinnern an die zahlreichen Frauen aus den russischen Republiken, die sich nach dem Zusammenbruch der Sowjetunion als Sextouristinnen in der Türkei verdingten und dort als sogenannte 'Nataschas' berühmt-berüchtigt wurden: Im Bild wird der käufliche Sex zum »vertrockneten Ast« zwischen ihren Beinen. Daß sie »auf einem Delphinrücken« reiten, verleiht dem Ganzen etwas Versöhnliches. Ein weiteres märchenhaftes Element ist die »Kutsche«, in der sich das lyrische Ich schlafend umherfahren läßt.

Das Gedicht ist eine poetische Traumreise an Orte europäischer Gegenwart und Geschichte, an klar benannte Orte und an

Topographien des Unterbewußten. Ein anonymer »jemand« (vgl.
Z. 28–31) ist da unterwegs und sucht nach dem »Frühling« – ist das
ein Wanderer zwischen den Welten, ein Träumer, oder ein
Derwisch? Er scheint das lyrische Ich jedenfalls nicht sonderlich zu
interessieren, denn es zieht weiter und schläft, bis es zuhause
ankommt. Der Grund für das Schlafen ist in eine
Schlüsselmetapher gefaßt, die uns am Anfang des Gedichts schon
begegnete (»da Poesie keiner Worte bedarf«), die hier aber
umgekehrt wird: »da Worte keiner Poesie bedürfen [. . .] « heißt es
nun. War das, was jemand »aus dem Koffer« vorliest, also nicht
poetisch? Wenn das Ich anscheinend endlich 'ankommt' im
eigenen Zimmer, und die Post öffnet, begegnen wir der zentralen
Metapher zum dritten Mal, und wieder ist sie abgewandelt: »da
Erinnern zuhause keiner Worte bedarf«.

Das Ich geht im Traum auf Reisen, beobachtet, nimmt Eindrücke
wahr, und begegnet Menschen immer nach dem gleichen Muster:
Sie fragen nach dem Weg, und das Ich gibt Auskunft. Ist es ein
Allwissender auf der Route des Ostmeridians? Die Traumlandschaft umfaßt ein riesiges Gebiet, »ein Meer und zwei Erdteile
weit«, und scheint doch nichts anderes zu sein als eine imaginäre
Karte der Erinnerung. Diese Erinnerung ist der Schlüssel zum
Traum, zur Reise, zur Poesie; und sie ist nicht mit Worten zu
fassen. Hier lotet das lyrische Ich das aus, was Şenocak in einem
literarischen Essay als seinen »Schreibmythos« bezeichnet. Dieser
Mythos ist nicht konkret greifbar, sondern entsteht im Unterbewußtsein, in jener twilight zone, die immer wieder in Şenocaks
Texten als Chiffre auftaucht. Im Interview in diesem Band
bezeichnet sich Şenocak als »Zwischengeneration« und verneint im
Übrigen die Frage nach irgendeiner Generationszugehörigkeit.[19] Ist
das Gedicht vielleicht die poetische Beschreibung dieser »Zwischengeneration« als »schlafende Generation«?

'Die Pilotin'

Im Gedicht 'Die Pilotin' (Ş, 11–12) ist das lyrische Ich nun weiblich
– und »anders«. Mit diesem Auftakt wird das Grundthema
angeschlagen: Es geht um das Selbstporträt einer Frau, deren
Traum das Fliegen ist. Fliegen als Grundthema bedeutet jedoch
mehr als nur der klassische Menschheitstraum. Wir denken sofort
an die Erzählung 'Fliegen' aus dem Band *Der Mann im Unterhemd*,
wo ein Detektiv ein verschwundenes türkisches Mädchen sucht

und es nach etlichen falschen Fährten schließlich hoch oben in den Lüften als Stewardess findet. Ist das Gedicht vielleicht eine lyrische Erklärung dessen, was die untergetauchte Stewardess bewegt? In der Erzählung sagt diese: »Auch ich bin auf der Suche, hier zwischen Frankfurt und Istanbul. Nach etwas, das zu mir gehört und das keiner sehen kann. Ich will nichts anderes als fliegen.«[20] Das Ich des Gedichts hat sich einen Kindheitstraum erfüllt: »ich wußte schon als Kind daß ich eines Tages fliegen würde / fliegen ohne Engel zu sein ich lebte ganz nach diesem Wunsch« (Z. 16–17). Sie ist Pilotin und nicht Stewardess, aber die Flugführung funktioniert nicht im herkömmlichen Sinn, sondern liegt im Bereich der sexuellen Befreiung: Die Pilotin ist eine »Lust-mechanikerin« ihrer eigenen Flugmaschine, und das Abheben in die Lüfte scheint wenn schon, dann ein gemeinsamer Akt zu werden, der erst noch bevorsteht. Fliegen ist hier eine Chiffre für einen Existenzzustand jenseits des konventionellen Lebens. Darauf verweisen auch die Topographien des Gedichts, die mit »unterirdisch« und »in der Nacht« Sphären zitieren, die auch in vielen Erzählungen aus dem Band *Der Mann im Unterhemd* vor-herrschen.

Die Pilotin deutet diese Art des Doppellebens freimütig an: »ich bin kein Engel«, sagt sie ebenso selbstbewußt, wie dies die Lisa-Figur aus *Der Mann im Unterhemd* tun würde. Wer aber sind diese »Engel«? Sind sie ein Gegenpol zu der Pilotin und ihren »Zug-vögeln«? Sind es tugendhafte Existenzen, die den Sprung ins andere Leben nicht schaffen, oder Überbringer von Botschaften? »Engel verpassen ihren Flug« heißt es zweimal lakonisch in dem Gedicht, und damit scheint schon alles gesagt. Die Engel-Metapher, gemeinsam mit dem Begriff der »Köchin«, verweist auf eine andere frühere Erzählung. In 'Die Frau bleibt Engel und der Mann Koch' (*MiU*, 105–10) streiten sich ein Mann und eine Frau um die Trennung, die sie will und er nicht. Der verbale Geschlechterkampf endet mit seinem Sieg: Der Mann als »Koch« darf sein »blutrotes, schlachtfrisches Fleisch« (und das wäre die Frau!) abermals »zubereiten«, und alles bleibt beim alten, wie der Titel der Geschichte verrät. Die Pilotin des Gedichts war ebenfalls eine »Hilfsköchin«, doch ist sie von diesem Metier zur Pilotin aufgestiegen: Şenocak überwindet hier seine eigene Metapher.

'Männergeschichte', 'Rede an die Übernächtigte'

Perspektivenwechsel im Gedicht 'Männergeschichte' (*Ş*, 13): In dreizehn Versen wird hier von anonymer Warte aus die Entwicklungsgeschichte der Menschheit als 'Geschichte der Männer' erzählt. Und diese ist nicht sonderlich ruhmreich: Sie beginnt mit dem Erfinden der Schrift und endet im Analphabetismus. Was ging da schief? Es geht um etwas, was wir bereits von Şenocak kennen, nämlich um den zentralen Mythos der Schrift, der Sprache und der Bücher. All dies ist im Gedicht eine Domäne von Männern. »Erfunden« aber wurde die Schrift »am Frauenleib«: dem Intellekt ist der weibliche Körper, und alles was er symbolisiert – Fruchtbarkeit, Sexualität, Wärme – als Pendant dazugestellt. Ohne das Eine kein Anderes. Die Männer der Geschichte jedoch verbannen das Weibliche, unterdrücken die Frau, ersetzen sie durch das »Traumweib«, verhüllen es – und ziehen als ahnungslose Analphabeten letztlich doch nur den Kürzeren.

Ein lakonisches Gedicht, das in wenigen Versen gekonnt die Entwicklungsgeschichte der Menschheit (of *man*kind!) nachzieht: Geschlechterkampf und Sprachgewalt (im Vertauschen der Zeichen und Unlesbarmachen der Schrift), Religionsphilosophie, Dogmenstreit, Aufklärung und Bildersturm, Hexenverbrennung, Erschaffung der Frau als Lustobjekt und ihre Unterdrückung. Das Spektrum reicht von der Antike über die Aufklärung, vom Existenzialismus und Kapitalismus bis zum Fundamentalismus, ohne sich je in solcherlei Terminologien zu verlieren. Stattdessen bleibt das Gedicht universal. Philosophisch-ironisch schildert es die selbstorganisierte Vertreibung des Mannes aus dem Paradies und sein Umherirren auf der Suche nach jenem verlorenen Glück des Urweiblichen.

Das Gedicht 'Männergeschichte' erinnert stark an die Gedanken in Şenocaks neuen Essays aus dem Band *Zungenentfernung*: Die Analphabeten, das könnten auch jene religiösen Eiferer sein, die der Vater im Text 'Der Bart' (*Zunge*, 69–73) mitleidig als 'die Bärtigen« bezeichnet. Sie könnten Nachkommen jener Urahnen sein, die 'Auf Reittieren' (*Zunge*, 16–17) vom Osten nach Westen zogen, also vom Ursprung in Richtung Moderne. Vielleicht aber steckt in dem Gedicht weniger eine Kritik an irregeleiteten Männern als mehr eine Frage. Şenocak stellt sie sich ebenfalls im bereits erwähnten Essay 'Welcher Mythos schreibt mich?' Es ist die

Frage nach dem Ursprung des Schreibens. Ähnlich den »Zweifelnde(n) der Schrift« aus dem Gedicht ist auch das Ich des Essays (das ich mit Şenocak gleichsetzen würde) auf der Suche nach der Sprache seines Schreibens, und ähnlich wie die Männer des Gedichts findet er sich in einem Widerspruch: »die Sprache meines Vaters war kalt, die meiner Mutter warm, wieder zerbrach eine sicher geglaubte Polarität, eine dichotomische Struktur. Schrieb ich den Eros eher der Mystik zu, wie man es erwartete, verschwand er in der erkalteten Sprache alter Texte, vertraute ich ihn der weiblichen Wärme an, wurde seine Sprache unverständlich« (*Zunge*, 101). Wie auch in den Gedichten 'Schlafende Generation' und 'Die Pilotin' sind hier die Protagonisten Umherirrende, Suchende, Ortlose: Die Entwicklungsgeschichte der Männer erscheint wie der Auszug aus dem Paradies. Die Männer sind keine Helden mehr, wie sie noch im 'Futuristen-Epilog' von Karpat und Şenocak auftreten. Auch nicht unbekümmert-viril, wie die »nach Angstschweiß riechenden Männer« aus früheren Gedichtzyklen.[21] Vielmehr sind sie den Engeln ähnlich, die ihren Flug verpaßt haben.

Ein solcher Mann mag auch der »Sternendeuter« aus dem Gedicht 'Rede an die Übernächtigte' (Ş, 15) sein: Er ist Rationalist, Positivist, und glaubt und tradiert nur das, was er sieht. Und da er den Himmel für nicht bedeckt hält, übersieht er die mythologischen Leuchtzeichen: Sterne, wie beispielsweise die angeredete »Übernächtigte« einer ist. Sie ist im Versteck, nur für das sprechende Ich sichtbar – und somit in Sicherheit.

'Solitude'

Während der Sternendeuter den Blick nach oben richtet, blickt ein Astronaut im Gedicht 'Solitude' (Ş, 14) von weit oben auf die Erde herab – und erkennt dort einen »Bruder«. Auch dieser einsame Ruderer auf dem Meer ist fern jeder Zivilisation, entrückt, wie ein Eremit, nur ist es eine große Weite, in der er sich verliert. Eine eigenartige Stimmung spiegelt sich in diesem sechzehn-zeiligen Gedicht, dessen Titel programmatisch ist: Solitude als Einsamkeit der Individuen. Auch das »Mammut« ist ein einsames Überbleibsel aus der Urzeit, einsam mit den Erinnerungen, die es als »Jahrtausendespeicher« hütet (Z. 4). Wer kann diese Erinnerungen schon entziffern? Und was sind sie noch wert, wenn die »Mammutzähne« fehlen, die andernorts als »Mahnmal« dienen (Z. 7–9)?

Şenocak spielt mehrfach auf die Schöpfung an, wenn er Berge, Meere, Fossilien und »Brandwunden« zum Gegenstand des Gedichtes macht. Dabei erhalten diese Begriffe religiösen Charakter: Die »Brandwunden« assoziieren die Wunden Christi, ebenso wie die Sünden der Umweltverschmutzung und den »Qualm«, den das lyrische Ich im Gedicht 'Die schlafende Generation' bei der Fahrt durch den Balkan wahrnimmt (die Sünden des Krieges also). Solitude macht sich breit angesichts des Laufs der Zeiten, und das sprechende Ich des Gedichts wird zum einsamen Beobachter, hoch oben im All, oder auf dem Ozean, immer jedoch fernab von allen anderen. Alles, was es hört, ist das »Ticken der Mammutuhr«, in der Unendlichkeit von Raum und Zeit.

Dieses sehr mystisch anmutende Gedicht wirft die Frage auf, wer dieses einsame Ich sein könnte. Şenocak selbst gibt einen Hinweis, nämlich auf einen Essay, der den Gedichttitel zitiert: 'Solitude: ein Begriff und seine Varianten' (*Zunge*, 73–4). Weniger für die Beschreibung eines Zustands der Isolierung zu gebrauchen, drücke »Solitude« eher eine von kommunizierenden Menschen geteilte Einsamkeit aus, schreibt Şenocak dort (*Zunge*, 73). Der »diasporische Intellektuelle« sei demnach eine Hauptfigur der »Solitude«, einer türkischen »solitude« allzumal. »"solitude"«, so schließt Şenocak seinen Essay, »läßt keinen Dialog zu. "solitude" ist Selbstgespräch. "solitude" ist Identität im eigentlichen Sinne und kann auf keinen anderen übertragen werden als auf einen selbst.« (*Zunge*, 74). Dieses Auf-sich-selbst-Geworfensein faßt der Lyriker Şenocak im Gedicht in eine Metapher: Hier sind Weltraum, Ozean und Mammutuhr Chiffren einer unendlichen Einsamkeit.

Die fünf neuen Gedichte Şenocaks ähneln denen der 'Wortschatzinsel' in Vielem. Auch hier sind die Topographien nicht klar festgelegt, sondern verschimmen ins Märchenhafte, Unterbewußte, in den Traum und in die Nacht. Auch hier geht es um das Begegnen von Menschen, häufig von Männern und Frauen, und um die Liebe. Genauso stark ist jedoch wieder die Stimme des lyrischen Ichs zu hören, die sich auf der Suche befindet: Nach dem eigenen Mythos, nach der Erinnerung.

Poetry on its Way to Language and Myth

Das Ich ist unterwegs in Şenocaks neuester Lyrik, so wie ein Derwisch auf Wanderschaft, und wir können mühelos konstatieren, daß Şenocaks jüngste Lyrik mystische Einflüsse trägt. Diese Mystik hat jedoch weniger mit Mittelalter zu tun als mehr mit Mythos: Şenocak ist unterwegs zum eigenen Schreibmythos. Dieser scheint in zahlreichen intertextuellen Verbindungen zwischen der Lyrik, der literarischen Prosa und den Essays durch. Die Topographien des Mythos sind ortlos, märchenhaft und traumhaft: Sie sind auf Wortschatzinseln verborgen oder in Durchgangsstationen zu erhaschen: In Träumen, aus denen man erwacht, in Bahnhöfen, auf denen sich Menschen begegnen, an Flugplätzen, wo Flüge nicht erreicht werden. »Mein Schreibmythos war geboren«, sagt Şenocak in seinem betreffenden Essay, und gebraucht eine Chiffre, die wir bereits aus der Lyrik kennen: »Er entstand an der Bruchstelle zwischen Ratio und Mystik, am Hauptbahnhof des Eros, wo Kommen und Gehen das Lebenselixier aller ist, die schon lange nicht mehr auf die Ankunft der Engel warten« (*Zunge*, 101). In diesem Essay und in vielen anderen mit autoreflexiver Thematik, besonders in *Zungenentfernung*, aber auch in der literarischen Prosa, finden wir Querverbindungen zur Lyrik Şenocaks – und umgekehrt. Diese Intertextualität ist vom Autor durchaus gewollt.

Ich bleibe bei meinem Mantra: Zafer Şenocak ist nach wie vor und immer noch Lyriker. Die anfängliche Befürchtung, der Dichter habe sich aus der Poesie zurückgezogen, erweist sich als unbegründet. Vielmehr hat er die Lyrik in die anderen Genres mit hinein genommen. Vielleicht, weil das lyrische Genre am stärksten in Bilder und Metaphern zu bringen vermag, was den Schreibmythos ausmacht. Auch wenn im Gegensatz zur Lyrik der frühen 1990er Jahre die Sprache klarer und knapper geworden zu sein scheint, die Kraft der Metaphern leuchtet ungebrochen hell. Es muß allerdings festgestellt werden, daß der Lyriker Zafer Şenocak im letzten Jahrzehnt ziemlich »unbehelligt« geblieben ist. »Was kümmert's mich?« ruft uns dieser, seinen Dichterkollegen Yunus Emre zitierend, jedoch gelassen zu. Und reist unbeirrt weiter auf den Pfaden der Lyrik – . . . poetry on its way!

Anmerkungen

[1] Vgl. den Beitrag von Matthias Konzett, Kapitel 5 in diesem Band.
[2] Darunter: 'Gedichte', in *Sprache im technischen Zeitalter*, 3 (1995); 'Elf Gedichte', in *Sirene*, 19 (1997); 'Satelliten', in *Das Gedicht*, 5 (Oktober 1997);

'In den Inzesthäusern Europas', in *Das Argument,* 222 (1997); 'Balladen aus dem Gedächtnis', in *Sirene,* 20/21 (1999); 'Gedichte', in *Das Gedicht,* 7 (1999/2000). Unterdessen feierte die Übersetzung des dritten Lyrikbandes, *La Mer verticale* (1999) in Frankreich einen beachtlichen Erfolg. Das dortige Vorwort des französischen Schriftstellers Pierre Pachet ist in diesen Band mitaufgenommen. Im Millenniumsjahr erschien in der Türkei zum zweiten Mal eine Übersetzung Şenocak'scher Lyrik, nämlich *Fernwehanstalten,* in der Übersetzung von Menekşe Toprak, unter dem Titel *Taşa ve Kemiğe Yazılıdır* (Istanbul, İyi Şeyler, 2000), die von der Literaturkritik aufmerksam rezipiert wurde. In den USA erschienen einzelne, neuere Gedichte in der amerikanischen Übersetzung von Elizabeth Oehlkers Wright: s. Bibliographie (Kapitel 13), 5.1.2.1. In naher Zukunft ist wohl auch eine Lyrik-Publikation in den USA zu erwarten, da Elizabeth Oehlkers Wright im Jahr 2003 eine Förderung des National Endowment for the Arts erhält für die Übersetzung von *Fernwehanstalten.* Siehe auch Bibliographie im Anhang.

[3] Zur Prosa-Tetralogie zählen *Der Mann im Unterhemd* (1995; *MiU*), die Romane *Die Prärie* (1997; *P*) und *Gefährliche Verwandtschaft* (1998; *GV*) sowie *Der Erottomane - Ein Findelbuch* (1999, *E*). Siehe auch Bibliographie.

[4] Die Bezeichnung 'Futuristen-Epilog' stammt von den Autoren selbst; die Texte wurden jedoch bislang nicht als Trilogie-Ausgabe, sondern nur jeweils einzeln veröffentlicht: als erster Text *nâzım hikmet: auf dem schiff zum mars* (München, Babel, 1998), zweitens *Tanzende der Elektrik* (1999) und als dritter Text das in der von Jamal Tuschick herausgegebenen Anthologie *Morgen Land* (Frankfurt am Main, Fischer, 2000) erschienene Poem 'wie den vater nicht töten'. Diese drei szenischen Poeme sind gedacht als 'Epilog' auf die Konzepte des 'neuen Menschen', so wie ihn die Futuristen zu Beginn des 20. Jahrhunderts verkündet haben. Interessant ist dabei die Wahl der 'Futuristen': Mit dem Lyriker Nâzım Hikmet im ersten und dem Republikgründer Mustafa Kemal Pascha im dritten Text werden zwei türkische Ikonen ins Zentrum der Dichtung gerückt; der zweite Text widmet sich dem persischen Mystiker Mevlana Celaleddin Rumi und dem russischen Kubofuturisten Velimir Chlebnikov. Der 'Epilog' ist dabei jeweils eine Mischung aus ironischer Hommage und Persiflage. Diese drei diffizilen Poeme werden ausführlich in meiner Dissertation behandelt, die voraussichtlich Ende 2003 erscheint. Eine ausführliche Interpretation des ersten Poems *nâzım hikmet: auf dem Schiff zum mars* ist: K.Y., 'Nâzıms Enkel schreiben weiter', in Monika Carbe und Wolfgang Riemann (Hrsg.), *Hundert Jahre Nâzım Hikmet: 1902–1963* (Hildesheim, Zürich, New York, Olms, 2002), 180–211.

[5] Den Begriff der 'Metropolenlyrik' habe ich in verschiedenen Aufsätzen verwendet; etwa in 'Topographien im "tropischen Deutschland" –

Türkisch-deutsche Literatur nach der Wiedervereinigung', in Ursula E. Beitter (Hrsg.), *Literatur und Identität. Deutsch-deutsche Befindlichkeiten und die multikulturelle Gesellschaft* (New York, Peter Lang, 2000), 303–39; 'Zafer Şenocak. Autoren-Artikel', in *KLG* 58, Neulieferung 1998 (dieser Artikel wird derzeit aktualisiert und erscheint ca. Mitte 2003); sowie in 'Das Empire schreibt zurück – Die deutschsprachige Migrationsliteratur', in Thomas Böhm und Martin Hielscher (Hrsg.), *Weltliteratur 2001. Vom Nobelpreis bis zum Comic* (Köln, Könemann, 2001), 118–37. Ausführlich wird die 'Metropolenlyrik' in meiner Dissertation diskutiert. Auch Sargut Şölçün und Timour Muhidine gehen auf den Kontext Stadt und Dichtung bei Şenocak ein (s. Bibliographie, Kapitel 13).

⁶ Der Text 'Jenseits der Landessprache' (*Zunge*, 87–90) bietet eine Art Poetik in 22 Sentenzen. Zuerst erschienen in *Sirene*, 15/16 (1996) 171–4.

⁷ Die in diesem Band, Kapitel 1 erschienenen Gedichte werden im folgenden mit 'Ş' und Seitenangabe zitiert. Einzelne Gedichte erschienen bereits vorab, wie z.B. 'Fernweh' und 'Der Tänzer'; vgl. Anm. 2.

⁸ Die Licht- und Sonnenmetapher spielt in den Poemen des 'Futuristen-Epilogs' ebenfalls eine zentrale Rolle; vgl. K.Y., 'Nâzıms Enkel'.

⁹ Die entsprechende Erzählung wäre 'Die Frau bleibt Engel und der Mann Koch' (*MiU*, 105–10). Vgl. auch die Ausführungen zum Gedicht 'Die Pilotin' später im Text.

¹⁰ Siehe in diesem Band, Kapitel 11.

¹¹ Und dort gibt der Titel 'wie den vater nicht töten' bereits einen Hinweis auf das im Text verborgene Vatermord-Motiv, das allerdings abgewandelt ist, weil dort der Vater vom Übervater ermordet wird.

¹² Der Dreizeiler (die Verfasserin zählt übrigens nur Zeilen, keine Erbsen!) erschien in der Erstveröffentlichung in *Das Gedicht*, 7 (1999) noch unter dem Titel 'Der Tänzer'. In derselben Zeitschrift (4, Oktober 1996) fand ein Lyrik-Streit statt (vgl. Ulrich Beil, 'Läßt sich über Lyrik streiten?' 69ff.), in der auch Şenocak seine Position bekannt gibt: 'Sechs Winkelzüge, um der deutschsprachigen Poesie auf die Schliche zu kommen' (80). Ob das Gedicht kurz oder lang sein solle, erinnere ihn, so Şenocak ironisch im VI. Winkelzug, »an die aus meiner Sicht müßige Frage nach der Länge des männlichen Gliedes«. Sein launischer Rat: »Wie es halt so kommt. Jedem das Seine. Je nachdem, was man damit anstellen will, hat mal dies, mal jenes Vorteile«.

¹³ Bei Şenocak ist der Vatermord häufiger als Überspringen des Vaters in der Generationslinie zu finden: So beginnt der Enkel in 'Das Heft', einer Erzählung in *MiU*, zu schreiben, nachdem er ein Heft des toten Großvaters in die Hand genommen hat. In *Gefährliche Verwandtschaft* löst die Erbschaft der verschlüsselten Tagebücher des verstorbenen Großvaters nach einiger Erinnerungsarbeit endlich den Schreibprozeß bei Sascha aus.

[14] Vergleiche dazu auch Leslie A. Adelsons Gedanken zu dem Begriff 'house of words' in ihrem Beitrag in diesem Band, Kapitel 11.

[15] Passend dazu lauten die Titel einiger Zyklen aus den letzten beiden Gedichtbänden: 'Archivare in Istanbul' (*SM*, 7ff.), 'Portraits in Handschriften und Versatzstücken' (*SM*, 43ff.) oder 'Geschrieben auf Stein und Knochen' (*FA*, 75ff.).

[16] Der Essay 'Welcher Mythos schreibt mich?' erschien zuerst unter dem Titel 'Der Schriftsteller ist ein Archäologe' in *Die Welt*, 5. Juni 1999.

[17] 'Zeile(n)' wird im folgenden als 'Z.' abgekürzt.

[18] Diese 'twilight zone' wird auch andernorts poetisch chiffriert. So spricht z.B. Sascha Muhteschem im Roman *Gefährliche Verwandtschaft* vom Übergang zwischen Tag und Nacht als einer Zeit, in der »Geschichten beginnen zu sprechen« (*GV*, 93).

[19] Tom Cheesman, '»Einfach eine neue Form«: Gespräch mit Zafer Şenocak', Kapitel 3 in diesem Band.

[20] *MiU*, 7–21 (20).

[21] Hier meine ich das Gedicht III des Zyklus 'Lu' (*FA*, 27).

11

Against Between: A Manifesto[1]

LESLIE A. ADELSON

A world-renowned author once described 'a migrant's vision' in terms of a 'triple disruption' that occurs when migrants lose their place in the world, enter into a language that is alien to them and find themselves 'surrounded by beings whose social behavior and codes are very unlike, and sometimes even offensive to' their own. The author in question then proceeds to explain how the creative work of a somewhat lesser known author – let's call him Y – is informed by such 'a migrant's vision':

> This is what the triple disruption of reality teaches migrants: that reality is an artefact, that it does not exist until it is made, and that like any other artefact, it can be made well or badly, and that it can also, of course, be unmade. What [Y] learned on his journey across the frontiers of history was Doubt. Now he distrusts all those who claim to possess absolute forms of knowledge; he suspects all total explanations, all systems of thought which purport to be complete. Amongst [. . .] writers, he is quintessentially the artist of uncertainty.[2]

Readers may be surprised to learn that the world-renowned author is none other than Salman Rushdie, and 'the artist of uncertainty' to whom he ascribes 'a migrant's vision' is Günter Grass.

Both writers will be familiar to readers of this volume, but probably not in the relationship in which they stand here. I do not begin with this odd inversion of expected categories because I want to celebrate Grass as the transnational or post-colonial author par excellence, but because what we need at the present juncture is *more* doubt about existing forms of knowledge, *more* uncertainty about presumed truths and *more* vibrant curiosity about a unique historical moment in German culture. The comments that follow revolve around questions too seldom asked: What does it mean to contemplate the Turkish presence in German culture today? What can German literature written by authors of Turkish descent tell us about a tectonic shift, partly in the lives of Turkish immigrants, but, more importantly, in the ground of German culture itself? What can the cultural labour of reading and writing literary texts teach us that political debates and demographic statistics only obscure? Where can Turks be located on the map of German culture at the onset of the twenty-first century?

In 2000, the president of Germany gave a landmark speech in Berlin's Haus der Kulturen der Welt, calling for a radical reorganization of thought in all arenas of social and political life in response to the changing face of the German nation: 'Wir müssen in allen Bereichen des gesellschaftlichen Lebens und des politischen und staatlichen Handelns umdenken.'³ President Rau most likely did not have literature in mind when he said this, but emergent literatures certainly are one important site of cultural reorientation. More than a mere repository of treasured or controversial works of art, a nation's culture is also an activity, a creative engagement with a rapidly changing present. It actively seeks to negotiate changing values and attitudes toward a changing world.⁴ This important labour of culture is currently being undertaken, in ways that have yet to be grasped, by authors usually presumed to be outside German culture, even if they have somehow managed to reside on German territory or acquire German citizenship. 'Between two worlds' is the place customarily reserved for these authors and their texts on the cultural map of our time, but the trope of 'betweenness' often functions literally like a reservation designed to contain, restrain and impede new knowledge, not enable it. For reasons that I hope to make clear, then, this essay is my manifesto *against between*.⁵

The notion that Turks in Germany are suspended on a bridge 'between two worlds' carries with it a number of misperceptions that thwart understanding, even as they claim to promote it.

1. The 'dialogue of cultures' that Johannes Rau and other public figures call for may be useful, even necessary, in the socio-political realm, but it fails completely, oddly enough, in the imaginative realm of social production that is often taken to represent culture. Whoever mines literary texts of the 1990s and beyond for evidence

of mutually exclusive collective identities in communicative dialogue with one another is not reading this literature for its most significant innovations. This is especially true for literature written in German by authors whose cultural imagination has been profoundly influenced by many years of living, working, studying and dreaming in the Federal Republic of Germany.

2. Despite wide recognition that political science and literary interpretation rely on different terms, media and analytical procedures, the growing and diverse field of Turco-German literature may well be the only sector in literary studies today where an entrenched sociological positivism continues to hold sway. This positivist approach presumes that literature reflects empirical truths about migrants' lives and that authors' biographies explain their texts so well that reading them is virtually superfluous. This saves readers and critics much time. Meanwhile, the literary elephant in the room goes unremarked.

3. The sociological thrust of this positivism is an epistemological holdover from the late 1970s and 1980s, when an emergent 'guest-worker' literature focused on the economic exploitation of and xenophobic disdain for the underprivileged. These tropes still circulate in the reception of migrants' literature today, especially when it is written by someone presumed to represent the culture of Turkey. Aras Ören and Güney Dal are best known for their literary reflections on the 'guest-worker' experience, for example, and they both continue to write in Turkish despite their long-time residence in Germany. But few people know that Ören explicitly conceived several of his novels from the 1980s on as being 'Auf der Suche nach der gegenwärtigen Zeit', that is, as a pseudo-Proustian series of literary reflections on the modernist legacy for an as yet uncharted, but shared, Turco-German present. Even fewer people know that the narrator of Güney Dal's tale of an industrial strike and a mutant migrant in the mid-1970s characterized foreign labourers as 'ein[en] Teil lebendiger Erinnerung', a piece of 'living memory' of Germans' own class history.[6] If the sociological tensions of this earlier period cannot be reduced to an absolute cultural divide between things German and things Turkish, they are even less useful for assessing the significance of a literature that has grown only more diverse since unification.

4. The imaginary bridge 'between two worlds' is designed to keep discrete worlds apart as much as it pretends to bring them

together. Migrants are at best imagined as suspended on this bridge in perpetuity; critics do not seem to have enough imagination to picture them actually crossing the bridge and landing anywhere new. This has to do in turn with the national contours that are ascribed to these ostensible 'worlds' linked by a bridge of dubious stability. In this model, the Federal Republic of Germany may change and the Republic of Turkey may change (though this is usually dismissed as unlikely), but what is not allowed to change is the notion that Turks and Germans are separated by an absolute cultural divide. Where does this leave Turco-German writers in Germany? It is absurd to assume today that they always and necessarily and only represent the national culture of Turkey.[7] The Turkish diaspora and its lines of affiliation cannot be traced or contained by the borders of the Turkish Republic, certainly not by these alone. Beyond the Cold War, German culture is already forever changed, and Turco-German literature is part and parcel of *this* cultural transformation.

5. Zafer Şenocak calls for 'so etwas wie eine negative Hermeneutik' that could perhaps heal 'die Wunden der Verständigung', wounds inflicted by a public obsession, right and left, with Self and Other.[8] Such a negative hermeneutic, again in Zafer Şenocak's words, 'critically interrogates what is presumed to be understood'.[9] In this sense we do not need more understanding of different cultures if our understanding only fixes them *as* utterly different cultures. Instead of reifying different cultures as fundamentally foreign, we need to understand culture itself differently.[10] Cultural contact today is not an 'intercultural encounter' that takes place between German culture and something outside it, but something happening *within* German culture between the German past and the German present. Turco-German literature has been making forays into this unfamiliar territory for some time now, but the imaginative complexity of this cultural endeavour has gone largely unrecognized to date.

6. In this context the spatial configuration of cultural labour also needs to be understood in a radically different way. Creative writing and critical thought certainly make reference to concrete places in the world, where people and nations have loved, lost, struggled and died. These places haunt human imagination, but the imagined spaces of cultural labour cannot be mapped or measured with surveyor's tools. The discursive model that repeatedly

situates Turks and other migrants 'between two worlds' relies too schematically and too rigidly on territorial concepts of 'home', 'Heimat'. Even the notion that 'language' becomes a 'home' for those in exile or diaspora presupposes that a territorial 'home' is the place of authenticity, from which language as 'home' can only distinguish itself in sorrow or celebration. Searching for traces of 'home' in contemporary cultural production is therefore a misguided venture. Creative thought is not bounded by geographical or political borders. The Turco-German literary texts that demand the most of their readers do not reflect 'Orte des Denkens' in any predictably national or ethnic sense. Instead they are 'Orte des Umdenkens', that is to say, imaginative sites where cultural orientation is being radically rethought.

7. In a series of aphorisms called 'Jenseits der Landessprache', Zafer Şenocak writes, 'Dazwischen bin ich nicht, denn ich habe die Richtung verloren'.[11] Here the military language of embattled camps – familiar to us from Samuel Huntington's *Clash of Civilizations*[12] – alternates with the disorienting language of lyrical reflection: 'Lieder und Salven wechseln sich ab'.[13] This disorientation that arises when familiar categories are left behind becomes the very ground on which critical readers reorient themselves anew. Lest I be misunderstood, this is not a celebration of violent circumstances that deprive people of the homes, lives and relations that matter most to them. A postmodern embrace of 'nomadic' fantasies is not what I propose. What I do have in mind is an epistemological reorientation to which migrants' literature contributes at a crucial juncture in an uncharted German present. It is surely no coincidence that two of the most complex writers in this field, Zafer Şenocak and Yoko Tawada, cite the great wordsmith Paul Celan as one of their literary muses. For the Japanese-born Tawada, the 'between' of Celan's poetry does not mark a border ('Grenze') between two distinct worlds but a threshold ('Schwelle'), a site where consciousness of something new flashes into view. She describes a poem by Celan as 'Zwischenraum', a *transitional* space. This is not the bridge 'between two worlds' on which Turks are so often thought to be suspended. For, as Tawada elaborates, 'Der Zwischenraum ist kein geschlossenes Zimmer, sondern er ist der Raum unter einem Tor. / Ich fing an, Celans Gedichte wie Tore zu betrachten und nicht etwa wie Häuser, in denen die Bedeutung wie ein Besitz aufbewahrt wird'.[14] For Tawada,

reading Celan, then, the word is a site of opening, a threshold that beckons. Turco-German literature too is a threshold that beckons, not a tired bridge 'between two worlds'. Entering this threshold space is an imaginative challenge that has yet to be widely met, and much critical work remains to be done.

How might such a manifesto inform concrete literary analysis? Here I must limit myself to a discussion of spatial relations, 'Orte des Umdenkens', in two explosive publications from 1995: Feridun Zaimoğlu's *Kanak Sprak: 24 Mißtöne vom Rande der Gesellschaft* and Zafer Şenocak's *Der Mann im Unterhemd*. German political discourse of the 1980s and the post-unification citizenship debates of the early 1990s were often fuelled by the social, legal and cultural assumption that Turks entering and then claiming German space constituted, if not an act of aggression, then at least an act of transgression. From this vantage point both authors might be considered second-generation transgressors, since they were born in Turkey and moved to the Federal Republic as very young children. In post-colonial terminology they might be called diasporic intellectuals, though this all too convenient designation tells us little about the specific significance of their work.

Three years younger than Şenocak, Zaimoğlu moved to the Federal Republic at the age of four in 1968. After studying art and medicine, he helped establish the Turkish literary journal *Argos*. *Kanak Sprak* was his first more widely reviewed publication, one that propelled him to cult stardom as the avant-garde of what he calls 'Kanak Attack'. Subsequent provocative publications such as *Abschaum* and *Koppstoff: Kanaka Sprak vom Rande der Gesellschaft* have sparked media events, public debate and film production.[15]

If spatial relations have figured prominently in various discussions of centre and periphery, metropolis and margin, West and East, North and South, and Self and Other, the prevalence of border metaphors speaks to the need for a critical language that could explain how and why it is that individuals, groups, nations and cultures seem to rub each other raw with the friction of difference. When these phenomena and contexts literally share borders, the geographical trope seems plausible enough. But how eagerly should we embrace the discourse of border skirmishes when our attention turns to the function of Turco-German culture in the Federal Republic today, to a culture whose perimeters can be neither easily defined nor readily localized? In the aphorisms cited earlier, 'beyond the language of the land', Şenocak writes: 'Das Denken wird zum Haus, in dem man sich versammelt, sich verbündet und von dem aus man gemeinsam singt und schiesst.'[16] If critical attention shifts away from borderlands and national boundaries to imagined houses and other social spaces of Turco-German culture, what insights flash into view?

The 'Mißtöne vom Rande der Gesellschaft' that comprise *Kanak Sprak* derive from interviews conducted with young Turkish-German men whom, with few exceptions, neither a Turkish nor a German mainstream would accept. Two rappers are represented, as are a transsexual, a gigolo, a junkie in the process of shooting up, a prostitute, a patient in a psychiatric hospital and others. Short, disparate, individual texts are linked, not by consistently delineated characters that elicit reader identification, but by architectures or spaces of transgression, especially those involving scatology, criminality, sexuality and gender.

Whereas Şenocak's prose is pointedly literary and phantasmatic, Zaimoğlu claims to write in the spirit of 'demystification', to point the way to 'a new realism' (*Kanak Sprak*, 17) and to dismantle the xenophilic myth of the loveable oppressed Turk, to decry the '"Müllkutscher-Prosa", die den Kanaken auf die Opferrolle festlegt' (*Kanak Sprak*, 12). For Zaimoğlu, 'Turk' is a derogatory term reserved for those who are 'socially acceptable', capable of integration. This group does not interest him in the least: he proudly proclaims, 'Hier hat allein der Kanake das Wort' (*Kanak Sprak*, 18).

Zaimoğlu presents his cast of characters as a kind of underworld, a substratum of reality that reflects a deeper truth about contemporary German society. This topography of above and below coincides with a discourse of transgressive bodies that foregrounds – and sometimes privileges – 'dreck'. Although this can refer to gross physical matter or to a metaphorical 'Dreck am Stecken', Zaimoğlu's discourse links flesh, filth, dirt, shit and history in curious ways. One interviewee complains that Germans do not see him as a human being with a bodily presence:

Da haun die tarife längst nimmer hin, dir kommt's vor, als wärst du'n fraß oder eher schon stinkiger abfall oder so ne blechdose, wo man wegkickt, und's scheppert wie krawall. Schlimm is, daß die alemannen dich nischt für ne müde mark sehn, du bist gar nischt da, du kannst da antippen und sagen: mann, mich gibt's schon seit ner urlangen zeit, faß man an, daß du merkst, da is fleisch und knochen, für die biste gar nischt, luft und weniger als schnuppe luft, du hast eben kein sektor, wo man dich ordnen könnt, das sieht denn aus, wie wenn ne olle leiche rumliegt, und die machen mit nem stück kreide nen umriß. Im umriß ist denn nix wenn se'n kadaver wegtragen, da siehste 'n strichmänneken aus teppich [. . .] (*Kanak Sprak*, 118–9)

The gigolo, on the other hand, asserts that those Germans whom he services see him only as 'eine fleischbestellung' (*Kanak Sprak*, 70). Their fantasies about his flesh are a kind of 'dreck' that he feels he must keep from clinging to his soul: 'sonst hältst du die sache mit der liebe für ne infamie' (72). Prompted by his recollections of a German 'christenlady' who liked to call him 'du mein schöner jude' (70), the gigolo expounds on his theory about German fantasies and the Jewish undead:

hier's land ist bis zum letzten erdenfleck vollgesogen mit totem jude-nunschuldsfleisch, das die arschgeigen gekillt haben und schnell man grob innen graben geschmissen oder zu asche verwandelt und wegge-fegt. Also rächt sich's verscharrte fleisch und klumpt als geist und viele geister in den lebenden, wo die man'n sprung wegkriegen oder'n komplex oder'n seelenausschlag, also sagt mir die theorie, daß so ne lady, wo die man mich ficken tat, sich was geholt hat, ohne daß sie's natürlich weiß, was geschnappt vonner leiche tief unten im schlamm schlimm gemeuchelt. (*Kanak Sprak*, 71–2)[17]

This theory is echoed by the poet in the book, who claims that 'kanaken' have 'den blick für das, was sich hinter den kulissen abspielt' (110). 'Solange dieses land uns den wirklichen eintritt verwehrt, werden wir die anomalien und perversionen dieses lan-des wie ein schwamm aufsaugen und den dreck ausspucken. Die beschmutzten kennen keine ästhetik' (113–4). These images of transgressive Turkish men both occupying and theorizing the space of the abject in German society complicate any merely so-ciological notion of spatial hierarchies. Complex histories are as much at stake as social conflicts in these discursive palimpsests.

The gigolo is positioned both as being 'dreck' and as articulating the meaning of 'dreck'· in contemporary German culture. Both functions rely on the gigolo inhabiting the subspace of the 'Kanake' that Zaimoğlu ascribes to him. Şenocak's literary reflections on Turco-German epistemologies, on the other hand, make hardly any pointed references to *being* Turkish or German or to inhabiting any kind of delimitable Turkish or German space. Not that *Der Mann im Unterhemd* is devoid of 'dreck'. Yet Şenocak's scenarios of fantasy, desire, humiliation, torture and lust do not highlight the gross physical matter connoted by 'dreck' so much as the irrecuperable *traces* of gross physical matter that haunt his prose.

Der Mann im Unterhemd offers no master narrative of twentieth-century German spaces, but neither does it comprise the victim narrative that much migrants' literature has been presumed to be. Neither the narrating voices of the text nor the narrated figures function as characters inviting reader identification. Instead they function as elusive personae: 'keine Person', 'nur ein Bild' (*MiU*, 48). The body that might otherwise be said to occupy space is dissolved into less tangible but nonetheless visceral components. 'Es beginnt in der Haltlosigkeit der Nacht – die Umsetzung der Zeit in Fleisch, die Auflösung des Fleisches in seine Bestandteile, Angst und Lust' (*MiU*, 74). While fear and desire propel Şenocak's tales, these psychological affects cannot be attributed to individual characters, let alone ethnic groups or national communities. Instead they function as ubiquitous but non-specific atmospheric elements, lending a disquieting texture to the spaces of the narrative.

Der Mann im Unterhemd confounds the analytical imagination. Şenocak writes against a facile notion of Turkish spaces in German history and culture, spaces that xenophobes and xenophiles all too glibly demarcate as distinct from properly German spaces of our time. This is a book about the riddle of invisibility (*MiU*, 7), about the hidden nooks and crannies of cultural imagination. The book's many references to the bridges and canals of Berlin, and to the murders, suicides and other sorts of deaths associated with them, highlight structures that define urban spaces but also allow those spaces to exceed their structural limits. The canals, we read, owe the dead 'Gedächtnisgräber' (*MiU*, 36):

> Die Kanäle aber tun so, als wäre nichts passiert, als lägen noch heute nicht die Spiegelbilder verzweifelter Gesichter auf ihren Wassern, den Ratten sich zum Fraß anbietend. Aber auch Ratten können die Geschichte nicht tilgen. Sie nagen an den Körpern, nicht an ihren Schatten. (*MiU*, 36)

The shadow that exceeds the body of the dead, the shadow that even rats cannot devour, signifies a dilemma that is epistemological and historical. This is not about ethnic identity politics. This dilemma is how to tell transnational, transgenerational time. How does Şenocak render transnational Turco-German history intelligible in such a way that Turks in Germany are recognized, firstly, as having a history, and, secondly, are not seen as having only or even primarily an ethnic or national history?

Although none of the personae in these texts are characters in the conventional literary sense, two figures are attributed with familial genealogies. The masochistic prostitute of 1932, whose morphium-addicted lover is one of the canal dead, murdered by brownshirts, has a granddaughter who is a cane fetishist and Artaud admirer in the present. Grandmother and granddaughter bear the same name, as do almost all the named female personae in the text. The male persona of the writer has in one story an Ottoman grandfather who does his own writing in Arabic script on the streets of Istanbul and only later retreats into 'das kleinste und hinterste Zimmer im Parterre des Hauses' (*MiU*, 133). This dark and nearly windowless room is called 'das blinde Zimmer' by the children of the household. The grandson who will become the writer of the text plays at imitating his grandfather's script in the grandfather's attic, but he dreams of being locked in 'the blind room' and forced to write (*MiU*, 132–3). When he inherits the grandfather's notebooks, he inherits 'das Haus seiner Wörter'.

Both genealogies concern elusive, at times forbidden, fantasies, rather than predictable linear histories or discrete cultural traditions. It is on the level of the phantasmatic that these genealogies touch. The site of these encounters is invariably spatialized without the space of the phantasm being in any way delimited as national or ethnic. The house of words that the writer inherits does not coincide with the actual family homestead in Istanbul. One piece begins, 'Es ist eine dumme Angewohnheit von Schriftstellern, von dem Haus zu erzählen, in dem sie wohnen' (*MiU*, 23). A later text distinguishes between the writer's house of residence and 'das verbrannte Haus in seinem Kopf' (*MiU*, 78).

Such distinctions between referential and phantasmatic spaces of history make it all the more difficult to sustain the fiction of in-betweenness which critics have been wont to celebrate in discussing Turkish-German literature. Even the one story that situates a dark Turkish criminal element at the bottom of a spatial hierarchy in Berlin toys with readerly notions of ethnic identity or sociological referentiality. In this instance the narrating persona occupies an apartment on the second floor of a multi-storey building that he describes as 'ein ordentliches Haus' (*MiU*, 29) where even the 'Treppenhaus' is 'regelmäßig geputzt' (*MiU*, 30). The Turco-German narrator lives across the hall from a 'Superdeutsche' who speaks ill of the dark-skinned criminals who reside on the ground floor beneath her because their language, Turkish, is one she wants rather fiercely to forget (*MiU*, 24). As the building rises above and on top of the Turkish-speaking smugglers, the residents get progressively lighter. 'In den oberen Etagen wohnen nur Weiße. Je höher man steigt, desto weißer werden sie. Unterm Dach wohnt ein Albinoehepaar' (*MiU*, 28). This seeming allusion to racialized hierarchies and sociological referentiality is belied by the text's concluding emphasis on the smugglers' dreams. The Turkish 'Superdeutsche' above them is convinced that they dream of raising donkeys in Berlin for a sausage factory. Here the narrator intervenes:

> Die Geschäfte der Dunklen sind die Träume der Weißen und umgekehrt, denke ich mir. Die Phantasie ist ein windgeschützter Umschlagplatz für ungedeckte Wechsel, ausgestellt auf ein Datum nach dem Tod des Träumers. Aber keine noch so kostspielige Sanierung wird die Farbordnung in unserem Haus verändern. (*MiU*, 30)

This house of words is a phantasm about phantasms. Yet I have tried to argue that *Der Mann im Unterhemd* is also about the spaces of historical narrative. How can this be? Specific references to identifiable persons or events in either German or Turkish history are infrequent and indirect. We encounter the German grandmother just before the onset of the Third Reich, and the allusion to brownshirts hints at a larger national history. Elsewhere the text refers to the national unification of 1990 as something that has driven real smugglers even farther underground, precisely because the language of secrets is now traded like a commodity on the open market (*MiU*, 27–8). The Ottoman grandfather in Istanbul who bequeaths his notebooks to the writing persona of the text suggests a historical divide of sorts between the Ottoman Empire ended by the founding of the Republic of Turkey in 1923, and Atatürk's subsequent sweeping language reform. The narrator also invokes a more recent historical referent when he recalls a classmate disappeared by (presumably) Turkish soldiers (*MiU*, 123), a riddle of invisibility that leads the narrator to reflect, 'Ich begreife, wie etwas durch Verschwinden wächst' (*MiU*, 125). These minimal references to decisive phases of German and Turkish national histories at best stake out a loose framework for conjuring the phantasms of history, without telling a story that moves in predictable fashion from one space or time to another.

The spaces of Şenocak's phantasms range from the domestic to the urban, from island brothels to torture cellars, from thresholds to windows, bridges to stairs. His convoluted mapping of domestic and urban spaces situates this work in a transnational history of modernity and modernism. As Anthony Vidler has remarked elsewhere:

> the house has provided a site for endless representations of haunting, doubling, dismembering, and other terrors in literature and art. On another level, the labyrinthine spaces of the modern city have been construed as the source of modern anxiety, from revolution and epidemic to phobia and alienation.[18]

Whereas Vidler is concerned with the ways in which postmodern architecture strips the classical bourgeois body of its privileged place in constructed spaces,[19] one could extrapolate from Vidler to suggest that Şenocak's phantasmatic architectures of transgression cannot be read reductively in terms of sociology, ethnicity or national identities. The house of words through which we move here diverges significantly from the more familiar trope of language as *Heimat* that has shaped much of the discussion on Turco-German literature to date. This house of words is both particular and transnational. The phantasmatic space of *this* German culture suggests analytical alternatives to the presumption of an all too rigid Turkish–German divide. Şenocak's configuration of transnationalism is less about national and ethnic 'identities' than it is about the textures and architectures of changing historical experience, which is no less *imagined* than it is *lived*. This work breaks the spell that an obsession with multicultural identity 'between two worlds' continues to cast on cultural studies of the Other.

Notes

[1] The manifesto that comprises the first half of this article was first presented at a conference convened by the Haus der Kulturen der Welt in Berlin, 2–4 June 2000, on the question 'Where and what is home in the 21st century?' It was delivered in the context of a panel on 'Orte des Denkens: Sprache und Bilder'. Portions of the second half of the present article overlap with sections of Leslie A. Adelson, 'Touching tales of Turks, Germans, and Jews: cultural alterity, historical narrative, and literary riddles for the 1990s', *New German Critique*, 80 (2000), 93–124. 'Touching tales' offers more detailed analytical reflections on historical narrative and figural referentiality in Zafer Şenocak's literary prose, while the present manifesto focuses on different concepts of cultural space and the competing methodologies they engender. 'Against between: a manifesto' also appears in Salah Hassan and Iftikhar Dadi (eds), *Unpacking Europe: Towards a Critical Reading* (Rotterdam, NAi Publishers, 2001), 244–55.

[2] Salman Rushdie, 'Günter Grass', *Imaginary Homelands: Essays and Criticism 1981–1991* (London, Granta [Penguin], 1991), 273–81 (277–80).

[3] Johannes Rau, 'Berliner Rede: Ohne Angst und Träumereien: Gemeinsam in Deutschland leben', Haus der Kulturen der Welt [Berlin], 12 May 2000; www.bundespraesident.de/reden/rau/de/00_01512.htm.

[4] See Agnes Heller's concept of the 'present-present age' as elaborated in *A Theory of History* (London, Routledge and Kegan Paul, 1982), 44, and discussed in my *Making Bodies, Making History: Feminism and German Identity* (Lincoln and London, University of Nebraska Press, 1993), 24.

[5] This manifesto is written as a pointed intervention in a particular field of political and scholarly rhetoric in Germany at a particular historical juncture in the development of contemporary German studies on an international scale. The trope of 'betweenness' may well be useful in other contexts, but they are not the author's present concern.

[6] Güney Dal, *Wenn Ali die Glocken läuten hört*, trans. Brigitte Schreiber-Grabitz (Berlin, Edition der 2, 1979), 92. So far published in German in Aras Ören's series 'Auf der Suche nach der gegenwärtigen Zeit' are: (I) *Eine verspätete Abrechnung oder Der Aufstieg der Gündoğdus*, trans. Zafer Şenocak and Eva Hund (Frankfurt am Main, Dağyeli, 1988); (II) *Granatapfelblüte*, trans. Eva Hund and Zafer Şenocak (Berlin, Elefanten Press, 1998); (III) *Sehnsucht nach Hollywood*, trans. Deniz Göktürk (Berlin, Espresso, 1999); (V) *Berlin Savignyplatz*, trans. Deniz Göktürk (Berlin, Elefanten Press, 1995); (VI) *Unerwarteter Besuch*, trans. Deniz Göktürk (Berlin, Elefanten Press, 1997). *Bitte nix Polizei* (Düsseldorf, Claassen, 1981; repr. Berlin, Fischer, 1983) is the precursor to this series.

⁷ See Leslie A. Adelson, 'Coordinates of orientation: an introduction', *ATG*, xxiv; and Zafer Şenocak and Bülent Tulay, 'Germany – home for Turks?', *ATG*, 1–9. For the German original of this second essay, see *Atlas*, 9–19.

⁸ For English-language commentary on this, see Adelson, 'Coordinates', *ATG*, xxix; Şenocak, 'The poet and the deserters: Salman Rushdie between the fronts', *ATG*, 37–42 (= *Hitler*, 21–8); 'Which myth writes me?', *ATG*, 77–82 (= *Zunge*, 97–103); and 'Beyond the language of the land', *ATG*, 66–8 (= *Zunge*, 87–90). The phrase 'so etwas wie eine negative Hermeneutik' appears in *Hitler*, 28 and *Zunge*, 103; 'Wunden der Verständigung' in *Zunge*, 90.

⁹ *Zunge*, 103; *ATG*, 82.

¹⁰ Adelson, 'Coordinates', *ATG*, xxxv.

¹¹ *Zunge*, 87–90 (88); *ATG*, 66–8 (67).

¹² Samuel P. Huntington, *The Clash of Civilizations and the Remaking of World Order* (New York, Simon and Shuster, 1996).

¹³ *Zunge*, 87; *ATG*, 66.

¹⁴ Yoko Tawada, 'Das Tor des Übersetzers oder Celan liest Japanisch', *Talisman* (Tübingen, Konkursbuch, 1996), 129–30.

¹⁵ Feridun Zaimoğlu, *Kanak Sprak: 24 Mißtöne vom Rande der Gesellschaft* (Hamburg, Rotbuch, 1995) (cited below as *Kanak Sprak*); *Abschaum: Die wahre Geschichte des Ertan Ongun* (Hamburg, Rotbuch, 1997) (filmed as *Kanak Attack!*, dir. Lars Becker, 2000); *Koppstoff: Kanaka Sprak vom Rande der Gesellschaft* (Hamburg, Rotbuch, 1998). For commentary, see Tom Cheesman, 'Akçam–Zaimoğlu–Kanak Attak: Turkish lives and letters in German', *German Life and Letters*, 60, 2 (April 2002), 180–95.

¹⁶ 'Jenseits der Landessprache', *ATG*, 66; *Zunge*, 87.

¹⁷ For further commentary on Zaimoğlu's *Kanak Sprak*, see 'Touching tales', where my English translations of these idiosyncratic passages first appeared (117).

¹⁸ *The Architectural Uncanny: Essays in the Modern Unhomely* (Cambridge MA, MIT Press, 1992), ix.

¹⁹ *The Architectural Uncanny*, xii.

12

Ş/ß: Zafer Şenocak and
the Civilization of Clashes[1]

TOM CHEESMAN

Manchmal habe ich mich im Ç Quadrat,
manchmal im Ş Quadrat,
meistens jedoch im Ğ Quadrat rumgetrieben.
Doch das wußtest Du nicht.
Du suchtest mich in den falschen Quadraten.
Ich war nie dort.
    Ich war nie im Q Quadrat.
(Hasan Özdemir, 'Mannhaus')[2]

Barthesians may be excused at once. 'Ş/ß' alludes to the celebrated essays on Balzac's *Sarrassine*,[3] but only in order to foreground the imbrication of cultural codes in Şenocak's texts, and in globalized society more broadly. The 'hook', 'comma' or 'beard', the cedilla on the initial letter of his surname, causes much trouble to western European typesetters and computer users.[4] This special character is a small but significant token of the Turkish diaspora presence in German society. 'Hoş geldiniz, yeni vatandaşlar' ('Welcome, new fellow-citizens'), ran the top line on the front page of the mass-market *Bild-Zeitung* on 16 October 1998, above the huge shock headline: '900.000 Türken bald Deutsche?' The new government had announced a major reform of the citizenship law, proposing to grant dual citizenship to some children born in Germany of foreign parents, and to reduce the residence requirement for naturalization from fifteen to eight years.[5] The first ever use of Turkish letters in Europe's biggest selling daily paper signalled a willing act of integration, from which the main headline implicitly – and palpably – recoiled. Further left on the political spectrum, and far down the league in terms of circulation figures, the banner of *perşembe*

('Thursday'), a short-lived weekly bilingual supplement to *die tageszeitung*, used tiny letters 'ch' in place of the cedilla, by way of helping monoglot Germans pronounce the name.[6]

Another recent reform, spelling reform, has decreased the incidence of the sz ligature in German texts, possibly a step towards expunging ß entirely and bringing the German signary into line with a Euro-American Latin alphabetic standard. On the other hand, the enlargement of the Europe Union is bringing several new character sets into the EU's common currency, and the long-drawn-out process of arrival of migrants and their offspring, during and since the Cold War, is having the same effect. German's ß sets the language apart from others, but Turkish's ş, along with ç, ğ, dotless ı and capital İ, now claim a possibly permanent place within German scriptory space on the strength of the numbers of bilingual, Turkish-writing and Turkish-reading residents. How long before the standard German character set includes these as 'New German' letters, just as Hasan Özdemir, in the long poem 'Mannhaus', has inscribed some of them in the cultural topography of post-Napoleonic Mannheim?

In the last decade, Şenocak's work has insistently raised questions about the possibility of German and European adaptation to the presence of Turks, and indeed Turkey, in Europe. At the time of writing, the Justice and Development Party – a self-declared conservative, secular party with roots in the banned Islamic Virtue Party – has just won the general election, and the vexed question of Turkey's accession to the EU has been raised more acutely than ever. Valérie Giscard D'Estaing, chair of a convention on the future of the Union, was reported by the BBC as telling *Le Monde* 'that Turkey's capital was not in Europe, 95% of its population lived outside Europe, and it was "not a European country". Asked what the effect of including Turkey in a future wave of European enlargement would be, he said: "In my opinion, it would be the end of Europe."'[7] For many, the cohesion of European identity requires strong borders to the south and east, in order to divide 'self' – the putative heirs to the Greek, Roman and Christian civilizational traditions – sharply from all 'others'. That can mean Orthodox Christians, and most certainly means non-Christians. Even if Turkey puts its house in order on questions of human rights and achieves economic stability, it may never be admitted to political Europe. Where does this leave the millions of Turks, and people of

Turkish descent, living in the European diaspora? More importantly perhaps, as American foreign policy makers are warning,
the construction of the EU as a 'Christian club' exacerbates perceptions of a 'clash of civilizations' between the West and the rest, the
global North and South, and especially between capitalist secular-
ism and Islamic fundamentalism.

The punning title of Şenocak's most recent collection of essays
and essayistic fictions, *Zungenentfernung: Bericht aus der Quarantänestation*, refers at once to the cruelty of being violently deprived
of a voice and to the gulf of silence that lies between two languages. After more than forty years of mass migration to Germany
from Turkey, the Turkish-speaker in Germany remains a stock
figure of mute powerlessness, while the distance between German
and Turkish views of the world seems to grow rather than shrink
with their intensifying contact. More than most German-language
writers of Turkish background, Şenocak is an 'axial' writer, one
who participates in the literary cultures and cultural politics of
both (and third) nations, addresses readers in both (and third) nations, draws on the literary traditions of both (and third) nations.[8]
Not so much a spokesman for the Turkish minority in Germany as
a critical commentator upon it, and upon the policies of both states,
Şenocak – who in 1993 co-edited a volume proclaiming the 'end of
patience' among German Turks[9] – now decries the enduring condition of quarantine in which they dwell, regardless of cosmetic
changes to the citizenship law. After September 2001, the readiness
on the part of Germans to regard German Turks or Turkish Germans as equals, rather than provisionally tolerated colonized sub-
jects, has not increased. Şenocak's reflections on relations between
Turkey, Germany and the Turkish diaspora in Germany have only
become more urgent as the notion of 'clash of civilizations' increasingly seems to be a Western policy maxim.

Not only Turks but migrant and post-migrant Muslims in general live in Europe as a barely tolerated but fast-growing minority.
Except in the largest metropoles, people 'of colour' – and in north-
western Europe this includes Turks – are 'visible others' whose
belonging here is constantly called into question in one way or
another. Yet Turkey was never colonized, is a member of NATO
and the Council of Europe, and certainly belongs to Europe as far
as the football and pop music industries are concerned. As the
successor state to the Ottoman Empire, with a mostly Sunni Mus-

lim population, and as a staunch ally of the USA, Turkey is often viewed with hostile suspicion not only in central Europe – where talk of the Turks at the gates of Vienna (1683!) is still common – but throughout the Middle East and the Arab world. Şenocak was far from being the first to note that difficult questions of identity and belonging are not only posed for Turks when they come (or indeed are born) into western Europe: 'seit einhundertfünfzig Jahren streckt sich das Land [Türkei] zwischen Moderne und Tradition, Morgen- und Abendland. Ein Spagat, der den türkischen Dichter deutscher Zunge auf eine geteilte Identität vorbereitet. Aber auch Muskelkater verursacht. Seine Zunge ist an vielen Stellen taub.' These 'taube Stellen' are the 'Tabus' and 'Stereotypen', crippling accretions of cultural history, which need to be excised painfully to enable a new speech to emerge, a 'bastardisierte Sprache' which can be shared by the whites, the European conquerers, the 'blacks' of Africa, the Americas and Asia, and the new 'schwarzen Weiße', the Europeans of ultra-European heritages (*Hitler*, 31–2). For every such utopian invocation, however, we find a wry expression of despair: 'Solche Phantasien habe ich nur, wenn ich gut gelaunt bin', remarks Sascha Muhteschem, after putting forward the notion of a German-Jewish-Turkish trialogue as a means of superceding the exhausted dialogues between opposed ethnicities (*GV*, 90).

Many more nuanced fantasies, holding the balance between bewilderment and optimism, are found in Zafer Şenocak's work, especially in the hybrid essay-poem or essay-fiction which is perhaps his most distinctive literary form. This chapter will focus on two such texts from *Zungenentfernung*. This volume opens with a section entitled 'Gedächtnisfragmente', short texts which raise questions about what V. S. Naipaul called the enigma of arrival.[10] The first of these fragments is a quasi-autobiographical sketch, 'Der Griff hat einen Sprung' (*Zunge*, 9–12). The narrator recalls his first childhood visit to Germany, preceding by several years the family's migration to Germany, and he touches humorously on questions of integration. It was the flavour of German milk and chocolate that immediately won him over to the new country:

Hätten alle Gastarbeiter ihre Kinder am ersten Abend in Deutschland mit Milch und Schokolade gefüttert und sie am nächsten Morgen in Lederhosen gesteckt, hätten wir heute keine Probleme mit der Integration. Aber meine Eltern waren keine Gastarbeiter. Das erklärt vielleicht ihre Affinität zur kalten Milch, zur Milkaschokolade und zu

Lederhosen. Sie hatten gar keine Berührungsangst mit der deutschen
Kultur. (*Zunge*, 9)

Şenocak's own social background is like his narrator's, and very
unlike that of most Turkish child-migrants from rural, working-
class backgrounds. As urbane intellectuals, his parents were never
anxious about him 'losing his Turkishness', or about the effects of
being exposed to a non-Muslim environment.

The narrator's recollections, it emerges, have been sparked by a
recent visit to his parents in Hamburg (the narrator, like the
author, grew up from an early age in Munich, but now lives in
Berlin). His father, who refers to their retirement move from Munich to Hamburg as their 'migration' from Bavaria to Germany, is an
avid collector of the celebrated Solingen knives. Filial visits must
always include an inspection of the latest acquisition. This time,
however, the son spots a crack in the handle of the new knife. It
will have to be returned. The father laments that German workmanship (he uses the talismanic phrase in Global English, 'Made in
Germany') is not what it used to be. The mother sarcastically re-
plies that the goods are probably manufactured in Poland anyway,
and merely packaged in Germany. This sparks a row, which soon
gets out of hand, as they both lose sight of what they were arguing
about. The narrator comments: 'Ich finde schon, daß wir eine gut
integrierte Familie sind' (as if such family rows were more a German than a Turkish characteristic). The piece closes with irritated
reflections on the contemporary obsession with cultural identity,
the anxious discrimination between 'self' and 'other', the fear of
losing or being robbed of one's cultural birthright; and on the un-
reliability of memories, for example, of flavours – our deceptive
recollection of how much better things used to be, in our childhood, back then.

Like much of Şenocak's writing, this text is unclassifiable and
richly suggestive. Neither autobiography nor sheer fiction, neither
story nor essay, its central metaphor – the Solingen-brand knife –
encapsulates several dimensions of Turco-German shared history.
The international reputation of Solingen's steel blade manufactur-
ers goes back over a century. Their cutting, chopping, slicing and
stabbing implements were admired by many in Turkey, long before the recruitment of 'guest workers' began in 1961. Their fact-
ories then became major employers of 'guest workers', and they
continue to employ many Turkish workers today, as well as other

non-Germans. But in May 1993 Solingen hit the international headlines when four young members of a Turkish family, and a family friend, all women and girls, were killed when their house was set on fire in the night by a group of German youths. In many discourses 'Solingen' – often paired with 'Mölln'[11] – now refers only and always to that event: the name has become a byword for German nationalist extremist violence, at least as much as for German quality workmanship. The phrase 'Solingen brand' has become a sinister interlingual pun.

Search in Google for 'Solingen Messer Türken', and the search engine presents two-line extracts from hundreds of websites, in which one seems to overhear an agonistic public-private conversation going on in all accents of German:

> ... der Italiener (nicht, daß ich was gegen Türken und ... Endlich, nach 45 Minuten läßt er Messer und ... Aus Solingen, hartvergoldet, 24 Karat, geschmiedet aus einem .../... Die Greueltaten von Mölln und Solingen, wo bei ... würde ich ihm sofort eine reinschlagen, aber die Türken ... immer in Gruppen da, außerdem haben die alle Messer .../... Der Alltag von Jugendlichen in Solingen Reportage 25 ... von ihnen wird wenige Tage später sterben – die Türken ... Der Türke, der mit dem Messer zugestochen hat .../... mich mit der Kultur eines Schwarzafrikaners oder eines Türken ... So gewählt reden Sie mit einem Messer in der ... Sie zu Brandanschlägen wie in Mölln oder Solingen .../... Wie zB in Solingen. ... Strömt herbei ihr fremden Scharen, immer rein in unser Land, ob's Türken ... ja, dann hat er frohen Mut, |:und wenn das Judenblut vom Messer ...[12]

The associative chains glimpsed here – Turk, Italian, black African, Jew; Turkish gangs, neo-nazi gangs; weapons, songs[13] – go to make up the discursive context in which Şenocak writes his short 'fragment of memory', mingling private (pseudo-) recollections with allusions to German(-Turkish) public history and demotic xenophobic lore.

The stereotypical male Turk in the German popular imaginary is a 'Messerstecher', armed for street fighting and mugging, and ready to defend family honour at the merest hint of an insult. Reports of knives and knifings are legion where 'Turks' are present, or more precisely, the fear of them: 'immer in Gruppen da, außerdem haben die alle Messer'. Hence, after 1993, a Turkish man in Germany who collects Solingen knives is a highly disturbing figure, one who seems to fetishize weapons of Turkish self-defence –

or maybe pre-emptive aggression – while also commemorating one of the biggest single tragedies in the series of nationalist and racist outrages that scarred the first years of German unification.

Yet the narrator's father is presented as a collector quite innocent of any such ethno-political motives. Instead, he is an enthusiastic Germanophile whose sorrow turns to anger in response to his wife's offhand talk of corporate globalization. Şenocak wrote elsewhere in 2000: 'Einst war Deutschland ein Symbol für eine harte Währung und für zuverlässige Produkte. Jetzt kommt "Made in Germany" aus Malaysia und die bewährte Währung gibt es nur noch ein paar Monate. Harte Zeiten für die deutsche Seele' (*Zunge*, 64).[14] And the story of the knife is embedded in a story about milk – about the wonderful flavour of German as compared with Turkish milk, in childhood memory, and about the loss of that flavour in the adult narrator's present. Once he associated this loss with his move from Munich to Berlin, but on returning to Munich he finds the milk equally tasteless in both places. This is presumably the result of industrial homogenization, another feature of globalization: the erasure of local cultural difference, accompanied by a seemingly inevitable hypostatization of difference at the level of 'identity politics'.

When the parents migrated to Germany, learning a new language and culture was a game, 'eine Maskerade'. Now, as the argument sparked by the knife reveals, it is 'bitterer Ernst': 'Längst geht es nicht mehr um eine Maskerade, sondern um eine Art Vaterlandsverteidigung, wenn von eigener und fremder Kultur die Rede ist.' But the narrator clings to a pre-identitarian past: 'Die Worte eigen und fremd sind mir eigentlich immer fremd geblieben. Vor allem wenn sie von Menschen ausgesprochen werden, die ich gut zu kennen glaube. Aus ihrem Mund klingen diese Worte irgendwie falsch. Jedenfalls für meine Ohren. Vielleicht habe ich auch einen Hörfehler' (*Zunge*, 11). Like Sascha in *Die Prärie* and *Gefährliche Verwandtschaft*, this narrator is at odds with – would ideally be deaf to – the prevailing discourse of cultural identity and 'clash of civilizations', a discourse he now even hears from intimates. So the crack in the knife's handle seems to symbolize the combined impact of identity politics and globalization, of 'Solingen 1993' and Germany's loss of economic security on a politically innocent Turkish Germanophilia derived from admiration for German technology, philosophy and productivity. By noticing the crack, the son shatters the father's personal transcultural idyll of integration into the German order. The mother rubs salt in the wound by alluding to the problems of 'Standort Deutschland'.[15] 'Made in Germany' can no longer be trusted either to be true or to mean a promise of excellence, and hence of economic security. For migrants who have made a home in Germany, one which events in Solingen and Mölln showed to be far less safe than their native German neighbours' homes, such changes in the meaning and value of 'Germany' are unsettling reminders of their ambiguous status as outsider-insiders, which makes them all too liable to become victims of mob scapegoating.

A term like 'Vaterland', the narrator notes, is no longer spoken aloud but only thought about in the silence of one's study. People no longer say '"mein Vaterland ist Deutschland," sondern "ich komme aus Deutschland," so als würde man gerade aus der Küche kommen' (*Zunge*, 11). Perhaps with a knife. Perhaps with a glass of milk. The domesticated, politically corrected language of new nationhood breeds new discursive monsters – 'Leitkultur', 'Integration' – which reassert atavistic fears of occupation and theft sparked by any immigrants, especially visibly different ones.

However, the strength of the position which Şenocak has developed over the past decade of work as a transnational public intellectual lies partly in his refusal merely to castigate the natives for their failure to face the realities of immigration, though he does this often enough: Germany 'wünscht sich einen gläsernen Einwanderer, in dessen Gefäß man deutsches Blut spritzen kann'. And: 'Die Deutschen haben die Türken in Ruhe gelassen, über drei Jahrzehnte lang. Dann auf einmal zündeten sie ihre Häuser an.'[16] Şenocak is no less acute on the ways in which the migrants' adaptation to their environment, based on their cultural traditions, exacerbates the conflict:

> Das tragischerweise ideale Pendant zu[r] verunsicherten deutschen Identität ist der türkische Einwanderer. [. . .] Die Türken sind von der Mentalität her Siedler, die sich wenig um die Identitätsängste der Deutschen kümmern. [. . .] Es ist immer eine Unverfrorenheit, wenn der Gast sich ungefragt niederlässt. Die Sorgen und Nöte der Deutschen sind ihnen schnuppe. (*SE*)

A fatal absence of elective affinity has meant that settlers or sojourners from Turkey feel themselves to be 'längst angekommen' in a Germany 'dessen Menschen und Geschichte sich so lange vor ihm verborgen gehalten haben, bis er das Gefühl gewinnen konnte, das Land sei ein dünn besiedelter Landstrich, der nur auf Landnahme wartet. Das wird sich weder durch Gesetze noch durch öffentliche Debatten ändern' (*SE*).

If neither lawmakers nor opinion-formers can alter the nature of the cultural baggages both sides carry, if the Turks are 'längst zu Hause in Deutschland' but are on the whole indifferent to the economic and social as well as cultural concerns of the Germans (and far more provoking in this indifference than in their religious and other 'difference') and if German politicians and media fail to do more than reflect the natives' atavistic fears, then, Şenocak asks: 'Kann man von diesem fast toten Punkt aus weiterdenken?' (*SE*).

In such political essays Şenocak does not hesitate to generalize about the presumed essential mentality of entire nationalities and about the conflict between these collective blocs. He repeatedly points out that these stereotypes are fully real in people's minds, however much based on mutual misapprehensions, ignorance, fear and, not least, the organized amnesia of national histories. But in fiction or autofiction, in poetry and drama, and especially in the hybrid texts like 'Der Griff hat einen Sprung' which fuse these genres with the essay, he cites such generalizations only in order to subvert or ridicule them. In the 'essay-hybrids' he excavates individual experience in transcultural 'contact zones', where belongings and longings are multiple, contingent and changeable. Thus 'Der Griff hat einen Sprung' reads like something Sascha Muhteschem might have written. The way the very public and political matter of national(ist) discourses and violence is connected to private and personal memory and fantasy recalls Sascha's sardonic remarks in *Die Prärie* about 'gender-patriotism' among writers: 'Heute schreibt jeder über sein eigenes Geschlecht, als handelte es sich dabei um das Vaterland, dessen Verteidigung ansteht. Ein obskurer Geschlechtspatriotismus macht sich breit' (*P*, 9). If identities are plural, many-layered and partially fluid, then so too are identity crises. Crises of nationhood are always also crises of gender and sexuality, as well as crises of family relations and family histories. And vice versa.[17] It is in the interplay between personal and mass fantasies and fears, or between geopolitics, macroeconomics and individual psychology, that the nature of the conflicts between settlers and natives, as well as within the minds and behaviours of individuals in both groups, can be discerned – conflicts which pose for constantly growing numbers of people the question: am I on one side or two? Or even: is there a third side I can join (yet)?

Şenocak's co-edited bilingual volume *Deutsche Türken: Das Ende der Geduld* (1993) went to press before 'Solingen 1993' happened. A decade later, patience is still demanded from those among Germany's Turks who do care about their place in German life. There have been considerable improvements in the material position of many, perhaps most, Turks in Germany (though rates of unemployment and lack of qualifications among young Turkish Germans remain extremely high), and there is a growing visibility of Turkish artistic, media, political and professional personalities. But visibly or audibly different citizens and denizens of Germany remain barely tolerated or treated with condescension in many circles. 'Ausländerfreie Zonen' are a reality in several Länder and cities. The option of dual citizenship has vanished from the political agenda, despite being widely regarded among migrants of all generations as an essential token of recognition of the dignity of difference within a pluralist German society and, more especially, of the vital contribution made by now elderly 'guest workers' to the economic miracle of the 1960s and 1970s. None of the chancellor candidates in 2002 put forward any proposals on the topics of immigration and integration that included foreign denizens and naturalized Germans as addressees rather than objects of their discourse. Instead, Stoiber's campaign culminated with a proposal to deal at a stroke with Islamist militancy by deporting 3,000 people, apparently without due process; Schröder was able to describe coolly how the state was dealing with the problem within the law.

Neither addressed the sorts of questions raised by Şenocak, in an article published in *Die Welt* on 15 September 2001,[18] about the long-term failure of governments in the West to acknowledge the transnational problem of Islamist militancy, to develop appropriate countermeasures at the level of intelligence and security as well as foreign and aid policy, and, in particular, to help Turkey – long a front line in the struggle between Islamist extremism and democracy – to tackle the problem. These failures, Şenocak argued, are rooted in a naive, complacent approach to 'tolerance' and 'multiculturalism', coupled with short-lived and wholly counterproductive military 'Strafaktionen' against some Islamic countries.

But it is not only that extremists are using Islam as a cover for activities which threaten 'die innere Sicherheit unseres Landes' and indeed world peace. Worse, Islam itself 'bildet den Bodensatz für die Gewalt, die in seinem Namen verübt wird', through the Koranic distinction between the inviolability of Muslims' lives and the violability of the lives of others. His polemic against the Islamic belief system culminates in an attack on the position of women: 'Die Verhüllung, egal ob als Schutz oder Unterdrückung interpretiert, ist das Symbol der intakten Tradition, der funktionierenden Hierarchien, die Scheidelinie zur freien Welt'. Modern Islam 'fordert nicht nur Unterwerfung, er ist im Sinne des Wortes gleichbedeutend mit Unterwerfung. Eine missinterpretierte, ihrem humanen Ansatz beraubte Religion, die niemandem mehr schadet als denen, die an sie glauben'.

Şenocak often highlights the distinction between the humane, tolerant and sensual impulses of early Islam and its widespread reduction, in the era of European or Euro-American colonization and neo-colonization, to a brutally repressive ideology of millennial resistance to Western hegemony. The fantasy essay-fiction, 'Der Bart' (*Zunge*, 69–72), explores these issues by focusing on one outward sign of Islamic masculinity, the beard – an underexplored area, as compared with the headscarf or veil of Muslim women.[19] Indeed, for this narrator, women's self-covering corresponds to the male beard as a form of compensation based on presumable beard-envy:

> Sie verdecken dabei nicht nur ihren Körper, sondern auch die Leere in ihren Herzen. Das hat mit Tradition nur wenig zu tun. Das ist Biologie. Die Frauen suchen sich einen Ersatz für den fehlenden Bart. Die leeren Herzen und die leeren Gedächtnisse bilden eine perfekte Trauergemeinde. (*Zunge*, 71)

The headscarf fashion among Muslim young women is provocatively dismissed as a sign of their lack of any identity grounded in tradition, memory or feeling.[20]

This text marginalizes women, then. Its focus (as in 'Der Griff hat einen Sprung', and as in much of the recent poetry)[21] is the relationship between the text's evidently male 'ich' and the father. 'Der Bart' opens with (and ends with an echo of) the remembered words of the deceased bearded father, words which sum up a tradition of ascetic piety: 'Die andere Welt betritt man nicht mit

Schuhen.' This is now a lost tradition, expressed only in the vacant continuity of outward signs which have lost their significance. The bearded men of today are amnesiacs and hypocrites. The father's beard betokened his secret knowledge, his living memory of spiritual heritage. He stood in a long line of bearded men. But the multiple caesuras in recent cultural history have broken that line:

> Wo das Tragen von Bärten in einem so engen Verhältnis zu Erinnerungen steht, ist das Vergessen einfach. Man rasiert den Bart ab und ist seinen Erinnerungen los. Die Bartträger von heute sind tragische Figuren. Aus dem Wunsch sich zu erinnern wächst ein Bart, der doch nichts anderes symbolisiert als die Amnesie, an der sie leiden. (*Zunge*, 70)

The text makes no specific reference to any religion, but it is clearly particularly pertinent to Islam. It implies that contemporary Islam, emasculated by two hundred years of subjugation under direct or indirect European rule, can produce no more than 'Karikaturen' (*Zunge*, 69) of the father's faith.

Indeed, in Turkey, republican secularization, language reform, globalization, and the rise of the transnational Islamist radicalism of western-educated students, typically engineers,[22] have successively demolished all organic links with the Islamic past. In the Kemalist Republic, the beard – like the veil – became a political symbol of religious (or ultra-nationalist, or ultra-leftist) opposition to the regime. Atatürk banned civil servants from wearing beards, and bearded (or veiled) students can still be banned from campuses or excluded from examinations. The beard of AKP president Recep Tayyip Erdoğan is seen as a token of his Islamist sympathies. Ultra-nationalists and left-wing revolutionaries sport their own styles – the former a beard with two pointed tips, recalling the crescent, and the latter a bushy moustache in the Alevite Bektaşi mode. 'In letzter Zeit hat die Zahl der Bärtigen auf der Straße zugenommen. Sogar im Fernsehen treten Bärtige auf', remarks the narrator of 'Der Bart'. This may be true in western Europe, due chiefly to the adoption of Islam as a political identity by disaffected males.[23] Yet, in the course of the 1990s, the proportion of beardless males in Turkey reportedly rose from 23 to 54 per cent. According to journalists, this is a sign of globalization (the 'globalization' which also goes by the name of 'westernization' or even 'Americanization').[24]

The narrator's father suffered for his beard: he was jailed. But: 'Nicht das Tragen eines Bartes hatte meinen Vater hinter Gitter gebracht, sondern die Gedanken, auf denen sein Bart wuchs' (*Zunge*, 69). Both the secret thoughts and the beard were for him 'eine Angelegenheit des Kopfes'. Nowadays, however, all such symbolic and secret things 'für die wir keinen Namen haben' are a matter, instead, for eyes and for mirrors, 'eine Angelegenheit der Augen, die die Gestalt des Betrachters im Spiegel erkennen' (*Zunge*, 69–70). Here the postmodern culture of self-referential, narcissistic spectacles and depthless surfaces is counterposed – perhaps nostalgically, perhaps rather more ironically – to an era of authenticity embodied by the father, with his brave resistance to torture by specialists in beards. What has intervened is, simply and tragically, forgetting, a general amnesia: 'Die Erde, auf der man lebt, ist keine Zeugin mehr für das eigene Leben, wenn man keine Erinnerungen mehr hat' (*Zunge*, 70). 'Bald wollen alle Männer des Volkes einen Bart, obwohl ihnen die Erinnerungen ausgehen. So geht das Geheimnis des Bartes für immer verloren' (*Zunge*, 71). 'Im Gedächtnis wird um jedes Wort gerungen' (*Zunge*, 70). 'Sprache in unseren Tagen ist ein Trauerspiel. Sie taugt nicht mal zum Ritual' (*Zunge*, 71). And more personally: 'An diesen Satz kann ich mich noch erinnern. Ich weiß nicht mehr, ob er von mir oder von meinem Vater stammt' (*Zunge*, 71). A final one-sentence paragraph underscores the conclusion that the narrator has indeed failed to reconnect his own language, faith and existence with those of the vanished father: as if 'die andere Welt' were a real place, he writes: 'Vielleicht läuft mein Vater heute noch am Ufer entlang, um vom Wasser zu erfahren, wo jener Ort ist, den man nicht mit Schuhen betritt' (*Zunge*, 72). Only one who is utterly severed from traditions of ascetic piety could write this half-mocking, half-nostalgic sentence.

'Der Bart' and 'Der Griff hat einen Sprung' – and numerous other more recent texts including several of the poems printed in this volume – have in common a set of concerns with cultural transmission or tradition, which is encapsulated in the writing subject's relationship with an ageing, vanished or anachronistic father. The narrator or lyric voice seems to wish to reconstruct the father's world view, his language, if only properly to escape from its overweening power, but cannot. Whether the father represents the broken continuity of Islamic mysticism or the vanquished pride and optimism of Turkish migrant pioneers in Germany, he partakes in the full, resonant gravity of patriarchal symbolism shared by all Europe's religious cultures, and he has become a sign of the evacuation of meaning from all such cultures.

In the course of the prose fiction tetralogy, the topography of Şenocak's imagined world expanded from the enclosed Berlin–Istanbul–Frankfurt axis of 'Fliegen', the opening story in *Der Mann im Unterhemd*, to the gruesomely dystopian global perspective of the story 'Das Haus im Süden' towards the end of *Der Erottomane*, where rich Americans order sex-murder victims in packing crates from civil war zones in the planetary South (*E*, 82–94). Şenocak's concern with the inadequacy of contemporary languages, his analysis of amnesia as the root cause of this inadequacy and his ambition to create a new language against the odds have remained constant. As he writes in the 'Wortschatzinsel' cycle, 'deine Augen sind schwach geworden Vater / nimm deine Hände aus meiner Sprache / damit ich mein eigenes Haus bauen kann'.

Notes

[1] This chapter is partly based on research carried out for a collaborative, multi-disciplinary project on 'Axial Writing', funded by the ESRC within the Transnational Communities research programme (award number L214252030, 1998–2002). The term 'axial writing' refers to work by mobile creative intellectuals who have a foot and a voice in two or more countries connected by long-standing axes of transnational migration. Details at www.transcomm.ox.ac.uk/wwwroot/cheesman.htm

[2] *Das trockene Wasser. Gedichte* (Berlin, Das Arabische Buch, 1998), 10–21 (15–16).

[3] Barthes, *S/Z: essais* (Paris, Seuil, 1970).

[4] Şenocak's name appears as 'Enocak' in my 'Polyglot politics: hip hop in Germany', *Debatte* 6/2 (1998), 191–214, and in a review of *Zunge* in the online edition of the *Neue Zürcher Zeitung* (29 January 2002). He is both 'Üenocak' and 'Ûenocak' in Moray McGowan, '"The Bridge of the Golden Horn": Istanbul, Europe and the "fractured gaze from the West" in Turkish writing in Germany', *Yearbook of European Studies* 15 (2000), 53–70. Many of his articles in the online edition of *die tageszeitung* are indexed as by 'Zafer 'enocak'. A quick Internet search also turns up ?enocak, $enocak, jenocak and, of course, Senocak. It took this editor several days of work to

find a combination of software and hardware capable of producing the required glyphs in the prescribed font.

[5] The law that was eventually passed, after much bitter controversy, was far more restrictive.

[6] *perşembe* appeared with *die tageszeitung* from September 2000 to July 2001, and continued independently until March 2002.

[7] http://news.bbc.co.uk/2/hi/europe/2420697.stm (8 November 2002).

[8] On 'axial writing', see note 1 above. An axial writer may be claimed by two (or more) literary cultures, or may be marginalized in each. Axial cultural traffic is rarely balanced. 'Der türkische Schriftsteller kennt Goethe, Schiller, Hölderlin, Benn, Trakl, Eich, Celan, Bachmann, Kafka, Camus. Und der deutsche Schriftsteller? Kennt er Cansever, Uyar, Süreya? Hat er je den Namen Ibnül Emin gehört?' (from 'Bastardisierte Sprache', *Hitler*, 31). Here the inclusion of Camus among 'German' writers also underlines the absurdity of national demarcations.

[9] Claus Leggewie and Zafer Şenocak (eds), *Deutsche Türken / Türk Almanlar: Das Ende der Geduld / Sabrın sonu* (Reinbek, Rowohlt, 1993).

[10] V. S. Naipaul, *The Enigma of Arrival* (Harmondsworth, Penguin, 1987).

[11] A Turkish woman, her young daughter and niece died in an arson attack on two houses in Mölln on 22 November 1992. Two German youths were later convicted. This was the first such dramatic attack in (former) west Germany, following several in the former GDR.

[12] Google search engine, accessed 29 September 2002.

[13] Cf. 'Das Denken wird zum Haus [...] von dem aus man gemeinsam singt und schießt. Lieder und Salven wechseln sich ab' ('Jenseits der Landessprache', *Zunge,* 87; see commentary by Adelson in this volume).

[14] 'Perspektiven der Mitte', first published as 'Mittelpunkt der Welt?' in *perşembe*, 5, in *die tageszeitung*, 5 October 2000.

[15] In October 1997 Günter Grass attacked the German state's treatment of Turkish migrants, including Kurdish asylum seekers, in a speech to the Börsenverein des deutschen Buchhandels in honour of Yaşar Kemal (recipient of the Börsenverein's Peace Prize). Here Grass rehearsed the critique of amoral German capitalism delivered in his Dresden speech of June 1997, published as *Rede über den Standort* (Göttingen, Steidl, 1997).

[16] 'Siedler und Einheimische', *die tageszeitung*, 5 April 2002. Here cited henceforth as *SE*.

[17] On the interplay between state legislation and personal subjectivities, see John Bornemann, *Belonging in the Two Berlins: Kin, State, Nation* (Cambridge, Cambridge University Press, 1992).

[18] 'Der Feind in unserer Mitte', *Die Welt*, 15 September 2001.

[19] Typing 'Islam' and 'veil' into Google produces over 45,000 results, 'Islam' and 'beard' only 28,000. I have looked in vain for scholarship on the contemporary (cross-)cultural significance of male facial hair.

[20] For a searching discussion of the significance of the veil in Germany and Turkey, see Ruth Mandel, 'Turkish headscarves and the "foreigner problem": constructing difference through emblems of identity', *New German Critique*, 46 (1989), 27–46.

[21] Cf. Karin Yeşilada's essay, chapter 10 in this volume.

[22] See the prescient essay on political Islamism, written in September 1993, 'Ingenieure des Glaubens' (*Hitler*, 6–20); also the pages satirizing Islamist and Kurdish private television stations in Berlin, in *GV*, 49–50.

[23] For well-informed commentary on the identity choices of a specific young Turkish man raised in Germany, see Werner Schiffauer, 'Islamism in the diaspora: the fascination of political Islam among second-generation German Turks', ESRC Transnational Communities Research Programme, Working Paper 99–06, at www.transcomm.ox.ac.uk

[24] Report by Jan Keetman, 'Bart ab, Schnauzer weg: Auch am Bosporus gehen die Uhren mittlerweile anders', *Die Presse*, 23 August 2001, at www.muslima-aktiv.de/news/muslimasww/bart_ab.htm

13

Bibliographie

KARIN E. YEŞILADA

Diese Bibliographie umfaßt Primär- und Sekundärliteratur seit 1983. Sie ist die bislang umfassendste zu Şenocak, da sie auch Titel der Sekundärliteratur im Ausland berücksichtigt und an Aktualität und Vollständigkeit über meinen Eintrag im *Kritischen Lexikon zur deutschsprachigen Gegenwartsliteratur* (*KLG*) sowie über die Autorenartikel von Konzett und Şölçün herausgeht. Die hier im Band publizierten Arbeiten sind aufgenommen worden, ebenso wie angekündigte Neuerscheinungen für 2003.

Gegliedert ist die Bibliographie länderspezifisch und jeweils nach Genre. Alle Rubriken sind chronologisch aufsteigend angelegt. Nach dem deutschsprachigen Raum (1. und 2.) unterscheidet sie die Rezeption sukzessive nach Ländern, in denen Zafer Şenocak in zeitlicher Folge rezipiert wurde, und zwar Türkei (3.), Frankreich (4.), USA und Kanada (5.), Großbritannien (6.), und weitere Länder (7.). Während die Rubrik 'Buchausgaben' (1.1.) nach Genres untergliedert ist, listet sie unter Ausland (3.–7.) noch alle Genres gesammelt. Rezensionen und wissenschaftliche Aufsätze sind ebenfalls jeweils gesammelt gelistet. Bei den türkischen Titeln habe ich deutsche Übersetzungen zum Verständnis hinzugefügt.

Die Rubrik 'Einzelveröffentlichungen' (1.2.) verzeichnet vor allem Texte, die noch nicht in Buchpublikationen enthalten sind, z.B. neue Lyrik (weitgehend ab 1994). Essays dagegen sind nahezu komplett aufgelistet, um die Quellenforschung einzelner Debatten zu ermöglichen (hier hat Leslie A. Adelson im Apparat der amerikanischen Ausgabe der Essays, *Atlas of a Tropical Germany* [*ATG*], bereits umfangreiche Vorarbeit geleistet). Sofern einzelne Texte in den Essaybänden erschienen, wurden diese stichwortartig in Klammern hinzugefügt (vgl. Abkürzungsverzeichnis oben S. xi). Alle bis zu Redaktionsschluß erschienenen aktuellen Essays in

2003 sind ebenfalls verzeichnet. Neben den allgemeinen Essays habe ich auch eine Rubrik zur 'Poetik' eröffnet, die es erlauben soll, Şenocaks poetologische Anmerkungen systematisch zu verfolgen. Interviews sind nach Ländern unterschieden und chronologisch aufsteigend aufgeführt.

Eine Unterteilung der Bibliographie nach Ländern ist insofern ambivalent, als dadurch öfters Doppelnennungen nötig werden. Im Zeitalter der globalen Vernetzung sind Informationen häufig international zugänglich und Publikationsorte international. Andererseits macht die vorliegende Gliederung eine Übersicht über die Rezeption Şenocaks in den einzelnen Ländern deutlich. Auch werden spezifische Publikationsprozesse sichtbar (so erschienen z.B. Şenocaks Texte im türkischen Original nicht etwa in der Türkei, sondern in der Berliner Zeitschrift *Şiir-lik*). Vielleicht ist die länderspezifische Unterscheidung der Rezeption in einer zukünftigen Bibliographie obsolet; zu diesem Zeitpunkt erscheint sie mir jedoch sehr aufschlußreich, denn sie ermöglicht es, den Schriftsteller Zafer Şenocak als interkulturellen Autor zu recherchieren und seine Rezeption in den jeweiligen Ländern, in denen seine Texte als Übersetzungen erschienen sind, zu verfolgen.

Ich danke Zafer Şenocak, Tom Cheesman, Leslie A. Adelson und Elizabeth Oehlkers Wright für die Unterstützung bei der Recherche.

München, 14. Januar 2003

INHALT

1. **Primärliteratur deutschsprachiger Raum**
1.1.   Buchausgaben und Herausgaben
1.1.1.   Lyrik
1.1.2.   Prosa
1.1.3.   Essays
1.1.4.   Herausgabe von Buchpublikationen
1.2.   Einzelveröffentlichungen
1.2.1.   Lyrik
1.2.2.   Prosa
1.2.3.   Poetik
1.2.4.   Essays, Artikel (ohne Poetik)
1.3.   Übersetzungen von Zafer Şenocak
1.4.   Interviews

2. **Sekundärliteratur deutschsprachiger Raum**
2.1.   Bibliographien
2.2.   Rezensionen
2.3.   Wissenschaftliche Aufsätze

3. **Rezeption Türkei**
3.1.   Primärliteratur in türk. Übersetzung und auf Türkisch
3.1.1.   Buchausgaben
3.1.2.   Einzelveröffentlichungen in türk. Übersetzung
3.1.2.1. Lyrik
3.1.2.2. Prosa
3.1.2.3. Essays
3.1.3.   Interviews
3.2.   Sekundärliteratur Türkei: Rezensionen und wiss. Aufsätze

4. **Rezeption Frankreich**
4.1.   Primärliteratur in franz. Übersetzung
4.1.1.   Buchausgaben
4.1.2.   Einzelveröffentlichungen in franz. Übersetzung
4.1.2.1. Lyrik
4.1.2.2. Prosa
4.1.2.3. Essays
4.1.3.   Interviews
4.2.   Sekundärliteratur Frankreich: Rezensionen

5. Rezeption USA und Kanada

5.1.   Primärliteratur in amer.-engl. Übersetzung

5.1.1.   Buchausgaben

5.1.2.   Einzelveröffentlichungen in amer.-engl. Übersetzung

5.1.2.1.   Lyrik

5.1.2.2.   Prosa

5.1.2.3.   Essays

5.1.3.   Interviews

5.2.   Sekundärliteratur USA: Rezensionen und wiss. Aufsätze

6. Rezeption Großbritannien

6.1.   Primärliteratur in engl. Übersetzung und auf Deutsch

6.1.1.   Buchveröffentlichungen: keine

6.1.2.   Einzelveröffentlichungen in engl. Übersetzung

6.1.2.1.   Lyrik (auf Deutsch)

6.1.2.2.   Prosa

6.1.2.3.   Essays, Artikel

6.1.2.4.   Einzelveröffentlichungen im Internet

6.1.3.   Interviews

6.2.   Sekundärliteratur Großbritannien

6.2.1.   Buchpublikationen

6.2.2.   Rezensionen und wiss. Aufsätze

7. Rezeption in anderen Ländern

7.1.   Primärliteratur in Übersetzung

7.1.1.   Buchausgaben

7.1.2.   Einzelveröffentlichungen

7.1.2.1.   Lyrik

7.1.2.2.   Prosa

7.1.2.3.   Essays

7.1.3.   Interviews

7.2.   Sekundärliteratur

1. Primärliteratur deutschsprachiger Raum

1.1. Buchausgaben und Herausgaben

1.1.1. Lyrik

Elektrisches Blau. Gedichte (München, Hohoff, 1983) [Ströme: neue Literatur 2].

Verkauf der Morgenstimmungen am Markt. Gedichte (München, Edition Literazette, 1983) [Haidhauser Werkstat(t)texte 4].

Flammentropfen. Gedichte (Frankfurt am Main, Dağyeli, 1985).

Ritual der Jugend. Gedichte (Frankfurt am Main, Dağyeli, 1987).

Das senkrechte Meer. Gedichte (Berlin, Babel, 1991) [Berliner Edition].

Fernwehanstalten. Gedichte (Berlin, Babel, 1994) [Berliner Edition].

Zusammen mit Berkan Karpat: *Nâzım Hikmet: Auf dem Schiff zum Mars* (München, Babel, 1998) [Babel Bibliothek Intermedia].

Zusammen mit Berkan Karpat: *Tanzende der Elektrik. Szenisches Poem* (München, Berlin, Cambridge [USA], Verlag im Gleisbau, 1999).

1.1.2. Prosa

Der Mann im Unterhemd (Berlin, Babel, 1995).

Die Prärie (Hamburg, Rotbuch, 1997).

Gefährliche Verwandtschaft. Roman (München, Babel, 1998).

Der Erottomane. Ein Findelbuch (München, Babel, 1999).

1.1.3. Essays

Atlas des tropischen Deutschland. Essays (Berlin, Babel, 1992, 2. Auflage 1993) [Berliner Edition].

War Hitler Araber? IrreFührungen an den Rand Europas. Essays (Berlin, Babel, 1994) [Berliner Edition].

Zungenentfernung. Bericht aus der Quarantänestation. Essays (München, Babel, 2001).

1.1.4. Herausgabe von Buchpublikationen

Jedem Wort gehört ein Himmel. Türkei literarisch, hg. v. Deniz Göktürk und Z.Ş. (Berlin, Babel, 1991) [Türkei literarisch].

Deutsche Türken – Das Ende der Geduld. Türk Almanlar – Sabrın Sonu, zweispr. dt.-türk., hg. v. Claus Leggewie und Z.Ş. (Reinbek bei Hamburg, Rowohlt, 1993) [rororo aktuell 13426].

Der gebrochene Blick nach Westen. Positionen und Perspektiven türkischer Kultur, hg. v. Z.Ş. (Berlin, Babel, 1994) [Türkise Reihe].

1.2. Einzelveröffentlichungen

[In Deutschland erschienene türkischsprachige Originaltexte und Übersetzungen sind hier ebenfalls aufgelistet.]

1.2.1. Lyrik

[Frühere Lyrik ist bereits in den Buchpublikationen enthalten. Siehe auch unter 4.1.2.1. und 6.1.2.1.]

Gedichte, in *Literatur im Kreienhoop*, hg. v. Manfred Dierks und Alfred Mensak (München und Hamburg, Knaus, 1986), 125–53.

Gedichte, *Ad Libitum*, 24 (1992), 217–33.

Gedichte, *Das Argument*, 1 (Januar/Februar 1994), 4.

Gedichte, *Sprache im technischen Zeitalter*, 3 (1995), 24–8.

'Yakın bir yer' [türk. Original], *Şiir-Lik*, 34 (Dezember 1996), 7.

'Die Wassersucher' [11 Gedichte], *Sirene*, 19 (1997), 111–18.

'İlk Söz' [türk. Original], *Şiir-Lik*, 36 (Februar 1997), 3.

'Bahçe Motifi' [türk. Original], *Şiir-Lik*, 38 (April 1997), 7.

'Mendil Motifi' [türk. Original], *Şiir-Lik*, 40 (Juni 1997), 6.

'Kapı Motifi' [türk. Original], *Şiir-Lik*, 43 (Oktober 1997), 7.

'Satelliten', *Das Gedicht*, 5 (Oktober 1997), 44.

'Wir aschmüden Wortklauber' [aus: Miniaturen. Unveröff. Manuskript], in Irmgard Ackermann (hg.), *Fremde AugenBlicke. Mehrkulturelle Literatur in Deutschland* (Bonn, Internationes, 1996), 147 [auch in der engl. Übersetzung: Irmgard Ackermann (hg.), *Foreign Viewpoints: Multicultural Literature in Germany* (Bonn, Internationes, 1999), 143].

'In den Inzesthäusern Europas' [Gedicht], *Das Argument*, 222 (1997), 608.

'Balladen aus dem Gedächtnis' [8 Gedichte], *Sirene*, 20/21 (1999), 25–8.

Gedichte, *Das Gedicht*, 7 (1999/2000), 48.

Zusammen mit Berkan Karpat: 'wie den vater nicht töten. Ein Sprechlabyrinth', in Jamal Tuschick (hg.), *Morgen Land. Neueste deutsche Literatur* (Frankfurt am Main, Fischer, 2000), 179–90.

1.2.2. Prosa

'Fliegen', aus d. Türk. übers. v. Eva Hummel, in Thomas Wörtche (hg.), *Neon-schatten. Geschichten aus der bösen Stadt* (Bergisch Gladbach, Bastei-Lübbe, 1994), 275–86 [auch in *MiU*].

'Samuel-Emil-Nordpol-Otto-Cäsar-Anton-Kaufmann', in Bahman Nirumand (hg.), *Deutsche Zustände. Dialog über ein gefährdetes Land* (Reinbek bei Hamburg, Rowohlt, 1993), 11–8.

'Lebenslauf', in Irmgard Ackermann (hg.), *Fremde AugenBlicke. Mehrkulturelle Literatur in Deutschland* (Bonn, Internationes, 1996), 144–6 [auch in der engl. Übersetzung: Irmgard Ackermann (hg.), *Foreign Viewpoints: Multicultural Literature in Germany* (Bonn, Internationes, 1999), 140–2].

'Warten auf Liebe', Vorabdruck aus *P*, in *die tageszeitung*, 5. August 1997, 15.

'Ben ve Öteki Çocuk', ins Türk. übers. v. Yeni Memet, *Şiir-Lik*, 45 (November 1997), 5 [= 'Ich bin das andere Kind'].

'Ich bin das andere Kind / Jenseits der Landessprache / Samuel-Emil-Nordpol-Otto-Cäsar-Anton-Kaufmann', in Walter Dostal, Helmut A. Niederle und Karl R. Wernhart (hg.), *Wir und die Anderen. Islam, Literatur und Migration* (Wien, WUV-Universitäts-Verlag, 1999), 287–94.

'Den Direktor küßt man nicht', Auszug aus *GV*, in Elisabeth Tworek (hg.), *Bayerisches Lesebuch* (München, Beck, 1999), 376–80.

1.2.3. Poetik

'Plädoyer für eine Brückenliteratur', in Irmgard Ackermann und Harald Weinrich (hg.), *Eine nicht nur deutsche Literatur. Zur Standortbestimmung der 'Ausländerliteratur'* (München und Zürich, Piper, 1986), 65–9.

'Vor-Wörter – Versuche über Poesie', *Sirene*, 2 (1988), 59–80.

'Zwischen Herz und Haut', Dankesrede zur Verleihung des Adelbert-von-Chamisso-Förderpreises 1988, *Atlas des tropischen Deutschland* (Berlin, Babel, 1991), 97–101.

'"... der Mensch, / der's mitanhört ... "', Vortrag auf dem Paul-Celan-Colloquium, Paris 1995, *Sirene*, 15/16 (1996), 166–70 [auch in *Zunge*].

'Jenseits der Landessprache', *Sirene*, 15/16 (1996), 171–4 [auch in *Zunge*].

'Sechs Winkelzüge, um der deutschsprachigen Poesie der Gegenwart auf die Schliche zu kommen', *Das Gedicht*, 4 (Oktober 1996), 80 [Serie: Läßt sich über Lyrik streiten? Positionen].

'Der Schriftsteller ist ein Archäologe. Ein Essay über Schreiben in Deutschland und überhaupt', *Die Welt* [*Die literarische Welt*], 5. Juni 1999 [auch in *ATG* und *Zunge*].

'Hände weg von meiner Biographie!', *Der Tagesspiegel*, 6. Juni 2001 [auch in *Zunge*].

'Meine drei Begegnungen mit Nâzım Hikmet', in Monika Carbe und Wolfgang Riemann (hg.), *Hundert Jahre Nâzım Hikmet: 1902–1963* (Hildesheim, Zürich, New York, Olms, 2002), 84–9.

1.2.4. Essays, Artikel (ohne Poetik)

'"Ein Lied auf des Volkes Zunge" – Anmerkungen zu Pir Sultan Abdal (ca. 1520–1560)', *Sirene*, 1 (1988), 52–7.

Zusammen mit Deniz Göktürk: 'Singen die Vögel an der Pforte noch? Moderne türkische Literatur im europäischen Blick', Vorwort zu: Deniz Göktürk und Zafer Şenocak (hg.), *Jedem Wort gehört ein Himmel. Türkei literarisch* (Berlin, Babel, 1991), 7–15.

'Pir Sultan Abdal', 'Yunus Emre', 'Orhan Veli Kanık', 'Behçet Necatigil', vier Autoren-Beiträge, in Walter Jens (hg.), *Kindlers neues Literaturlexikon*, 20 Bände (München, Kindler Verlag, 1988–92), 8. Auflage.

'Einen anderen Duft als den der Rose. Über türkische Volks- und Divandichtung', *Der Deutschunterricht*, 5 (1993), 18–31.

Zusammen mit Zafer Toker und Bülent Tulay: 'Fünf nach zwölf. Die Straße ist verloren, aber noch nicht das ganze Land: Nach den Morden in Solingen ist die Anerkennung der doppelten Staatsbürgerschaft erstes politisches Gebot', *taz [die tageszeitung] Extra*, 30. Mai 1993, 1.

'Es reicht!', *Berliner Zeitung*, 1. Juni 1993.

'Kanzler Kohl, treten Sie zurück!', *die tageszeitung*, 3. Juni 1993.

'Kommunizierende Ohnmächte. Die Organisation der Türken in Deutschland', *[die tageszeitung] taz-journal*, 1 (1993), 69.

'Verlassenheit, die guttut. Deutschlands türkische Jugend will jetzt um ihre Rechte kämpfen', *[die tageszeitung] taz-journal*, 1 (1993), 93.

'Das Buch mit sieben Siegeln – Über die vergessene Tradition der Divandichtung', *Sirene*, 9 (1992), 28–63 [auch in *Hitler*, 34–47, als: 'Das Buch mit den sieben Siegeln – Über die vergessene Tradition der osmanischen Dichtung'].

'Der gebrochene Blick nach Westen', Einleitung zu Zafer Şenocak (hg.), *Der gebrochene Blick nach Westen. Positionen und Perspektiven türkischer Kultur* (Berlin, Babel, 1994), 7–16.

'Zwischen Orient und Okzident', *Die Zeit*, 26. Mai 1995.

'Gedanken zum 8. Mai 1995', in Heinz L. Arnold, Brigitte Sauzay und Rudolf von Thadden (hg.), *Vom Vergessen vom Gedenken. Erinnerungen und Erwartungen in Europa zum 8. Mai 1945* (Göttingen, Wallstein, 1995), 91–3 [auch in *Zunge*].

'Krieg und Frieden in Deutschland – Gedanken über die deutsch-türkische Zukunft', in Hilmar Hoffmann und Dieter Kramer (hg.), *Anderssein, ein Menschenrecht. Über die Vereinbarkeit universaler Normen mit kultureller und ethnischer Vielfalt* (Weinheim, Beltz Athenäum, 1995), 115–23 [auch in *ATG* und auf Türk.].

'Für eine autonome deutsch-türkische Identität', *Zeitschrift für Kulturaustausch*, 47, 1–2 (1997), 109–10 [Sonderheft: Türkei und Deutschland – Schwieriger Dialog].

'Deutscher oder was? Eine Reform des Staatsbürgerschaftsrechts ist notwendig, wird aber nicht dazu führen, daß sich die Mehrheit der Türken assimiliert', *Die Woche*, 7. November 1997.

'Fremdarbeit. Über die Gefahr einer deutsch-türkischen Teilung', *Vorwärts*, 8 (1998), 40.

'Schwieriger Geburtstag eines Sorgenkindes. Mustafa Kemal Atatürk plante in den 20er und 30er Jahren eine radikale Verwestlichung der Türkei. Dennoch ist ihr nicht der Anschluß an Europa gelungen. Im Wege stehen ihr dabei ein Demokratiedefizit und Menschenrechtsverletzungen', *Der Tagesspiegel*, 25. Oktober 1998.

'Die Heimat trägt der Mensch in sich. Gedanken zu einem typisch deutschen Begriff', *Die Stuttgarter Zeitung*, 21. November 1998 [auch in *Zunge*].

'Der Dinosaurier wankt – Der türkische Staat nach dem Beben / Dinozor sallanıyor – Depremden Sonra Türk Devleti' [zweispr. dt./türk., ins Türk. übers. v. Melike Bilgin], *Die Welt* [*Die literarische Welt*], 4. Sept. 1999.

'Mittelpunkt der Welt?', [*die tageszeitung*] perşembe, 5, 5. Oktober 2000, 2 [in *Zunge* als 'Perspektiven der Mitte'].

'Der Feind in unserer Mitte. Allzulange haben die westlichen Gesellschaften den radikalen Islam toleriert', *Die Welt*, 15. September 2001.

'Yabancı dilin yerlileri. Die Einheimischen der Fremdsprache: Das Verhältnis der Migranten zur deutschen Sprache ist Ausdruck für ihr Fremdbleiben in der deutschen Kultur. Mit der Fähigkeit, sich in das Andere hineinzuversetzen, verliert das Eigene den Charakter einer Festung', *die tageszeitung*, 30. Oktober 2001.

'Raus aus der Nische. Die Integration der Deutsch-Türken muss zu einer nationalen Aufgabe werden', *Der Tagesspiegel*, 3. November 2001.

'Der Islam in der Modernisierungskrise', *Universitas (Orientierung in der Wissenschaft)*, 668 (Februar 2002), 192–6.

'Siedler und Einheimische. Die Deutschen werden durch ein Zuwanderungsgesetz nicht offener, wenn sie weiterhin die Ausgangssituation ignorieren: Sie haben vor allem bei der Integration bisher versagt', *die tageszeitung*, 5. April 2002.

'Die Beschädigung des Islam. Statt mit durchdachter Selbstkritik reagieren die arabischen Gesellschaften zunehmend brutaler auf erlittene Demütigungen. Eine psychologische Analyse des Nahostkonflikts', *die tageszeitung*, 21. Juni 2002.

'Ist der Islam demokratiefähig?' [Zafer Şenocak, Christian H. Hoffmann, Oliver Schlumberger in der Kontroverse], *Universitas (Orientierung in der Wissenschaft)*, 672 (Juni 2002), 625–37 [besonders 625–9].

'Die Türkei wird fitgemacht für die Mitgliedschaft in der EU. Seitdem Ankara 1999 der Beitritt in die Union in Aussicht gestellt wurde, fanden kleine Revolutionen statt', *Die Welt*, 23. August 2002.

'Die neue Souveränität. Berliner Agenda (2): Schröder konnte den "deutschen Weg" verkünden, weil er kein Nationalist ist. Jetzt muss Rot-Grün den Weg mit durchdachten Konzepten beschreiten', *die tageszeitung*, 27. September 2002.

'Auf ewig anders? Auf dem Weg nach Europa (2): Wer die Kultur des EU-Anwärters Türkei für nicht vereinbar mit der europäischen Identität hält, lebt in einer Welt, die nicht mehr existiert', *die tageszeitung*, 25. November 2002.

'Am historischen Wendepunkt angelangt. Die Türkei hat eine neue Regierung, aber sie braucht ein neues System', *Die Welt*, 5. Dezember 2002.

'Europas Mission in der arabischen Welt. Von der Achse EU–Türkei–Israel könnte die Demokratisierung der Region ausgehen', *Die Welt*, 4. Januar 2003.

1.3. Übersetzungen von Zafer Şenocak

[Die folgenden Titel wurden von Zafer Şenocak aus dem Türkischen ins Deutsche übersetzt.]

Fethi Savaşçi, *München im Frühlingsregen. Erzählungen* (Frankfurt am Main, Dağyeli, 1986).

Yunus Emre, *Das Kummerrad / Dertli Dolap. Gedichte* (Frankfurt am Main, Dağyeli, 1986).

'Pir Sultan Abdal: 12 Gedichte', *Sirene*, 1 (1988), 58–83.

Aras Ören, *Eine verspätete Abrechnung oder Der Aufstieg der Gündoğdus. Roman*, Übersetzung zusammen mit Eva Hund (Frankfurt am Main, Dağyeli, 1988).

'Das Buch mit sieben Siegeln – Über die vergessene Tradition der Divandichtung. Gedichte von Fuzuli, Baki, Seyhülislam Yahya, Nedim, Yahya Kemal', *Sirene*, 9 (1992), 28–63.

Aras Ören, *Uhrmacher der Einsamkeit. Gedichte*, Übersetzung zusammen mit Eva Hund (Berlin, Mariannenpresse, 1993).

1.4. Interviews

Anonymus, 'Eine Synthese der gedanklichen Sättigung und der farbigen Gemütsstrahlung. Ein Interview mit Zafer Şenocak', *Dergi* (Duisburg), 6 (1987), 22–3.

Yeşilada, Karin E., 'Darf man Türken und Juden vergleichen, Herr Şenocak?', *Der Tagesspiegel*, 13./14. April 1995.

——, '"Das selbstzufriedene Deutschland hat sich als unsicheres und schnell beleidigtes Konstrukt geoutet"' [Interview zur Goldhagen-Debatte], *Süddeutsche Zeitung*, 19. August 1996.

——, '"Kendini beğenmiş, Almanya, kendine güveni olmayan ve çok alıngan bir yapı olarak teşhir oldu"' [Interview zur Goldhagen-Debatte in türk. Übers.], *Arkadaş*, 9 (1996), 3.

Ulun, Aydın, 'Yaşar Kemal kötü tarihçi' ['Yaşar Kemal ist ein schlechter Historiker'. Interview mit Zafer Şenocak], *Hürriyet* [Deutschlandausgabe], 13. November 1997.

Von Becker, Peter, 'Die Türkei muß sich aus ihrem Kokon lösen. Der deutsch-türkische Schriftsteller Zafer Şenocak über ein Land, das nur zu Europa gehören wird, wenn Europa sich ihm zuwendet', *Der Tagesspiegel*, 14. November 2002.

2. Sekundärliteratur deutschsprachiger Raum

2.1. Bibliographien

Yeşilada, Karin, 'Zafer Şenocak', in Heinz-Ludwig Arnold (hg.), *Kritisches Lexikon zur deutschsprachigen Gegenwartsliteratur (KLG)* (Göttingen, edition text+kritik, 1998), 58. Nachlieferung, A–D [Aktualisierung voraussichtlich 2003] [auch unter 2.3. genannt].

Adelson, Leslie A., 'Sources', 'Other Books by Zafer Şenocak', in *ATG*, vii–ix und 135–6 [auch unter 5.1.1. genannt].

Konzett, Matthias, 'Zafer Şenocak (1961–)', in Matthias Konzett (hg.), *Encyclopedia of German Literature* (Chicago und London, Fitzroy Dearborn und Routledge, 2000), 895–7 [Autorenartikel] [auch unter 5.2. genannt].

Şölçün, Sargut, 'Literatur der türkischen Minderheit', in Carmine Chiellino (hg.), *Interkulturelle Literatur in Deutschland. Ein Handbuch* (Stuttgart, Metzler, 2000), 135–52 (151), 470 [Artikel über Z.Ş. 151, Bibliographie 470] [auch unter 2.3. genannt].

2.2. Rezensionen

Pemsel, Klaus, 'Das Wort wird Stein. Ulrich J. Beil: *Guetaria*. Z.Ş.: *Elektrisches Blau*', *Ulcus Molle*, 4/5/6 (1983), 35.

Anonymus, 'Zafer Şenocak: Elektrisches Blau 2', *Die Zeit*, 22. Juni 1984.

Heise, Hans-Jürgen, 'Weg von der Diwan-Poesie. Stationen türkischer Lyrik', *Süddeutsche Zeitung*, 22./23. März 1986.

Anonymus, 'Erstochen hab ich den Mond', *Frankfurter Allgemeine Zeitung*, 21. April 1986 [zu *FT*].

Freund, Jutta, 'Zafer Şenocak: *flammentropfen*', Besprechung im *Hessischen Rundfunk*, Oktober 1986.

Knodt, Reinhard, 'Dichter-Derwisch. Aus dem Werk des Yunus Emre', *Süddeutsche Zeitung*, 21./22. März 1987.

Hohoff, Ulrich, 'Diktatur der Lichter. Autorenporträt: Zafer Şenocak', *Literatur in Bayern* (Juni 1987).

Buz, Metin, 'Zafer Şenocak und sein letztes Werk *Ritual der Jugend*', *Die Brücke*, 3 (Juni/Juli 1988).

Beil, Ulrich Johannes, 'Autor im Zwielicht', *Literatur in Bayern*, (April 1988) [Laudatio anläßlich der Verleihung des Adelbert-von-Chamisso-Förderpreises 1988].

Şölçün, Sargut, 'Geschichtsbewußtsein in poetischen Strukturen. Trifft einer in Berlin auf Istanbul . . . Ein literaturkritischer Versuch', *die tageszeitung*, 9. November 1991 [zu *SM*].

Schiffer, Reinhold, 'Deniz Göktürk und Zafer Şenocak (Hg.): *Jedem Wort gehört ein Himmel. Türkei literarisch*', *Materialia Turcica*, 16 (1992), 145–6.

Schmid, Thomas, 'Vom Mut zur Lücke in der Identität. Der türkische Autor Zafer Şenocak entwirft ein Bild der kulturellen Geographie

Deutschlands und diskutiert die Voraussetzungen für eine wirkliche multikulturelle Gesellschaft', *die tageszeitung*, 19. Dezember 1992 [zu *Atlas*].

Ambros, Peter, 'Zafer Şenocak: *Atlas des tropischen Deutschland*', Rundfunkbesprechung für *DS–Kultur*, 1993.

Wieking, Klaus, 'Wider das falsche Bewußtsein vom Fremden. Der *Atlas des tropischen Deutschland* deckt die Verlogenheit der "Ausländerdiskussion" auf', *Oranienburger Generalanzeiger*, 22. Januar 1993.

Wörtche, Thomas, 'Wie immer. Nur die besten Absichten. Z.Ş.: *Atlas des tropischen Deutschland*', *Frankfurter Rundschau*, 19. Februar 1993.

Freund, Jutta, 'Kuddelmuddel. Zafer Şenocak über Deutschland', *Frankfurter Allgemeine Zeitung*, 26. Juni 1993 [zu *Atlas*].

Gottschlich, Jürgen, 'Beim Namen nennen: Deutsche Türken', *die tageszeitung*, 25. September 1993 [zu *Deutsche Türken*].

Beil, Ulrich, 'Zafer Şenocak: *Fernwehanstalten*', *Das Gedicht*, 2 (1994), 129–30.

Heise, Hans-Jürgen, 'Ein Bildlyriker. Neues von Zafer Şenocak', *Süddeutsche Zeitung*, 12./13. März 1994 [zu *FA*].

Schmid, Thomas, 'Konspiration mit der Finsternis. IrreFührungen eines türkisch-deutschen Essayisten an den Rand Europas', *die tageszeitung*, 2. April 1994 [zu *Hitler*].

Wahrenberg, Achim, 'Können wir ohne Feindbild nicht leben? Orient und Okzident – Gedanken zu Zafer Şenocaks Buch *War Hitler Araber?*', *Märkische Allgemeine Zeitung*, 14. Mai 1994.

Menzler, Walter, 'Zafer Şenocak (Hrsg.): *Der gebrochene Blick nach Westen*', *Zeitschrift für Türkeistudien*, 2 (1994), 307–8.

Wulf, Dieter, 'Auf den Spuren kultureller Ignoranz. Zafer Şenocak hinterfragt das Verhältnis zwischen westeuropäischen und arabischen Intellektuellen', *Berliner Zeitung*, 10. Juni 1994 [zu *Hitler*].

Raddatz, Fritz, 'In mir zwei Welten. Deutschsprachige Literatur von Ausländern. Gibt es einen deutschen Rushdie? Bei uns leben mehr Immigranten, die deutsch schreiben, als die meisten wissen', *Die Zeit*, 24. Juni 1994 [Sammelrezension].

Karakuş, Mahmut, 'Zafer Şenocak in türkischer Übersetzung', *Diyalog*, 2 (1994), 231–4 [zu *RdJ*] [auch unter 3.2. genannt].

Carbe, Monika, 'Zafer Şenocak: *Der Mann im Unterhemd*', *Listen*, 40 (1995), 35.

Grünefeld, Hans-Dieter, 'Zafer Şenocak: *War Hitler Araber?*', *Zeitschrift für Kulturaustausch*, 1 (1995), 140.

Bakirdöğen, Ayhan, 'Kein Interesse, keine Erkenntnis', *Frankfurter Rundschau*, 27. Februar 1995 [zu *Der gebrochene Blick nach Westen*].

Spinnler, Rolf, 'Schlingpflanze in der Monokultur. Der deutsch-türkische Schriftsteller im Wilhelmspalais', *Stuttgarter Zeitung*, 3. Februar 1996.

Frischmuth, Barbara, 'Künstlerfragen: War Hitler Araber? Warum geht ein Türke nicht in die Oper?', *Die Presse*, 8. Februar 1996 [zu *Atlas* und *Hitler*].

Beil, Ulrich, 'Zafer Şenocaks ästhetische Subversion', in Irmgard Ackermann (hg.), *Fremde AugenBlicke. Mehrkulturelle Literatur in Deutschland* (Bonn, Internationes, 1996), 141–3 [auch in der engl. Übersetzung: Irmgard Ackermann (hg.), *Foreign Viewpoints: Multicultural Literature in Germany* (Bonn, Internationes, 1999), 137–9].

Grünefeld, Hans-Dieter, 'Männerängste', *Foglio* (Februar/März 1996) [zu *MiU*].

Greve, Martin, 'Genervt von Herkunftsfragen. Türkisch-deutsche Schriftsteller: Aras Ören, Zehra Çırak, Zafer Şenocak', *Zitty* (Berlin), 12 (1996), 28–31.

Glombitza, Birgit, 'Die Insekten auf dem Gedankenstrich. In *Die Prärie* spinnt Zafer Şenocak ironische Gedankenwolle rund um einen Autisten', *die tageszeitung* [Hamburger Ausgabe], 5. August 1997.

Anonymus, 'Die Heimat des Fremden. "Mein Schreibtisch ist der kleinste Irrgarten der Welt" ', *Handelsblatt*, 19./20. September 1997 [zu *P*].

Heise, Hans-Jürgen, 'Mit kalkuliertem Unschuldsblick. Prosa und Verse von Zafer Şenocak', *Süddeutsche Zeitung*, 23. Oktober 1997 [zu *P*].

Anonymus, 'Aufgelesen. Prospekte für Leser', *Frankfurter Rundschau*, 25. Oktober 1997 (zu *P*).

Grünefeld, Hans-Dieter, 'Der Autor als Sphinx', *Buchkultur*, 1 (1998), 54 [zu *P*].

Decker, Markus, 'Verwirrendes ums Fremde', *Mitteldeutsche Zeitung*, 24. November 1998 [zu *GV*].

Martin, Nicholas, '*Gefährliche Verwandtschaft*. Ein Roman über die Beziehung von Deutschen und Türken', *Frankfurter Rundschau*, 25. November 1998.

Carbe, Monika, '*Gefährliche Verwandtschaft*', *Listen*, 52 (Dezember 1998), 16.

Mair-Gummermann, Elisabeth, 'Şenocak, *Gefährliche Verwandtschaft*', *[Einkaufszentrale für Bibliotheken] ekz–Informationsdienst*, 7 (1999).

Gutschke, Irmtraut, 'Alles offen ohne Mauer. Zafer Şenocak: *Gefährliche Verwandtschaft*', *Neues Deutschland*, 8. Januar 1999.

Bialas, Dunja, 'Postmoderne Identitätssuche. Zafer Şenocak, *Gefährliche Verwandtschaft*', *Münchner Stadtmagazin*, Februar 1999.

Frischmuth, Barbara, 'Der Blick des Randgängers. Ein Roman von Zafer Şenocak', *Neue Zürcher Zeitung*, 7. April 1999 [zu *GV*].

Weber, Antje, 'Der Aufstand der Vorzeige-Exoten. Die Sprache der angeblich Sprachlosen: Wie die Kinder türkischer Einwanderer ihre Erfahrungen literarisch umsetzen', *Süddeutsche Zeitung*, 17./18. April 1999 [Sammelrezension mit Schwerpunkt Z.Ş.].

Bialas, Dunja, 'Ein Findelbuch. Zafer Şenocak: *Der Erottomane*', *Münchner Stadtmagazin* (Januar 2000), 68.

Yeşilada, Karin, 'Die jungen Wilden', *etap* (Berlin), 2 (2000), 70 (zu *E*).

Carbe, Monika, 'Mord im Halbdunkel. Zafer Şenocak: *Der Erottomane*', *Neue Zürcher Zeitung*, 7. März 2000.

Carbe, Monika, 'Vexierspiel mit der Identität', *Listen*, 57 (21. März 2000), 31 [zu *E*].

Mair-Gummermann, Elisabeth, 'Şenocak, *Der Erottomane*', *[Einkaufszentrale für Bibliotheken] ekz–Informationsdienst*, 7 (2000).

Grünefeld, Hans-Dieter, '*Der Erottomane*', *Buchkultur*, 67 (August–September 2000).

Carbe, Monika, 'In der "Quarantänestation". Vierzig Jahre Türken in Deutschland', *Neue Zürcher Zeitung*, 29. Januar 2002 [zu *Zunge*].

2.3. Wissenschaftliche Aufsätze

Horn, Dieter, 'Schreiben aus Betroffenheit. Die Migrantenliteratur in der Bundesrepublik', in Alfred J. Tumat (hg.), *Migration und Integration: ein Reader* (Baltmannsweiler, Pädagogischer Verlag Burgbücherei Schneider, 1986), 213–33.

Göktürk, Deniz, 'Muttikültürelle Zungenbrecher: Literatürken aus Deutschlands Nischen', *Sirene*, 12/13 (September 1994), 77–92.

Grünefeld, Hans-Dieter, 'Wahlheimatliteratur. Rezeption literarischer Texte der Migration', *Zeitschrift für Kulturaustausch*, 1 (1995), 105–12.

Waldhoff, Hans-Peter, 'Ein Übersetzer. Über die soziobiographische Genese eines transnationalen Denkstils', in Elçin Kürşat-Ahlers, Dursun Tan und Hans-Peter Waldhoff (hg.), *Brücken zwischen Zivilisationen. Zur Zivilisierung ethnisch-kultureller Differenzen und Machtungleichheiten. Das türkisch-deutsche Beispiel* (Frankfurt am Main, IKO-Verlag für Interkulturelle Kommunikation, 1997), 323–64.

Özoğuz, Yüksel, 'Zafer Şenocak – ein bikultureller Dichter', in Nilüfer Kuruyazıcı, Sabine Jahn, Ulrich Müller, Priska Steger, Klaus Zelewitz (hg.), *Schnittpunkte der Kulturen. Gesammelte Vorträge des Internationalen Symposions 17 –22. September 1996, Istanbul/Türkei* (Stuttgart, Akademischer Verlag, 1998), 144–53 [zu *FA* und *RdJ*] [auch unter 3.2. genannt].

Yeşilada, Karin, 'Zafer Şenocak', in Heinz-Ludwig Arnold (hg.), *Kritisches Lexikon zur deutschsprachigen Gegenwartsliteratur [KLG]* (Göttingen, edition text+kritik, 1998), 58. Nachlieferung, 1–6, A–D [Aktualisierung voraussichtlich 2003] [auch unter 2.1. genannt].

Şölçün, Sargut, 'Literatur der türkischen Minderheit', in Carmine Chiellino (hg.), *Interkulturelle Literatur in Deutschland. Ein Handbuch* (Stuttgart, Metzler, 2000), 135–52 [Artikel über Z.Ş. 151] [auch unter 2.1. genannt].

Yeşilada, Karin E., 'Topographien im "tropischen Deutschland" – Türkisch-deutsche Literatur nach der Wiedervereinigung', in Ursula E. Beitter (hg.), *Literatur und Identität. Deutsch-deutsche Befindlichkeiten und die multikulturelle Gesellschaft* (New York, Peter Lang, 2000), 303–39

[Loyola College in Maryland Berlin Seminar: Contemporary German Literature and Society, Bd. 3].

——, 'Das Empire schreibt zurück – Die deutschsprachige Migrationsliteratur', in Thomas Böhm und Martin Hielscher (hg.), *Weltliteratur 2001. Vom Nobelpreis bis zum Comic* (Köln, Könemann, 2001), 118–37.

——, 'Nâzıms Enkel schreiben weiter', in Monika Carbe und Wolfgang Riemann (hg.), *Hundert Jahre Nâzım Hikmet: 1902–1963* (Hildesheim, Zürich, New York, Olms, 2002), 180–211.

3. Rezeption Türkei

3.1. Primärliteratur in türk. Übersetzung und auf Türkisch

3.1.1. Buchausgaben
Gençlik Ayinleri, ins Türk. übers. v. Yüksel Özoğuz (Istanbul, Yapı Kredi Yayınları, 1994) [= *RdJ*].

Atletli Adam, ins Türk. übers. v. Mustafa Tüzel (Istanbul, Kabalcı Yayınevi, 1997) [= *MiU*].

Hitler Arap Mıydı?, ins Türk. übers. v. Mustafa Tüzel und Vedat Çorlu (Istanbul, Kabalcı Yayınevi, 1997) [= *Hitler*].

Taşa ve Kemiğe Yazılıdır. Şiirler, ins Türk. übers. v. Menekşe Toprak (Istanbul, İyi Şeyler Yayınevi, 2000) [= *FA*].

3.1.2. Einzelveröffentlichungen in türk. Übersetzung

3.1.2.1. Lyrik
'Kara Bahardan Önce Berlin' [mit Originaltext], ins Türk. übers. v. Mustafa Tüzel, *Fol Dergisi*, Nr. 7 (Dez. 1997), 40–7 [= 'Berlin vor dem schwarzen Frühling', *SM*].

3.1.2.2. Prosa
'Ev', ins Türk. übers. v. Vedat Çorlu, *Varlık*, 10 (1996), 53–5 [= 'Das Haus', *MiU*].

3.1.2.3. Essays
'Modern'de Savaş ve Barış', ins Türk. übers. v. Mustafa Tüzel, in Vedat Çorlu (hg.), *Dünya Kültürü. Felsefe, Sanat, Edebiyat ve Kültür Tarihi Üzerine Yazılar I* ['Weltkultur. Schriften zu Philosophie, Kunst, Literatur und Kulturgeschichte I'], (Istanbul, Kabalcı Yayınevi, 1996), 49–55 [= 'Krieg und Frieden in Deutschland'].

3.1.3. Interviews

Yüreklik, Güner, 'Yunus' Humanismus ist universell', *Bizim Almanca*, 20 (1986), 37–8 [Interview zu *Das Kummerrad*].

Ulun, Aydin, 'Imajlar ancak kültür üzerinden değişebilir' ['Die Bilder können sich erst über die Kultur verändern'], *Hürriyet*, 27. Februar 1992.

Gökhan, Halil, 'Almanya Bir Ülke Olmaktan Çok Bir Dildir' ['Deutschland ist mehr eine Sprache als ein Land'], *Kitap-lik*, 12 [November–Dezember 1994] [auch in amer.-engl. Übers. in *ATG*].

Emre, Gültekin, '"Edebiyat ötekine ulaşmaktır". Zafer Şenocak'la *Atletli Adam* üzerine' ['Literatur erreicht den Anderen. Über *Atletli Adam*'], *Cumhuriyet Kitap*, 20. März 1996.

Durgun, Duygu, 'Bir 'Kent gezgini'nin iç dünyasi. 1970'ten yana Almanya'da yaşayan yazar Zafer Şenocak'ın yapıtları Türkçede' ['Die Innenwelt eines Flaneurs. Über die Texte des seit 1970 in Deutschland lebenden Autors Z.Ş.'], *Cumhuriyet*, 20. Januar 1997, 15.

Yeşilada, Karin, 'Zafer Şenocak'la söyleşi', ins Türk. übers. v. Mustafa Tüzel, *Cumhuriyet Kitap*, 383, 19. Juni 1997, 1–2 [= Interview 'Kann man Türken und Juden vergleichen?'].

Tüzel, Mustafa, 'Zafer Şenocak'la söyleşi', *Varlık Kitap Eki*, 3 (1998), 11–13.

Ayer, İlhan, 'Avrupa'nın bilinç altındaki Türk imajı' ['Europas unterbewußtes Türkenbild'], *Cumhuriyet hafta*, 30. November 2001.

Emre, Gültekin, 'Dil yazarı seçer. Zafer Şenocak'la söyleşi' ['Die Sprache wählt den Dichter. Interview mit Z.Ş.'], *Kitap-lik*, 55 (September–Oktober 2002), 105–8.

3.2. Sekundärliteratur Türkei: Rezensionen und wiss. Aufsätze

Özoğuz, Yüksel, 'Almanca yazan bir türk şairi: Zafer Şenocak' ['Porträt eines deutschsprachigen türkischen Dichters'], *Gösteri* 144 (1992), 30–31.

Karakuş, Mahmut, 'Zafer Şenocak in türkischer Übersetzung', *Diyalog*, 2 (1994), 231–4 [zu *Gençlik Ayinleri*] [auch unter 2.2. genannt].

Emre, Gültekin, 'Gençlik Ayinleri'nin yolcusu Türkiye'de', *Cumhuriyet Kitap*, 260 (1995), 7 [zu *Gençlik Ayinleri*].

Yaşin, Mehmet, *Poeturka. Deneme* (Istanbul, Adam Yayınevi, 1995) [dort besonders 'Eski Türkiyelilerin Almanca Şiiri' ('Deutsche Lyrik ehemaliger Türken'), 57–64].

'Geçmişine göçemeyen bir yazar: Zafer Şenocak' [Themenheft Zafer Şenocak], *Cumhuriyet Kitap*, 383, 19. Juni 1997, 1, 4–5

Carbe, Monika, '*Atletli Adam* üzerinde', ins Türk. übers. v. Mustafa Tüzel, *Cumhuriyet Kitap*, 383, 19. Juni 1997, 4 [zu *Atletli Adam*].

Emre, Gültekin, 'Iki Kitabıyla Zafer Şenocak', *Cumhuriyet Kitap*, 383, 19. Juni 1997, 5 [zu *Hitler Arap Mıydı?* und *Atletli Adam*].

——, 'Zafer Şenocak'ın "Uçmak" Öyküsündeki Istanbul' ['Istanbul in der Erzählung "Uçmak"/"Fliegen"'], *Adam Öykü*, 11 (Juli/August 1997), 109–11.

Özoğuz, Yüksel, 'Zafer Şenocak – ein bikultureller Dichter', in Nilüfer Kuruyazıcı, Sabine Jahn, Ulrich Müller, Priska Steger, Klaus Zelewitz (hg.), *Schnittpunkte der Kulturen. Gesammelte Vorträge des Internationalen Symposions 17.–22. September 1996, Istanbul/Türkei* (Stuttgart, Akademischer Verlag, 1998), 144–53 [zu *FA* und *RdJ*] [auch unter 2.3. genannt].

Tökel, Dursun Ali, 'Hitler'in ırkından Divan şiirinden gizemine' ['Von Hitlers Abstammung zu den Geheimnissen der Divan-Lyrik'], *Dergah*, 1 (1998), 9f [zu *Hitler Arap Mıydı?*].

Özoğuz, Yüksel, 'İki kültürün kesiştiği noktada yeni bir şiir dili' ['Eine neue dichterische Sprache am Schnittpunkt der Kulturen': türk. Version von 1998, s.o.], in Nilüfer Kuruyazıcı und Mahmut Karakuş (hg.), *Gurbeti Vatan Edenler. Almanca Yazan Almanyalı Türkler* ['Die in der Fremde heimisch werden. Deutschschreibende Deutschtürken'] (Ankara, Kültür Bakanlığı, 2001), 201–8.

Yeşilada, Karin Emine, '"Göçmen İşçi Yazını" Ya da: How Turkish is it?' ('Deutschsprachige Migrantenliteratur, oder: How Turkish is it?'), ins Türk. übers. v. Mine Dal und Mustafa Tüzel, in Zehra İpşiroğlu (hg.), *Çağdaş Türk Yazını. Yazın öğrenimi için temel bir kaynak* ['Grundlagen zur Einführung in die zeitgenössische türkische Literatur'] (Istanbul, Adam, 2001), 207–43.

Özlü, Demir, 'Almanya'da bir yazar' ['Ein Autor in Deutschland'], *Adam Sanat* (Istanbul) [erscheint März 2003] [zu *GV*].

4. Rezeption Frankreich

4.1. Primärliteratur in franz. Übersetzung

4.1.1. Buchausgaben

La Mer verticale. Poèmes, ins Franz. übers. v. Timour Muhidine, préface de Pierre Pachet, postface de Timour Muhidine (Paris, L'Esprit des Péninsules, 1999) [= *SM*].

Parenté dangereuse. Roman, ins Franz. übers. v. Colette Strauss-Hiva (Paris, L'Esprit des Péninsules, 2000) [= *GV*].

L'Érottoman, ins Franz. übers. v. Colette Strauss-Hiva (Paris, L'Esprit des Péninsules, 2001) [= *E*].

4.1.2. Einzelveröffentlichungen in franz. Übersetzung

4.1.2.1. Lyrik

'Archivistes à Istanbul', ins Franz. übers. v. Timour Muhidine, *Dédale*, 5/6 (1997), 415–9 [= 'Archivare in Istanbul', *FA*].

'City Dwellers', aus d. Türk. ins Engl. übers. v. Yurdanur Salman, *Mediterraneans/Mediterranéans* [Ausgabe hg. v. Kenneth Brown u. Robert Waterhouse, *Istanbul, Many Worlds / Istanbul, monde pluriel*], 10 (Winter 1997–8), 63 [= 'Kentliler', unveröff. türk. Original].

4.1.2.2. Prosa

[keine Einzelveröffentlichungen]

4.1.2.3. Essays

'Une langue abâtardie', *Liber*, 15 (1993), 10–12 [= 'Die bastardisierte Sprache'].

'Dans la jungle des souvenirs', ins Franz. übers. v. Nicole Bary, *Études*, 391 (Juli/August 1999), 26–8 ['Im Dschungel der Erinnerungen'; nur auf franz. erschienen].

'Racines coupées', ins Franz. übers. v. Fernand Cambon, *Europe*, 861/862 (Januar/Februar 2001), 63–6 [= '"...der Mensch, / der's mit anhört ... "'].

'Mes trois rencontres avec Nâzım Hikmet', ins Franz. übers. v. Colette Strauss-Hiva, *Europe*, 878/879 (Juni/Juli 2002), 54–8 [= 'Meine drei Begegnungen mit Nâzım Hikmet'].

4.1.3. Interviews

Aday, Taner, 'Entretien avec Zafer Şenocak' [Gespräch mit Z.Ş.], *Oluşum/Genèse* (Nancy), 15 (1991).

Ciriez, Frédéric, 'L'Erottoman ou la langue comme puissance et impuissance sexuelle', *fnac café litteraire online*, 18 (März 2001), www.fnac.net/le_café_litteraire_2001/html/zafer_senocak_interview.html

4.2. Sekundärliteratur Frankreich: Rezensionen und Artikel

Muhidine, Timour, 'Nouvelles d'Allemagne – Zafer Şenocak: *Das senkrechte Meer* (*La Mer verticale*)', *Arabies*, 62 (1992), 83.

——, 'Zafer Şenocak', *Les Belles étrangères* (Mai 1993).

——, 'La province turque des lettres allemandes', *Le Monde diplomatique*, 8 (1993), 29 [Sammelrezension].

——, 'Au parapets de l'Europe. Postface', in Zafer Şenocak, *La Mer verticale. Poèmes* (Paris, L'Esprit des Péninsules, 1999), 113–6.

Pachet, Pierre, 'Istanbul, l'imagination même. Préface', in Zafer Şenocak, *La Mer verticale. Poèmes* (Paris, L'Esprit des Péninsules, 1999), S. 7–14 [auch auf engl., siehe unter 6.1.2.3.].

Anonymus (J.-F. K.-T.), 'Zafer Şenocak: *Parenté dangereuse*', *Documents. Revue des questions allemandes*, 5 (November–Dezember 2000).

Goldschmidt, Georges-Arthur, 'Şenocak, suite', *La Quinzaine littéraire*, 797 (1.–15. Dezember 2000), 6 [zu *Parenté dangereuse*].

Masson, Jean-Yves, 'Allemand d'origine turque', *La Quinzaine littéraire*, 797 (1.–15. Dezember 2000), 5–6 [zu *Parenté dangereuse*].

Rousset, D., 'Zafer Şenocak, *Parenté dangereuse*', *Diasporique*, 16 (Dezember 2000), 28.

Strauss-Hiva, Colette, 'Zafer Şenocak', in Kerstin Behre und Petra Metz (hg.), *Jetzt-Autoren: ils écrivent en allemand* (Paris, Pauvert, 2001), 228–32.

Muhidine, Timour, 'Zafer Şenocak, *Parenté dangereuse*', *europe. revue littéraire mensuelle* (Mai 2001), 370.

Dedet, Joséphine, 'Ils ont choisi l'allemand', *Jeune Afrique / L'intelligent*, 2109, 12.–18. Juni 2001, 56–7 [Sammelrezension].

Riera, Anne, 'Zafer Şenocak, *Parenté dangereuse*. La part manquante', *L'espace e-culture*, 29. März 2001, unter: www.melomix.com [auch in *Matricules des anges*, Angaben fehlen].

5. Rezeption USA und Kanada

5.1. Primärliteratur in amer.-engl. Übersetzung

5.1.1. Buchausgaben
Atlas of a Tropical Germany. Essays on Politics and Culture, 1990–1998, übers. und hg. v. Leslie A. Adelson (Lincoln und London, University of Nebraska Press, 2000) [auch unter 2.1. genannt; *ATG*].

5.1.2. Einzelveröffentlichungen in amer.-engl. Übersetzung

5.1.2.1. Lyrik
[Sämtliche Übersetzungen der aufgelisteten Lyrik ins Amerikanisch-Englische stammen von Elizabeth Oehlkers Wright.]

'Between Sea and Land I', 'Message in a Bottle I', *Another Chicago Magazine*, 7 (1996–7) [= 'Zwischen Meer und Land I', 'Flaschenpost', *FA*].

'Lu I–III', 'The Blue Notebook', 'The Tiger, The Woods and Us', *Dimension2*, 4;2 (May 1997) [= 'Lu I–III', 'Das blaue Heft', 'Der Tiger, der Wald und wir', *FA*].

'Door Languages I', *Language International*, 12 (2000) [= 'Türsprachen', *FA*].

'M', 'The Blinded', untitled: 'I had a stronger brother', *Agni Review* (Boston University), 53 (2001), 49–53.

'Spell', 'Self-Portrait', untitled: 'Beyond the sea there is a woman', in *Slope*, 11–12 (Juli–Oktober 2001), unter: www.slope.org [aus 'Balladen aus dem Gedächtnis'; mit Originaltexten].

'In the New World I, IV, VI, VIII', in *Perihelion*, 9 (Winter 2002), www.webdelsol.com/perihelion [= 'In der neuen Welt', *FA*].

5.1.2.2. Prosa

'Flying', ins Amer. übers. v. Judith Orban, *Descant* (Toronto), 24, 4 (Winter 1993–94), 111–9 [= 'Fliegen'].

'Man in the Undershirt', ins Amer. übers. v. Nancy Isenson, *Trafika* (New York und Prag), 5 (Autumn 1995), 7–19 [= 3 Texte aus *MiU*, darunter 'Lebenslauf', Nachdruck in: Irmgard Ackermann (hg.), *Foreign Viewpoints: Multicultural Literature in Germany* (Bonn, Internationes, 1999), 143–4; auch unter 1.2.2. genannt].

5.1.2.3. Essays

'Tradition and taboo', ins Amer. übers. v. Judith Orban, *Descant* (Toronto), 24, 4 (Winter 1993–94), 147–8 [= 'Tradition und Tabu'].

'War and peace in modernity: reflections on the German-Turkish future (1994)', ins Amer. übers. v. Martin Chalmers, *Cultural Studies*, 10, 2 (1996), 255–69 [= 'Krieg und Frieden in Deutschland' (1995); Einführung von Kevin Robins unter 5.2. genannt].

Zusammen mit Bülent Tulay, 'Germany – a *Heimat* for Turks?', in Antje Harnisch, Anne Marie Stokes and Friedemann Weidauer (hg. u. übers.), *Fringe Voices: An Anthology of Minority Writing in the Federal Republic of Germany* (Oxford und New York, Berg, 1998), 256–63 [auch in *ATG*].

'To my readers in the United States. Preface', in *ATG*, xxxix–xli.

'War and peace in modernity: reflections on the German-Turkish future (1994/1998)', ins Amer. übers. v. Martin Chalmers und Leslie A. Adelson, in *ATG*, 83–98 [= vom Autor erweiterte Fassung von 'Krieg und Frieden in Deutschland'].

'Which myth writes me?' ins Amer. übers. v. Leslie A. Adelson, in *ATG*, 77–82 [zuerst als Vortrag an der Ohio State University, 1996; auch in *Zunge*].

'Territories', ins Amer. übers. v. Leslie A. Adelson, in *ATG*, 74–6 [zuerst als Vortrag an der Ohio State University, 1996; auch in *Zunge*].

5.1.3. Interviews

Konzett, Matthias, 'Zafer Şenocak im Gespräch', *The German Quarterly* [erscheint Spring 2003].

5.2. Sekundärliteratur USA: Rezensionen und wiss. Aufsätze

Buruma, Ian, 'Outsiders', *The New York Review of Books*, 7 (April 1992) [Autorenporträt im Kontext Neonazismus in Deutschland].

Robins, Kevin, 'Introduction to Zafer Şenocak', *Cultural Studies*, 10, 2 (1996), 255–8.

Wyszpolski, Bondo, 'Exiled and uprooted', *Easy Reader* (L.A.), 22. August 1996 [Autorenporträt].

Adelson, Leslie A., 'Coordinates of orientation: an introduction', in *ATG*, xi–xxxvii.

——, 'Touching tales of Turks, Germans and Jews: cultural alterity, historical narrative, and literary riddles for the 1990s', *New German Critique*, 80 (2000), 93–124 [auch in Keith Bullivant und Bernhard Spies (hg.), *Literarisches Krisenbewußtsein: Ein Perzeptions- und Produktionsmuster im 20. Jahrhundert* (München, Iudicium, 2001), 216–49].

Konzett, Matthias, 'Zafer Şenocak (1961–)', in Matthias Konzett (hg.), *Encyclopedia of German Literature* (Chicago und London, Fitzroy Dearborn und Routledge, 2000), 895–7 [Autorenartikel] [auch unter 2.1. genannt].

Adelson, Leslie A., 'Against between: a manifesto', in Salah Hassan und Iftikhar Dadi (hg.), *Unpacking Europe. Towards a Critical Reading* (Rotterdam, NAI, 2001), 244–55.

Klaasen, Julie, 'Zafer Şenocak, *Atlas of a Tropical Germany*', *Colloquia Germanica*, 34, 3–4 (2001), 362–3.

Adelson, Leslie A., 'The Turkish turn in contemporary German literature and memory work', *The Germanic Review*, 77, 4 (Fall 2002), 326–38.

——, 'Back to the future: Turkish remembrances of the GDR and other phantom pasts', in Leslie A. Adelson (hg.), *The Cultural After-Life of East Germany: New Transnational Perspectives* (Washington DC, American Institute for Contemporary German Studies, 2002), 93–109 [Helen & Harry Gray Humanities Program Series 13].

Dollinger, Roland, 'Hybride Identitäten: Zafer Şenocaks Roman *Gefährliche Verwandtschaft*', *Seminar*, 38 (2002), 59–73.

Gerstenberger, Katharina, 'Difficult stories: generation, genealogy, gender in Zafer Şenocak's *Gefährliche Verwandtschaft* and Monika Maron's *Pawels Briefe*', in Stuart Taberner (hg.), *Recasting German Identity: Culture, Politics and Literature in the Berlin Republic* (Columbia S.C., Camden House, 2002), 235–49.

Segelcke, Elke, 'Die Frage nach kultureller Identität und nationaler Geschichte in den Werken deutschsprachiger AutorInnen der Gegenwart', *Glossen*, 15 (2002) [Sonderausgabe / Special Issue: Crosscurrents – German Literature(s) and the Search for Identity] [auch unter: www.dickinson.edu/glossen].

6. Rezeption Großbritannien

6.1. Primärliteratur in engl. Übersetzung und auf Deutsch

6.1.1. Buchveröffentlichungen
[keine Buchpublikationen]

6.1.2. Einzelveröffentlichungen

6.1.2.1. Lyrik
[siehe auch unter 6.1.2.4.]
'Gedichte' ['Wortschatzinsel'-Zyklus und andere], in Tom Cheesman und Karin E. Yeşilada (hg.), *Zafer Şenocak* (Cardiff, University of Wales Press, 2003), 1–15 [Contemporary German Writers].

6.1.2.2. Prosa
[siehe auch unter 6.1.2.4.]
'Flying', ins Engl. übers. v. Tom Cheesman, *Moving Worlds* (University of Leeds), 1 (2001), 89–96 [= 'Fliegen', *MiU*].
'Two Stories by Zafer Şenocak' ['Resumé' und 'On an Illegible Map'; = 'Lebenslauf' und 'Auf einer unlesbaren Karte', *MiU*], ins Engl. übers. v. Tom Cheesman, *Planet: The Welsh Internationalist*, 149 (Oktober/November 2001), 81–4 [Einführung unter 6.2.2. genannt].

6.1.2.3. Essays, Artikel
[siehe unter 6.1.2.4.]

6.1.2.4. Einzelveröffentlichungen im Internet
[Alle folgenden Titel wurden übersetzt von Tom Cheesman. Copyright der Übersetzungen beim Übersetzer. Die Texte sind abrufbar unter: www.swan.ac.uk/german/cheesman/senocak/zs1.htm]
Lyrik
Nazim Hikmet: On the Ship to Mars (verse drama, co-authored with Berkan Karpat); selected poems from *The Vertical Sea* and from *Sleep Reflexes*.
Prosa
Perilous Kinship [= GV]; selections from *The Man in a Vest* and *The Erottoman*; 'There's a Crack in the Handle'; 'Bastardised Language'; 'Dialogue on the Third Language: Germans, Turks and their Future'; 'Fear of Bilingualism'.
Interview
Z.Ş. interviewed by Frédéric Ciriez for *fnac: le cafe littéraire* (18 March 2001).

6.1.3. Interviews

[siehe auch unter 6.1.2.4.]

Cheesman, Tom, '»Einfach eine neue Form«: Gespräch mit Zafer Şenocak', in Tom Cheesman und Karin E. Yeşilada (hg.), *Zafer Şenocak* (Cardiff, University of Wales Press, 2003), 19–30 [Contemporary German Writers].

6.2. Sekundärliteratur Großbritannien

[Die Beiträge des vorliegenden Bandes wurden mitaufgenommen.]

6.2.1. Buchpublikationen

Cheesman, Tom und Karin E. Yeşilada (hg.), *Zafer Şenocak* (Cardiff, University of Wales Press, 2003) [Contemporary German Writers].

6.2.2. Rezensionen und wiss. Aufsätze

Cheesman, Tom und Göktürk, Deniz, 'German titles, Turkish names: The Cosmopolitan Will', *new books in german (nbg)*, (Autumn 1999), 22 [Sammelrezension] [auch unter: www.new-books-in-german.com/features.html].

Cheesman, Tom, 'Zafer Şenocak – TransEuropean internationalist', *Planet: The Welsh Internationalist*, 149 (October/November 2001), 78–80.

Adelson, Leslie A., 'Against between: a manifesto', in *Zafer Şenocak* (2003), 130–43.

Beil, Ulrich Johannes, 'Wider den Exotismus: Zafer Şenocaks west-östliche Moderne', in *Zafer Şenocak* (2003), 31–42.

Carbe, Monika, '*Der Erottomane*: Ein Vexierspiel mit der Identität', in *Zafer Şenocak* (2003), 80–90.

Cheesman, Tom, 'Ş/ß: Zafer Şenocak and the civilization of clashes', in *Zafer Şenocak* (2003), 144–57.

Jordan, James, 'Zafer Şenocak's essays and early prose fiction: from collective multiculturalism to fragmented cultural identities', in *Zafer Şenocak* (2003), 91–105.

Konzett, Matthias, 'Writing against the grain: Zafer Şenocak as public intellectual and writer', in *Zafer Şenocak* (2003), 43–60.

McGowan, Moray, 'Odysseus on the ottoman, or "the man in skirts": exploratory masculinities in the prose texts of Zafer Şenocak', in *Zafer Şenocak* (2003), 61–79.

Pachet, Pierre, 'Istanbul: imagination itself', aus d. Franz. ins Engl. übers. v. Tom Cheesman, in *Zafer Şenocak* (2003), 106–11.

Yeşilada, Karin E., 'Zafer Şenocak: outline biography', in *Zafer Şenocak* (2003), 16–18.

——, 'Poetry on its way – Aktuelle Zwischenstationen im lyrischen Werk Zafer Şenocaks', in *Zafer Şenocak* (2003), 112–29.

——, 'Bibliographie Zafer Şenocak 1983–2003', in *Zafer Şenocak* (2003), 158–84.

Hall, Katharina, '"Bekanntlich sind Dreiecksbeziehungen am kompliziertesten": Turkish, Jewish and German Identity in Zafer Şenocak's *Gefährliche Verwandtschaft*', *German Life and Letters*, 51, 1 (2003), 72-88.

7. Rezeption in anderen Ländern
[Wurde aus Platzgründen zusammengelegt; nur vorhandene Genres sind genannt. Hebräische Originaltitel konnten nicht wiedergegeben werden.]

7.1. Primärliteratur in Übersetzung

7.1.1. Buchausgaben
L'Erottomanno, ins Ital. übers. v. Elsa Luttazzi (Rom, Voland) [erscheint 2003].

7.1.2. Einzelveröffentlichungen

7.1.2.1. Lyrik
12 Gedichte [aus *RdJ*], ins Hebräische übers., in *Iton 77* [= *Iton le-sifrut uletarbut*, Tel-Aviv], 154–5 (1992), 34–5.
12 Gedichte [aus 'Die Wassersucher'], ins Spanische übers. v. Carme Gala, in *Nómadas de las Palabras* (Barcelona, Virus, 1997), 31–44.
12 Gedichte [aus 'Die Wassersucher'], ins Katalanische übers. v. Carme Gala, in *Nòmades de les Paraules* (Barcelona, Virus, 1997), 31–44.

7.1.2.2. Prosa
Auszug aus *GV*, ins Hebräische übers., in *Iton 77* [= *Iton le-sifrut ule-tarbut*, Tel-Aviv], 229 (1999), 10–13.

7.1.2.3. Essays
'Ubehaget ved kulturbegrebet', ins Dänische übers., in *Social Kritik* (Kopenhagen), 51 (Oktober 1997), 62–5 [= 'Das Unbehagen am Kulturbegriff', *Hitler*].

7.1.3. Interviews
Schwarzenstein, Tali, [Interview mit Z.Ş zu *GV*], ins Hebräische übers., in *Iton 77*, 229 (1999), 10–13.

7.2. Sekundärliteratur
van Uffelen, Kees, 'De problemen beginnen waar de islam wordt verketterd', *Forum 6* (Amsterdam), 1990.

Index

Aeschylus 108
Akçam, Dursun 105
Adelson, Leslie A. 44, 47, 60, 77, 115, 128, 158
Adorno, Theodor 45, 54–5, 77
Anderson, Benedict 57
Aristophanes 108
Aristotle 32
Arjouni, Jakob 60, 98
Artaud, Antonin 32
Auster, Paul 90

Bachmann, Ingeborg 50, 158
Bade, Klaus J. 97
Bakhtin, Mikhail 52
Balzac, Honoré de 144
Barthes, Roland 144
Baudelaire, Charles 108
Beil, Ulrich 112, 114, 128
Benn, Gottfried 158
Bialas, Dunja 86
Boccaccio, Giovanni 88
    Decameron 88
Born, Nicolas 20
Bornemann, John 158
Breton, André 108
Brinkmann, Rolf 20
Butler, Judith 64, 72

Camus, Albert 158
Canetti, Elias 63
Cansever, Edip 158
Castles, Stephen 97
Celan, Paul 36, 134
Chandler, Raymond 98
Chamisso, Adelbert von (Prize) 16, 32, 33

Chlebnikov, Velimir 127
Christ, Jesus 124
Curtius, Ernst Robert 35

Dal, Güney 64, 66, 77, 132
    Wenn Ali . . . 64, 66, 77
Defoe, Daniel
    Robinson Crusoe 24
DeLillo, Don 89–90
Donne, John 73
Dracula, Count 120
DuBois, W. E. B. 45

Eich, Günter 50, 158
Emin, İbnül 158
Emre, Yunus 33, 115, 126
Erdoğan, Recep Tayyip 155
Euripides 108

Frischmuth, Barbara 54, 102

Giscard D'Estaing, Valérie 145
Goethe, Johann Wolfgang 25, 158
Grass, Günter 44, 130, 158
Gökberg, Ülker 60
Göktürk, Deniz 17
Gür, Metin 105

Habermas, Jürgen 43, 48, 97
Hafiz, Shiraz 25
Heise, Hans–Jürgen 60, 100
Hemingway, Ernest 66
Herbert, Ulrich 97
Hikmet, Nâzım 89

Hijiya-Kirschnereit, Irmela 31,
37
Hölderlin, Friedrich 158
Huntington, Samuel 134
Huyssen, Andreas 48–9

Jakobson, Roman 35

Kafka, Franz 98, 158
'Die Verwandlung' 67
Kama Sutra (*Kamasutra*) 88
Karpat, Berkan 18, 112, 117,
124, 127
Kemal, Yaşar 158
Kemal, Mustafa ('Atatürk') 116,
127, 140, 155
Khlebnikov, Velimir 127
Kleist, Heinrich von 110
Kohl, Helmut 29
Kureishi, Hanif 49

Lacan, Jacques 64
Lautréamont 32, 107
Leggewie, Claus 17, 104, 158

Mandel, Ruth 159
Marco Polo 69
McGowan, Moray 77, 157
Meinecke, Thomas 64
Tomboy 64
Mohammed, Prophet 23, 82
Muhidine, Timour 111, 126
Muhteschem, Sascha 21, 51–4,
67, 99–103, 112, 116, 118, 128,
129, 147, 150, 152
Müller, Heiner 77

Naipaul, Vidia S. 147
Nietzsche, Friedrich 31
Nirumand, Bahman 17, 104

Odysseus 61, 76
Oelkers-Wright, Elizabeth 127
Ören, Aras 50, 78, 132
Özdamar, Emine Sevgi
*Das Leben ist eine Karawan-
serei . . .* 39–40, 93
Özdemir, Hasan 144, 145

Pamuk, Orhan 25
Pascha, Talat 53
Pirinçci, Akif 78
Plato 108
Polgar, Alfred 19

Rau, Johannes 131
Rex, John 97
Riemann, Wolfgang 78, 127
Rilke, Rainer Maria 22
Rimbaud, Arthur 32, 36
Roth, Joseph 56
Rumi, Mevlana Celaleddin 127
Rushdie, Salman 23, 49, 51, 82,
99, 130

Sade, Marquis de 69
Said, Edward 31, 39, 43, 93
Saint-Aubin, Authur F. 74
Sartre, Jean-Paul 45
Savaşçı, Fethi 79
Schiffauer, Werner 158
Schiller, Friedrich 158
Schlegel, Friedrich 89
Schmidt, Helmut 47–8
Schröder, Gerhart 153
Schwenger, Peter 66
Sedgwick, Eve Kosofsky 65
Şenocak, Zafer
*Atlas des tropischen Deutsch-
lands* 32, 36, 63, 91–5, 103
'Ein Türke geht nicht in
die Oper' 47, 49, 58

'Wann ist der Fremde zu Hause' 39–40, 46–9
'Zwischen Herz und Haut' 33–4
Das senkrechte Meer 35–6, 50, 62, 106–111, 112, 128
Der Erottomane 22, 41, 55–6, 61–2, 65, 68–76, 79, 80–91, 157
'Fridaynightfever' 65, 73, 82, 84, 85
'Das Haus im Süden' 79, 86, 89–90, 157
Der Mann im Unterhemd 21–3, 26, 51–2, 66, 71, 91, 97–99, 115, 121–2, 137–40
'Das Haus' 21, 139–40
'Das Haus des Schreibers' 22, 139–40
'Die unlesbare Karte' 28–9, 140
'Fliegen' 51, 97–8, 121–2, 157
'Lebenslauf' 23
'Rolling Stones' 66, 75
Die Prärie 26, 51–2, 66–8, 71, 75, 91, 99–100, 101, 112, 150, 152
Elektrisches Blau 50
Fernwehanstalten 35–6, 50, 64, 112, 128, 129
Flammentropfen 50
Gefährliche Verwandtschaft (*see* Muhteschem, Sascha) 19, 23, 26, 41, 52–4, 86, 91, 100–3, 116, 118, 128, 129, 147, 150, 159
Ritual der Jugend 33–4
'Samuel-Emil-Nordpol-Otto-Cäsar-Anton-...' 104–5

'Siedler und Einheimische' 151–2
Tetralogy (*MiU, P, GV, E*) x, 17–8, 26–8, 112, 113, 127
War Hitler Araber? 36–41, 42, 91, 95–6
'Das Buch mit den sieben Siegeln' 31–2
'Das Leben ist eine Karawanserei' 37–40, 93
'Ingenieure des Glaubens' 159
'Wortschatzinsel' 1–9, 112–18, 157
Zungenentfernung 146
'Berühren oder Begegnen?' 115
'Der Bart' 123, 154–6
'Der Griff hat einen Sprung' 147–52, 156
'Jenseits der Landessprache' 113–14, 134, 158
'Poetologische Skizze' 118
'Welcher Mythos schreibt mich?' 23, 102–3, 113–14, 117, 121, 123, 125–6
Sezgin, Hilal 50
Shildrick, Margot 62
Smith, Zadie 49
Socrates 108
Şölçün, Sargut 127
Soysal, Yasemin 57
Stoiber, Edmund 153
Strauss, Botho 48
Süreya, Cemal 158

Taylor, Charles 96–7
Tawada, Yoko 134
Teraoka, Arlene 105

Tieck, Ludwig 89
Toprak, Menekşe 126
Trakl, Georg 158
Travolta, John 73
Tulay, Bülent 16–17

Uyar, Turgut 158

Vidler, Anthony 141

Walser, Martin 48

Wallraff, Günter 92
   Ganz unten 92
Williams, Raymond 95

Yeşilada, Karin E. 89, 159
Yıldız, Bekir 78

Zaimoğlu, Feridun 135–7
   Kanak Sprak 135–7
Zaptçıoğlu, Dilek 50